ABORTION

QUESTIONS

&

ANSWERS

DR. AND MRS. J.C. WILLKE

This book is a successor to "Handbook on Abortion." First American edition published 1971, revised 1975, 1979, with 21st printing March 1983.

Other language editions include Latin American, Hiltz & Hayes, 1974; French, France Empire, Paris, 1974; Malayan, India, 1974; Continental Spanish, EUNSA, Pamplona 1975; Italian, Milano, 1978; Chinese, Hong Kong, 1978; Portuguese, Sao Paulo, 1980; Swedish, Jarfalla, 1980; German, Vorarlberg, 1982.

Hayes Publishing Company, Inc.
6304 Hamilton Avenue
Cincinnati, Ohio 45224
Phone (513) 681-7559

CONTENTS

PREFACE

Fourteen years ago, at the insistence of many people, particularly our college daughters, we wrote *HAND-BOOK ON ABORTION*. In question and answer format, it attempted to present all of the arguments for abortion and to answer them in a rational, medical, and scientific way. The first edition, in June 1971, numbered 141 pages and contained 42 scientific references arranged for the reader's convenience immediately following the answer to a question.

Its 1975 revision increased its size to 208 pages with 180 references, and the 1979 revision totalled 210 pages with 210 newer references. In 24 printings, *HANDBOOK ON ABORTION* sold over one million copies and was translated into ten languages.

But time moves on. Society's present questions remain, in many ways, unchanged; but we must constantly rethink our answers. In addition, a flood of new scientific information, particularly the explosion of detailed information about the other patient (the tiny one) through recent technology and modern research, reshapes our answers. Historical, legislative, and legal developments must also be incorporated into our thinking. A few earlier "facts" have been disproven. Many new facts have been confirmed by scientific studies.

Should we revise again on the framework and skeleton of the current edition? Our decision was not to. We thought we needed a totally new book. And so we started with blank paper and wrote afresh. Where are we today?

What questions are asked of us now? What information do people need?

It was an exciting adventure. Each topic, in turn, had us probing our own memories, our experiences, and digging deeply into over 40 fully packed file drawers to document our answers.

We have a new title, new sections and chapters probing entirely new areas, and new questions and answers. Except for a few classic papers, we have used new and updated scientific articles to support our answers. We tried to keep the book brief and concise. But it also had to be what was needed. And to fill those needs, it ended up larger and, we're convinced, far richer and more useful.

Whether this will again become the "bible" of the Right to Life movement, as our *HANDBOOK ON ABORTION* was so often called, remains to be seen. We live in a different time than 14 years ago. We need new tools. We offer this new book to you as our best effort to fill the continuing need of all pro-life activists and all men and women who have questions and need answers.

Jack and Barbara Willke

INTRODUCTION

Abortion: Where It Is Today

In the United States

Throughout the U.S.'s 200-year history, the developing baby in the womb had been protected by law. Then, in 1967, the first state legalized abortion for a few "hard cases."

In 1973 the U.S. Supreme Court decided that as long as the baby lived in the womb, he or she would henceforth be the property of the mother. Further, it became legal in all 50 states to destroy that property, for any and every reason, during the entire nine months of pregnancy, as long as a licensed physician did the abortion.

Now, almost every third baby conceived in America is killed by abortion, a total of over 1½ million babies a year.

For over a decade, the birth rate has been well under replacement level. Except that older people are living much longer and immigration is strong, our population would be declining.

Canada

The reversal of its previous protection of unborn human life came in Canada in 1969. Buried in a lengthy revision of the penal code was, to many people's surprise, the legalization of abortion.

It provided for "therapeutic abortion committees" in hospitals, which would have to pass on requests for abortion. In some areas these committees have conscientiously screened applications and limited approvals. In many other areas, particularly major metropolitan centers, approval is essentially automatic and abortions can be done on-demand. Today, every sixth baby conceived in Canada is killed in abortion and Canada's indigenous birth rate is also below replacement level.

Europe

The laws vary. Germany and Belgium still technically protect the unborn child, but abortionists go unpunished. In Holland a court legalized abortion. England protects the unborn only after 28 weeks gestation, while Ireland has just passed the world's first constitutional amendment protecting the unborn from the time of conception. Italy legalized abortion in a referendum. The Swiss cantons (counties) vary. Spain's Socialist party has legalized abortion, but the constitutionality of the law is under challenge. Portugal legalized abortion for a few "hard cases." France's Parliament has legalized early abortion, as has Scandinavia's. Most Eastern-block countries have sharply reversed their previous abortion-on-demand policies, principally because of dropping birth rates and damage to women.

Africa and Latin America

There is a lot of propaganda, and illegal abortions are being done, especially in Latin America, but no legalization.

Near East

There is *no* abortion in Moslem nations. In Israel the Moslem birth rate is far above that of the Jews, who permit abortion.

Asia

Abortions are widely practiced and legal, but customs, religion, and the need for large families widely alters the situation, depending on the area. China, particularly, is an open scandal, doing compulsory abortions into the third trimester after the first child. As many as ten million abortions were done in 1983, up to 90% of them coerced (M. Weisskopf articles, Jan. 6-8, 1985). Japan continues its 35-year pattern of abortion-on-demand, killing almost every other baby conceived in that nation.

Down Under

In Australia abortion is legal by Parliamentary action, with few restrictions in practice. Birth rates are below replacement level.

New Zealand's law is much tighter, with its Society to Protect the Unborn Child laboring mightily to hold it there.

The Bottom Line

Although many in other nations are unhappy about it, the fact is that what the United States does about abortion will deeply influence or even directly point the way for most other nations in the free world. Will America maintain its present course? The following pages will tell you why that course will almost certainly change.

PART I
The Questions

CHAPTER 1

The Questions

The first question in the entire abortion controversy is: "Is this human life?" or "When is this human life?" In order to answer it, we must first agree on the terms of the argument and its importance.

Define "Alive"
Alive means that this being is growing, developing, maturing, and replacing its own dying cells. It means not being dead.

Define "Human"
Human means one of the biological beings who belongs to the species Homo Sapiens. Such beings are unique from all other beings in that they have 46 *human* chromosomes in every cell. Such beings do not belong to the rabbit family, the carrot family, etc.

Define "Person"
Person is defined in at least a dozen different ways, according to the field or discipline in which you define it.

1

In theology it usually means when the soul is created. In law (in the U.S.), personhood begins at birth. Other countries have ruled that it begins at different ages. In medicine and natural science, person usually means when the being is alive and complete. In philosophy it has multiple meanings and shades of meanings.

We strongly suggest that no one use this term without first defining precisely what you mean by it; for, unless you do, any discussion of personhood is foolish.

Is this human life?

This is the question that must first be considered, pondered, discussed, and finally, answered. It cannot be brushed aside or ignored. It must be faced and met honestly. Upon its answer hinges the entire abortion question, as all other considerations pale to insignificance when compared with it. In a sense, nothing else really matters. If what is growing within the mother is not human life, if it is just a piece of tissue — a glob of protoplasm — then it deserves little respect or consideration, and the primary concern should be the mother's physical and mental health, her social well-being, and, at times, even her convenience.

But, if this is a human life, then we are faced with a second question — one that says yes or no to the entire abortion question.

What is this Second Question?

It is, "Should we give equal protection under the law to every human in this nation from the beginning of his life until each individual's natural death?"

Or, "Should we discriminate under the law against entire classes of living humans — fatally?"

Chapter 2 attempts to answer this question. Then, chapter 3 explores discrimination, and chapters 4, 5, and 6 examine protection.

For two millennia in our Western culture, written into our constitutions, specifically protected by our laws, and deeply imprinted into the hearts of all men and women,

2

there has existed the absolute value of honoring and protecting the right of each human to live. This has been an unalienable and unequivocal right. The only exception has been that of balancing a life for a life in certain situations or by due process of law.

- Never, in modern times — except by a small group of physicians in Hitler's Germany and by Stalin in Russia — has a price tag of economic or social usefulness been placed on an individual human life as the price of its continued existence.
- Never, in modern times — except by physicians in Hitler's Germany — has a certain physical perfection been required as a condition necessary for the continuation of that life.
- Never — since the law of paterfamilias in ancient Rome — has a major nation granted to a father or mother total dominion over the life or death of their child.
- Never, in modern times, has the state granted to one citizen the absolute legal right to have another killed in order to solve their own personal, social or economic problem.

And yet, if this is human life, the U.S. Supreme Court decision in America and permissive abortion laws in other nations do all of the above. They represent a complete about-face, a total rejection of one of the core values of Western man, and an acceptance of a new ethic in which life has only a relative value. No longer will every human have a right to live simply because he or she exists. Man will now be allowed to exist only if he measures up to certain standards of independence, physical perfection, or utilitarian usefulness to others. This is a momentous change that strikes at the root of Western civilization.

It makes no difference to vaguely assume that human life is more human post-born than pre-born. What is critical is to judge it to be — or not to be — human life. By a measure of "more" or "less" human, one can easily and logically justify infanticide and euthanasia. By the mea-

3

sure of economic and/or social usefulness, the ghastly atrocities of Hitlerian mass murders came to be.

One cannot help but be reminded of the anguished comment of a condemned Nazi judge, who said to an American judge after the Nuremburg trials, "I never knew it would come to this." The American judge answered simply, "It came to this the first time you condemned an innocent life."

Ponder well the words of George Santayana: "Those who do not remember the past are condemned to relive it."

Wm. Shirer, *The Rise and Fall of the Third Reich*, Simon & Schuster, 1959

Is this unborn being, growing within the mother, a human life? Make this judgment with the utmost care, scientific precision, and honesty. Upon it may hinge much of the basic freedom of many human lives in the years to come.

CHAPTER 2

When Does Human Life Begin?

If there is one function absolutely central to the duty of a nation-state, it is to protect the most precious possession of its citizens — their very lives. In order to make laws to protect their lives, it is necessary to determine when their lives begin. The question must be answered.

Where does one begin?

The question can be answered spiritually, philosophically, or biologically. Much of today's confusion arises from mixing these disciplines. Each is valid, but only one can be used to make law.

How is "Human Life" defined spiritually?

A religious, faith belief or spiritual definition usually sees the creation of the soul as the beginning of human life. The problem here is that believers differ in when they think the soul is created. There are, of course, other sincere people who do not believe there is a soul.

What is important is that in our secular nation, no one's religious, faith belief can be imposed on others through force of law. Therefore, we cannot use a religious definition of when human life begins as the basis for making laws.

How is "Human Life" defined philosophically?

In a myriad of ways. For example, this is not human life until birth or until there is: a certain level of consciousness; a certain degree of being wanted; a certain exchange of love; a certain humanization or culturalization; a certain degree of self-sufficiency or viability; a certain degree of physical development; a certain degree of physical or mental perfection; etc. Many sincere people define "human life" by these and other criteria, all of which have certain things in common:

- While admittedly arrived at through a certain reasoning process, all of the above remain theories.
- None can be proven factually by science.
- All individuals have a right to hold their own philosophic beliefs.
- People of good will can and do differ completely on the correctness of the philosophic beliefs mentioned.

Because these are non-provable theories and beliefs, they should be treated the same way as religious beliefs. Just as our nation should not impose religious, faith beliefs on others through force of law, so it should likewise not force philosophic beliefs and theories on others through force of law.

What of a biologic definition?

This is the area where there is no disagreement — the area where natural science has provided proven facts. The biologic details of human growth and development, from the single cell stage until death, are beyond dispute.

Any discussion of human life must first look to embryology, fetology, and medical science. What are the known facts? Only then can we honestly answer the central question of human life's beginning.

Part III on Fetal Development is the most important part of this book, for it explores in detail these biologic facts.

6

CHAPTER 3

The Second Question

There are only two questions that are basic to the entire abortion controversy. The first is, "Is this human life?" As we have seen in chapter 2 (and will further examine in Part III), the answer clearly is Yes. That answer is a medical and scientific one, for we cannot impose a religious or philosophic belief on the nation through force of law.

The second question is: "Should we grant equal protection by law to all living humans in our nation?" or, "Should we allow discrimination against entire classes of living humans?"

Has such discrimination ever been legal before? Yes, sadly so.

Race
The Nazi Holocaust was a terrifying example of legal racial discrimination. It began with the elimination of almost 300,000 Aryan German citizens who were "defective" and ended with the elimination of 6 million members of a race that was also judged to be "defective." (Add perhaps another 6 million Gypsies, Poles, war prisoners, etc.)

First, Jews were labeled subhuman through the use of names such as "vermin, garbage, subhuman, trash," etc. Then, legal personhood and equal protection by law were removed in 1936 by the Supreme Court of Germany. Finally, the killing began. Detailed documentation is available in *THE GERMAN EUTHANASIA PROGRAM*, Wertham, Hayes Publishing Co., Cincinnati ($1.25) and *The Abortion Holocaust*, Brennan, Landmark Press ($7.00).

Skin Color

In the U.S., from Colonial times, there was legal discrimination on the basis of skin color.

This ugly chapter in our history came to its legal climax with the Dred Scott decision by the U.S. Supreme Court in 1857, three years before Lincoln's election and the U.S. Civil War. In essence, it confirmed that black people had no legal rights and were the property of their owners. The analogy to abortion is direct. Complete details are available on this analogy in *ABORTION AND SLAVERY — HISTORY REPEATS*, Willke, Hayes Publishing Co., Cincinnati, 1984 ($3.50).

Age

If you are conceived in France, your life is legally protected after ten weeks of life. In Denmark, it is 12 weeks. In the State of Washington, life was protected at 16 weeks; Sweden was 20. In New York, it had been 24 weeks; England is 28; and presently in the U.S., life is legally protected only after birth. Nobel prize winner, Dr. James Watson, has suggested "three days after birth."

At first glance, one is likely to comment that all of the above disagree. But look closer at the ethic, the logic, and the criteria. They all agree. They agree that you can discriminate against an entire class of living humans on the basis of age. They just don't agree on which age.

But note well that in the U.S. today there are 3.5 taxpayers for every retired person who draws Social Security or other tax-funded pensions. By the year 2040, there will only be 1.5 taxpayers to support each retired person (assuming no rise in the current birth rate). Our nation (among others) is all but bankrupt now, largely due to such entitlement programs.

This will be a completely impossible economic situation. The answer could be rather simple and direct. Copy the ethic, the logic, and the criteria of today's fatal discrimination on the basis of age — only start at the other end of the spectrum.

Perhaps a court could rule that everyone over 80 years of age was no longer a legal person. Or maybe it would have to be lowered to 75 — or even to...?

Handicap

Handicap is one of the two most accepted reasons for abortion. But remember, before birth and after birth, it is the same patient and the same handicap. Is it any wonder that we are increasingly seeing the same "solution" after birth (killing by infanticide) as before birth (killing by abortion)?

Since when have we given doctors the right to kill the patient to "cure" the disease?

Place-of-Residence

This is abortion in the U.S. It is discrimination on the basis of place-of-residence. If the child in the womb can escape from his first place-of-residence (the womb) the day before his scheduled execution, his life is protected by full force of law. As long as he remains in the womb, however, he can be killed at his mother's request.

PART II
History

CHAPTER 4

Way Back When

In the ancient world, abortion was not common, but infanticide was widely practiced.

Why was this so?
Because abortion was so often fatal to the mother. The only methods known then were two: One method was to give certain poisons to the mother and hope the unborn child would die; often the mother did, too. The other method was to physically abuse the mother's abdomen to induce abortion, which sometimes fatally injured her.

And so?
Almost universally, the child was delivered and then killed if unwanted. Abortion was rare; infanticide was common.

What were the laws?
The early Christian church was very positive (see chapter 22). While its Fathers argued about formed and

unformed, the soul, etc., they completely condemned abortion and infanticide. Penalty for the sin of abortion ranged up to and beyond seven years of public penance.

J. Connery, *Abortion, the Development of the Roman Catholic Perspective*
Chicago: Loyola University Press, 1977, pp. 65-87

These penances were more stringent for abortion after quickening (then defined as after being formed), for most thought life didn't begin until after quickening.

What is quickening?

Originally, it meant "when formed," for this was when the soul was presumably created. Later, it came to mean when the mother "felt life," (its present meaning).

As ecclesiastical law gave way to civil law, English common law also condemned all abortion, but only as a misdemeanor before quickening, a felony after. This was because scientists "knew" that the baby was not yet alive before that time. After quickening, or when the mother "felt life," it was "known" that life was present and severe punishments were inflicted for late abortions. When "life came to the child," the child "came alive;" when the mother "felt life" or "felt the baby kick," then that life was given the fullest protection of the law.

When did they think that human life began?

In primitive times, there were many theories of how human life began and grew. Most scientists "knew" that the man planted the total new being in the nutrient womb of his wife's body. From this came the agrarian terms of "planting the seed," "fertile," "barren," etc.

When microscopes were developed, sperm were discovered (by Hamm in 1677). They were seen to be tadpole-like objects and not at all "little men." Even so, the books of those years show drawings of a little man curled up in the sperm's head, for they "knew" he was there. This was called a "Homunculus."

As the power of microscopes increased, it slowly became evident that there must be another explanation of life's beginnings. Perhaps the woman contributed something to this new being?

But few abortionists were punished. Why not?

In order to prove the crime of abortion, one must a) prove that the woman was pregnant and b) prove that this action killed the baby.

Until recent times, the only absolute proof of pregnancy was to feel fetal movement and/or to hear the fetal heart, which was at four to five months. After abortion, the only proof of pregnancy was to produce the baby's body — the corpus delecti. These were seldom available as evidence. Because of the inability to prove that an early pregnancy in fact existed, the crime usually couldn't be proven.

J. Dellapenna, *The History of Abortion, Technology, Morality, and Law,*
University of Pittsburgh Law Review, 1979

But abortions were common in the 19th century!

"Sometime after 1750, a new technique for inducing abortion was introduced. [It was a] major technological innovation," which involved inserting objects through the cervix into the uterus to initiate the abortion. It, too, had major risks to the mother, but was so much safer than the older, more lethal methods that it replaced them, and infanticide became rare.

ibid., above

Abortions did increase in the 19th century then?

Yes, many fold. In fact, they became very common.

J. Mohr, *Abortion in America,*
Oxford University Press, 1978

Then in 1827, Karl Ernst von Boar, in a scientific journal, postulated that both man and woman contribute to a process called conception. His was the first accurate description of the process of conception. This was observed in a rabbit in 1843 by Martin Berry, but not actually seen in a human until many years later.

By the 1850s the scientific and medical world came to fully accept the fact that the man and woman each contributed half to the creation of the new human being. This event was called conception or fertilization, and this stimulated the anti-abortion action of the doctors.

There was an anti-abortion movement then?

While abortions became common, the medical community was, at the same time, becoming aware of the newly discovered scientific fact that human life began at fertilization. It was at this time that members of the American Medical Association went to the state legislatures to testify and inform them of this scientific fact.

> "In 1859 the AMA protested that the quickening distinction allowed the fetus rights 'for civil purposes [but as] to its life as yet denies all protection.' They protested against this 'unwarrantable destruction of human life,' calling upon state legislatures to revise their abortion laws and requesting the state medical societies 'in pressing the subject.'"
>
> Roe vs. Wade,
> U.S. Supreme Court, 1973, VI, 6, p. 26

By 1871 the AMA report had summed up abortion: *"we had to deal with human life."* As the state lawmakers were taught the newly discovered scientific fact that human life didn't begin at quickening but rather at conception, the laws were changed. One by one, each state ruled that human life should be equally and fully protected by law, not from the time of quickening, but from its actual beginning at conception.

When were the new state laws passed?

Originally, the U.S. colonies, and then the states operated under English Common Law. Connecticut passed the first separate state law in 1821. By 1860, 85% of the population lived in states which had clearly prohibited abortion with new laws.

J. Dellapenna, *The History of Abortion, Technology, Morality, and Law,*
University of Pittsburgh Law Review, 1979

Quay, *Justifiable Abortion-Medical and Legal Foundations,*
49 Georgetown Univ. Law Review, 1960-1961

Besides clearly outlawing abortion, these laws and those passed after the Civil War moved the felony punishment from quickening back to conception. This was done primarily to protect new human life.

Pro-abortion people claim that there were other more important reasons.

Cyril Means, a law professor and legal counsel for the National Association for the Reform of Abortion Laws, wrote two works which suggested that the laws were passed to protect the health of the mother. (All other surgery was dangerous, too, but no other surgery was forbidden.)

C. Means, *The Law of New York and Abortion and Status of Foetus,* 14 NYLF, 1968, p. 411

C. Means, *The Phoenix of American Freedom,* 17 NYLF, 1971, p. 335

Justice Blackman, in writing the Roe vs. Wade Supreme Court decision, cited Means four times in an echo of his thinking. This version of the history of abortion evoked scathing criticism.

R. Byrn, *An American Tragedy,* 41 Fordham Law Review, p. 807, pp. 814-839, 1973

To counter this, the Ford and Rockefeller foundations funded a major study by James Mohr, whose book, *Abortion in America,* (Oxford Univ. Press, 1978), was a more sophisticated version of the same thesis. Mohr's historical study reported events only from 1800, ignored the past, and added other reasons. These included concern over the declining WASP (White Anglo-Saxon Protestant) birth rate, and the concern of the doctor-members of the AMA over competition from other medical practitioners.

Weren't these valid reasons?

Professor Joseph Dellapenna and others have almost totally discredited these attempts to rewrite history. The main reason was clearly that lawmakers wanted to protect human life from its biologic beginning.

J. Dellapenna, *Abortion and the Law, Roe's Distortion of the Historical Record*, A.U.L. Conference, Chicago, Apr. 1, 1984 (to be published).

What, then, did all these new state laws say?

Without exception, all states in the U.S. by mid- to late-19th century, protected the unborn from his/her life's beginning at conception and until birth. Abortionists, if convicted, were punished. For example, the records of Clinton Prison, Schenectady, NY, in March 1878, show the discharge of a Thomas Weed, with the notation: "Dr. Weed, the notorious abortionist, 6 years, 4 months, for the crime of abortion."

Signed by Henry Schripture of Albany,
Agent and Warden

Were women punished?

The definitive study on this gives the lie to Planned Parenthood's ads which claimed: "If you had a miscarriage you could be prosecuted for murder."

Washington Post
April 27, 1981

Studying two hundred years of legal history, the American Center for Bioethics concluded:

"No evidence was found to support the proposition that women were prosecuted for undergoing or soliciting abortions. The charge that spontaneous miscarriages could result in criminal prosecution is similarly unsupportable. There are no documented instances of prosecution of such women for murder or for any other species of homicide; nor is there evidence that states that had provisions enabling them to prosecute women for procuring abortions ever applied those laws. The vast majority of the courts were reluctant to implicate women, even in a secondary fashion, through complicity and conspiracy charges. Even in those rare instances where an abortionist persuaded the court to recognize the woman as his accomplice, charges were not filed against her. In short, women were *not* prosecuted for abortions. Abortionists were. The charges of Planned Parenthood and other "pro-choice" proponents are without factual basis. Given the American legal system's reliance on precedent, it is unlikely that enforcement of future criminal sanctions on abortion would deviate substantially from past enforcement patterns."

Women and Abortion, Prospects of Criminal Charges
Monograph, American Center for Bioethics,
422 C St., NE, Washington, DC 20002, Spring 1983

Under a Human Life Amendment, will women be punished?

We don't know of a single pro-life or pro-abortion leader, or church leader, or congressman, or state representative who would want this. The mother is the second victim; she needs help and love — not punishment. No, women would not be punished under a Human Life Amendment. Would the abortionist? Yes, he or she is the killer who took money and did the abortion.

The abortionist deserves punishment and would, in all probability, be punished, as in years past.

CHAPTER 5

Two Infamous Days in the U.S.A.

On March 6, 1857 the U.S. Supreme Court finally decided a very vexing question which had troubled the citizens of the United States for many years. In the landmark Dred Scott decision the court ruled once and for all that black people were not legal "persons" according to the U.S. Constitution. A slave was the property of the owner and could be bought and sold, used, or even killed by the owner at the owner's discretion. The ruling was final. It was by the highest court in the land.

Those who opposed slavery protested, but were met with the retort: "So you oppose slavery? It is against your moral, religious, and ethical convictions? Well, you don't have to own a slave, but don't impose your morality on the slave owner. He has the right to choose to own a slave. The Supreme Court has spoken. Slavery is legal."

But not for long. It took a bloody civil war to stop slavery. It took the 13th, 14th, and 15th Amendments to the Constitution to legally grant freedom, civil rights, and voting rights. From a socioeconomic view, we are still striving for full equality.

Then on January 22, 1973, the U.S. Supreme Court finally decided a very vexing question which had troubled the citizens of the United States for many years. In a landmark decision, the court ruled once and for all that unborn humans were not legal "persons" according to the U.S. Constitution. An unborn baby was the property of the owner (mother) and she could have the baby killed at her request because of her health (social distress). This could be done at any time until birth. The ruling was final. It was by the highest court in the land.

Those who opposed abortion protested, but were met with a retort that seemed an echo of slavery days. "So you oppose abortion? It is against your moral, religious, and ethical convictions? Well, you don't have to have an abortion, but don't impose your morality on the mother (the owner). She has the right to choose to have an abortion. The Supreme Court has spoken. Abortion is legal."

But not for long? That was over a decade ago. The goal of a Constitutional Amendment or reversal by the Court is still well ahead of us. But the pro-life movement continues to grow. It is now the largest grass-roots movement in the history of our nation.

Then, the discrimination was on the basis of skin color. Now, it is on the basis of age and place of residence (living in the womb).

SLAVERY	ABORTION
Dred Scott 1857 7-2 Decision	Roe vs. Wade 1973 7-2 Decision
Black Non-person	Unborn Non-person
Property of Owner	Property of Owner (Mother)
Choose To Buy-Sell-Kill	Choose To Keep Or Kill
Abolitionists Should Not Impose Morality On Slaveowner	Pro-lifers Should Not Impose Morality On Mother
Slavery Is Legal	Abortion Is Legal

CHAPTER 6

The Supreme Court Decision and Attempts to Reverse It

During the mid 1800s, all states tightened their laws, making abortion—from the time of fertilization on — a serious crime.

When did the laws change again?
- For over 100 years, and until 1967, all states fully protected all human life from conception except when the mother's life was threatened. Then the first permissive law was passed in Colorado.

- In June 1970, when New York passed the first abortion-on-demand law (24 week limit), it became the 16th state to allow abortion. Most of the others had allowed abortion only for very restrictive reasons.

- After that, in the next 2 years, only *one* more state legalized abortion (Florida because of a court order), while 33 states debated the issue in their legislatures. All 33 states voted against permitting abortion for any reason except to save the mother's life.

- In April 1972, New York repealed its law, but Governor Nelson Rockefeller vetoed the repeal, and the law remained in force.

What of the state courts?

In the late 1960s and early 1970s, pro-abortionists challenged the constitutionality of laws forbidding abortion in most states. In about one-third of the decisions, such laws were declared unconstitutional and varying degrees of abortions were permitted. (Most of these were states that had already legalized abortion in their legislatures.) Two-thirds of the state courts, however, declared existing laws to be constitutional.

Then there were referenda?

Yes. After the pro-abortionists were stopped in the legislatures and in the courts, they tried referenda in two states (abortion-on-demand until 20 weeks) in the November 1972 election.

- North Dakota, only 12% Catholic, voted 78% against abortion.
- Michigan, an industrial state (pre-polled at 60% pro-abortion), voted 63% against abortion.

The tide had turned?

Yes. It seemed obvious that most people did not want abortion. But, on January 22, 1973, the U.S. Supreme Court ruled.

Roe vs. Wade, U.S. Supreme Court
410 U.S. 113, 1973

Doe vs. Bolton, U.S. Supreme Court
410 U.S. 179, 1973

What was the ruling?

It struck down all laws against abortion which had in any way protected unborn babies. The ruling legalized abortion in all 50 states for the full nine months of pregnancy for social and economic reasons.

- It created a new basic constitutional right for women in the right to privacy, which the Supreme Court had created only a few years earlier. This right to privacy was "broad enough to encompass a woman's right to terminate her pregnancy."
- It stated that the law protects only legal "persons" and that "legal personhood does not exist pre-natally."
- It gave the state "a compelling interest in the protection of the pregnant woman's health."

The ruling authorized:
- No legal restrictions at all on abortion in the first three months.
- No restrictions from then until viability, except those needed to make the procedure safer for the mother.
- Abortion was allowed until birth if *one* licensed physician judged it necessary for the mother's "health."

How did the U.S. Supreme Court define "health?"
The Court said that abortion could be performed:
"...in the light of all factors — physical, emotional, psychological, familial, and the woman's age – relevant to the well being of the patient. All these factors may relate to health."

Doe vs. Bolton, U.S. Supreme Court,
No. 70-40, IV, p. 11, Jan. 1973

"Maternity or additional offspring may force upon the woman a distressful life and future. Psychological harm may be imminent. Mental and physical health may be taxed by child care. There is also the distress for all concerned associated with the unwanted child, and there is the problem of bringing a child into a family already unable, psychologically or otherwise, to care for it. In other cases the additional difficulties and continuing stigma of unwed motherhood may be involved. All these are factors that the woman and the responsible physician will consider in consultation."

Roe vs. Wade, U.S. Supreme Court,
No. 70-18, p. 38, Jan. 1973

But these reasons are social reasons, not health reasons.

That is the situation! The U.S. Supreme Court has specifically defined the word "health" to include a broad group of social and economic problems, as judged by the mother herself. It has further specifically forbidden any state to forbid abortion at any time prior to birth for these reasons, if the mother can find a doctor to do the abortion.

Then the United States has abortion-on-demand until birth?

Correct. This is the legal situation.

Give me some authoritative reference on that!

President Reagan, in his book, clearly states:

"Our nationwide policy of abortion-on-demand through all nine months of pregnancy was neither voted on by our people nor enacted by our legislators."

R. Reagan, *Abortion & the Conscience of the Nation*,
Thomas Nelson Publishers, 1984, p. 15

Also, the official report of the U.S. Senate Judiciary Committee, issued after extensive hearings on the Human Life Federalism Amendment (proposed by Senators Hatch and Eagleton), concluded:

"Thus, the [Judiciary] Committee observes that no significant legal barriers of any kind whatsoever exist today in the United States for a woman to obtain an abortion for any reason during any stage of her pregnancy."

Report, Committee on the Judiciary, U.S. Senate, on Senate Joint
Resolution 3, 98th Congress, 98-149, June 7, 1983, p. 6

How did the court justify its action?

It seems obvious that the court approached the issue with a clear conviction that "a woman must have this right" and tried to justify this right. They admitted their decision was not in the Constitution, but claimed that it was implied — that it was found in the emanations (i.e., vapors) from the penumbra (i.e., shadows) of the 14th Amendment. They used almost every pro-abortion argument available and totally ignored a vastly larger body of firm scientific facts which would have completely refuted these arguments

Specifically?

The most devastating was their judgment that, even though they didn't know when "life" begins, they would rule out all protection for this growing living human being on the basis of age and place-of-residence (the womb).

They justified this civil rights violation because the fetus had not yet reached *"the capability of meaningful life"*; that he or she was not a *"person in the whole sense"* [authors' italics].

Roe vs. Wade, U.S. Supreme Court
IX, p. 47; X, p. 48

All of the "foot-in-the-door" early euthanasia bills (living will, death with dignity) introduced so far, justify post-born extermination when the patient is no longer capable of "meaningful" life.

The Court found the right to abort in the right to privacy. What about the right of a woman to the privacy of her own body?

The U.S. Supreme Court decision is based on this. We think it is an entirely fallacious bit of reasoning.

If you, as a citizen, stand outside a door and listen to a mother battering her child, even to the point of killing him, what would you do? Would you respect the privacy of her home? You would not! You would open or break down the door and rescue the child. By virtue of her assault upon and abuse of another human person, she has surrendered her constitutional right to privacy in this case. The same analogy applies to abortion. The right of the child to live is greater than and supersedes any right that a woman may have to the privacy of her own body.

But a woman does have a right to her own body. Isn't the child, at least in the early stages of pregnancy, part of her body?

A woman's appendix, obviously a part of her body, can be removed for sufficient reason. The cells of the appendix, however, carry the identical genetic code that is present in every other cell in the mother's body. They are, for this reason, undeniably part of her body.

The single-celled fertilized ovum, or later developing embryonic human being within her uterus, cannot, by any stretch of the imagination, be considered part of her body. This new living being has a genetic code that is totally different from the cells of the mother's body. He or she is, in truth, a completely separate growing human being and can never be considered part of the mother's body.

Does she have a right to her own body? Yes. But this is not part of her own body. It is another person's body.

The Supreme Court also decided other related cases after this?

Yes. The main ones were:

• Spousal and parental consent was ruled unconstitutional. Prohibition of salt poisoning abortion on medical grounds was ruled unconstitutional.

Planned Parenthood vs. Danforth,
428 U.S. 52, 1976

• Viability is what the doctor says it is.

Colautti vs. Franklin,
429 U.S. 379, 1979

• The State is not required to fund "medically necessary" abortions for the poor.

Harris vs. McRae, 448 U.S. 297, 1980

• Informed consent is not required. A waiting period is unconstitutional. Mandatory hospitalization for second trimester abortions is unconstitutional. "Humane" disposal of fetal remains is unconstitutional.

City of Akron vs. Akron Center for Reproductive Health,
103 S. Ct. 2481, 1983

Aren't there any absolute legal requirements?

There are three. The woman must request it, a licensed doctor must agree to do it, and the pre-born baby must still live in the womb.

Can the U.S. Congress do anything at all?

Yes! Increasingly, the U.S. Congress has been passing pro-life bills:

• to cut off federal funding for Medicaid abortions (Hyde Amendment);

• to stop federal funding of abortions in Federal Employees' Health Insurance;

• to stop pro-abortion legal action by government lawyers;

• to limit fetal experimentation;

• to stop overseas aid for abortion;

• to stop funding of abortions in military hospitals;

• to aid pregnant women;

• to take abortion out of family planning aid.

The decision can only be reversed by an amendment to the U.S. Constitution?

Yes, unless the Supreme Court would reverse its decision.

How can such an amendment be passed?

There are two methods. For the last 16 amendments added to the Constitution, the proposed amendment first had to pass both Houses of the U.S. Congress by a two-thirds vote. In the other method, used for the first ten amendments (the Bill of Rights), a Constitutional Convention first approved the proposed amendments. In both cases, the proposed amendment(s) had to be ratified by three-fourths of the state legislatures.

Have pro-lifers tried either method?
Yes. They are working on both. The most recent vote in the Congress was in June 1983, when the Hatch-Eagleton Amendment was debated and voted on by the U.S. Senate.

Also, 19 states have voted to call a Constitutional Convention. The required number is 34.

What amendments have been proposed?
The original wording formulated in 1974 by the Legal Committee of the National Right to Life (NRLC) organization was:

THE NRLC HUMAN LIFE AMENDMENT
Section 1: With respect to the right to life, the word "person" as used in this article and in the Fifth and Fourteenth Articles of Amendment to the Constitution of the United States applies to all human beings irrespective of age, health, function, or condition of dependency, including their unborn offspring at every stage of their biologic development.

Section 2: No unborn person shall be deprived of life by any person; provided, however, that nothing in this article shall prohibit a law permitting only those medical procedures required to prevent the death of the mother.

Section 3: The Congress and the several States shall have power to enforce this article by appropriate legislation.

Later, another version was introduced which came to be called:

THE PARAMOUNT AMENDMENT

The Paramount right to life is vested in each human being from the moment of fertilization without regard to age, health, or condition of dependency.

Then, in 1981, these two versions were merged into a new NRLC Amendment often called:

THE NRLC UNITY HUMAN LIFE AMENDMENT

Section 1: The right to life is a paramount and most fundamental right of a person.

Section 2: With respect to the right to life guaranteed to persons by the Fifth and Fourteenth Articles of Amendment to the Constitution, the word "person" applies to all human beings, irrespective of age, health, function, or condition of dependency, including their unborn offspring at every state of their biological development including fertilization.

Section 3: No unborn person shall be deprived of life by any person; provided, however, that nothing in this article shall prohibit a law allowing justification to be shown for only those medical procedures required to prevent the death of either the pregnant woman or her unborn offspring as long as such law requires every reasonable effort be made to preserve the life of each.

Section 4: Congress and the several States shall have power to enforce this article by appropriate legislation.

The National Right to Life Political Action Committee will accept support for any of the three versions as criteria for endorsement of a candidate for public office.

Which of these three versions has the most support?

A measure of legislative support in the 98th Congress showed 26 senators cosponsoring the original NRLC, three senators cosponsoring the original Paramount, and seven senators cosponsoring the Unity Amendment.

Would all three reverse the Supreme Court decision?

Yes, but they would go further. Prior to the 1973 Supreme Court decision, the U.S. had a de facto states' rights situation under which each state could decide if it wanted to forbid or to permit abortion and to what degree.

These amendments would reverse the 1973 Supreme Court decision, but would also go further and mandate federal protection for the unborn in all 50 states.

Many legal experts had thought that such protection was already present in the 14th Amendment to the Constitution; but, as we know, in the late 1960s, 17 states passed laws to allow abortion for various reasons. Pro-life leaders do not want this to happen again. Accordingly, these amendments would revoke the pre-existing states' rights situation and mandate universal civil rights for all living humans — born or unborn.

But this is over a decade later and none of these amendments have been passed!

True. But support for such an amendment has steadily increased. In 1974 there were only 28 pro-life Senate votes. By 1979 there were 40. By 1983 there were 50, as demonstrated by the Hatch-Eagleton vote in June 1983.

But an amendment needs 67 votes!

That's the problem. Almost every third baby conceived in America (and every fifth baby in Canada) is killed by abortion. Even if the growth of pro-life strength continues, it could be another decade before such an amendment would be passed out of Congress. That was why two major steps-on-the-way, the Helms Human Life Bill (HLB) and the Hatch-Eagleton Constitutional Amendment were proposed. Neither would have done the entire job, but both, it was thought, would have reversed the abortion juggernaut and stopped part of the killing.

What was the Helms Human Life Bill?

The HLB was introduced in January 1981. It was a statute, not a Constitutional Amendment. Bills or statutes need only a majority vote to pass (unless filibustered, in which case 60 votes are needed). They can be challenged and are subject to Supreme Court review.

If passed by both Houses (President Reagan had said he would sign it), it would have declared that unborn humans were legal persons. If the high court judged this to be Constitutional, the Supreme Court would have, in effect, reversed its judgment of 1973. The HLB certainly would have applied to State abortions, but there was a question as to whether it would have stopped private abortions. The Court would have decided.

Was it passed?

It proved to be controversial within the pro-life movement. The National Right to Life Board endorsed it by a narrow margin eight months after it was introduced and by a two-thirds margin eight months after that. By the time it reached the Senate floor, there was full pro-life support for it. Stating that he had "only 35 or 40 votes" for its personhood feature, Senator Helms removed that section on the eve of the vote. It was still filibustered. Sixty votes for cloture were needed to stop a filibuster. The deciding vote on invoking cloture, in September 1982, only received 50 votes. It was then tabled on a 48-47 vote.

What was the Hatch-Eagleton Amendment?

This was to be the first of two Constitutional amendments. Facing the reality of the inability at this time to pass a full federal amendment, this was proposed as a major first step on the way. It stated: "A right to abortion is not secured by this Constitution."

What would it have done?

It would have reversed the Supreme Court decision and returned the nation to the "status quo ante;" that is, essentially, the condition prior to the 1973 Supreme Court decision, when each state had the power to forbid, but also, the power to permit abortion. It would also have reinstated certain Congressional powers to regulate abortions. Estimates varied, but it was thought that if such an amendment were passed and ratified, upwards of 25 states would have protected all unborn lives (except when the mother's life was in jeopardy); most of the rest of the states would have partially protected them, and only a few would have retained complete abortion-on-demand. Furthermore, through taxation, the commerce clause, and other regulations, the Federal Congress could have restricted abortion even further.

It was felt that this approach would have considerably more support and could probably be passed many years sooner than a full Federal Human Life Amendment. Then, some years later, as our nation continued to become more pro-life, a second amendment could be passed, completing the process and making protection a federal mandate.

But it was also controversial?

Yes, it was. It was introduced in September 1981 by conservative Republican Senator Orrin Hatch (UT), and liberal Democratic Senator Thomas Eagleton (MO). Like its earlier cousin, the HLB, it was also a new approach. As a Constitutional amendment, it could not have been struck down by the Court. But the Hatch-Eagleton, as a Constitutional Amendment, needed even more votes (67, as compared with the HLB's 60). And, if passed, it would have required ratification by three-fourths of the states.

The chief objection was that it was only a partial solution and many feared that a second amendment would never be passed. Proponents answered this by noting that they feared that a one-step amendment could not be passed in this decade and possibly not in this century. They felt that they could possibly stop over half of the killing and didn't do it. Further, they argued, a reversal of the court decision would re-establish a climate of protection and respect for life and make a second step possible.

There were a few legal scholars who questioned whether the wording would accomplish what its sponsors were convinced it would. The great majority of legal authorities (including pro-abortion ones), however, felt that it would effectively reverse the 1973 Supreme Court abortion decision.

But wasn't the "Hatch" a compromise?

Opinions differ. It was clear enough that all pro-life leaders still wanted all babies protected. There was no compromise on the basic ethic or ultimate goal. This was a change in legislative strategy, and some pro-lifers did believe this was a compromise.

But wouldn't the Hatch Amendment be allowing many abortions?

Some pro-lifers thought so. Supporters of the Amendment, however, pointed to the following reasoning: If, today, we have 100% abortion, and we have the power to stop 60% of them (but not the full 100%) and do so, are we "permitting" the 40% that remain? Hardly! We've taken one step, saved many lives, and begun the reversal process. We'll stop more abortions as soon as we have the strength to do so.

But it was defeated also?

The National Right to Life Board endorsed it by a narrow margin three months after its introduction and by a two-thirds vote four months later. After full debate, the Senate vote, in June 1983, was 49 votes for and 50 votes against, with one pro-life senator abstaining. It failed the two-thirds majority needed.

Were these two defeats crushing blows?

Not at all!

No pro-life leader realistically expected either the bill or the Constitutional Amendment to pass. Nevertheless, there were major social, legislative, and political reasons to bring both before the Senate for record votes. This was the first time that a major effort had brought a measure, the Hatch-Eagleton Amendment — one which would have reversed the Supreme Court decision — through a Senate subcommittee, then through the full Judiciary Committee, and on to a floor debate and vote by the full Senate. Just ten years after that fateful Supreme Court decision, the Senate split right down the middle, by far the strongest showing yet on such a major measure. Then, several months later, proving that the Right to Life movement had not lost its strength, the U.S. Congress reaffirmed the abortion funding restrictions of the Hyde Amendment to the Labor, Health and Human Services Annual Appropriation Bill, and then, for the first time, cut off the use of tax money to help pay for abortions done under the Federal Employees' Health Insurance program.

Will abortion ever be stopped through the legislative process?
Pro-life leaders grow more optimistic as the years go on. There is also a greater possibility that the Supreme Court could reverse the decision itself. As new justices are seated on the Court, it is entirely plausible that these new members could be instrumental in reversing the Supreme Court's 1973 decision.

Has the Supreme Court ever reversed one of its major decisions?
Yes! In the over 200-year history of the U.S.A., the Court has completely reversed its own major decisions over one hundred times.

PART III
Fetal Development

CHAPTER 7

Development in the Womb
The Beginning

When and where does fertilization occur?

Sperm enter the women's vagina, swim through the cavity of her uterus and out through her Fallopian tubes. The egg, breaking out of the shell of her ovary, is penetrated by one of the sperm. The 23 chromosomes of the sperm unite with the 23 chromosomes of the ovum, forming a new 46 chromosome cell. When this process of fertilization is complete, a new human being exists.

This is then only a single cell?

Yes. But a remarkable and unique one.

This cell is now either male or female.

The cell is unique, i.e., never before in the history of the world has this exact individual human existed. Never again in history will another exactly like this human exist.

The cell is complete, i.e., nothing else — no bits or pieces — will be added from this time until the old man or woman dies — nothing but nutrition and oxygen.

This being is programmed from within, moving forward in a self-controlled, ongoing process of growth, development, and replacement of his or her own dying cells.

This living being is dependent upon his or her mother for shelter and food, but in all other respects is a totally new, different, unique, and independent being.

How does it grow?

This single celled human being divides into two cells, each containing the same total and identical DNA message, the same total contents. Two becomes four, eight, sixteen, etc., as it moves down the Fallopian tube. Ultimately, each human being's body contains 30 million, million cells.

When sufficient cells are present, organ formation, body structure, and function begins. Cell doubling occurs only 45 times. That timing is as follows:

CELL DOUBLINGS	BY AGE	PERCENTAGE
8	by implantation	18%
30	by 8 weeks	66%
41	by birth	91%
44	by kindergarten	98%
45	by adulthood	100%

A. W. Liley, *The Tiniest Humans*,
CA: Sassone Press, p. 14

I've heard that another animal also has 46 chromosomes!

True, but not 46 *human* chromosomes. Different species have different types of chromosomes.

But what of a human with 47 chromosomes, doesn't this disprove your "humans have 46" statement?

Certain humans have 12 toes. Others are born with one arm. Are they human? They certainly are, but they are humans with an abnormality. A "Triple X" or a Down's

Syndrome human has an extra chromosome. Are they human? Yes, but humans with an abnormal number of chromosomes.

This tiny human moves down the Fallopian tube?

Yes, and at about one week of life, at the blastocyst stage of about 128 to 256 cells, it implants into the nutrient lining of the uterus. There, only three days later, this tiny male or female human sends a chemical-hormonal message into the mother's body, which stops her menstrual periods.

The new being controls her body?

Yes, for the balance of pregnancy. It is the developing baby who enlarges her breasts to prepare her for nursing and softens her pelvic bones in preparation for labor. It is even the baby who "determines his own birthday."

A. Liley, *A Case Against Abortion*, Liberal Studies,
Whitcombe & Tombs, 1971

Isn't the fertilized ovum only a potential human being?

No. This is not a *potential* human being; it is a human being with vast potential. One could say that the sperm and ovum, before their union, constitute a potential human being. Once their union is completed, however, they have become an actual human being.

What if this being dies soon after fertilization? Was it human then?

Human death can occur at any time during our journey through life. This could be minutes after fertilization or 95 years after fertilization. Human death is merely the end of human life.

There are those who claim that almost 40% are lost in the first week. If this is so, it would mean that there is a mortality rate of almost 40% in the first week of life. This is not relevant to the question of whether or not this is human life — any more than infant mortality is a justification for infanticide, or death in old age justifies euthanasia, or the death toll on the roads is an argument in favor of capital punishment. All it means is that the mortality rate in the first week of life may be 40%. (See table below for one measured estimate.)

HUMAN MORTALITY RATE, ESTIMATED 1983

Total fertilization:	10,000,000		
			Normal
— pre implantation loss	3,800,000	46%	mortality
— spontenous miscarriages	800,000		rate
Destined to be born:	5,600,000		
			Artificial
— Live births	3,600,000	33%	mortality
— Induced abortion	1,800,000		rate
After birth:			
— deaths in first month	30,000	1.2%	Mortality
— deaths in first year	50,000	0.7%	rate

Adapted from *Colloquy,*
Dorsey Labs, May 1980

I've heard the fertilized ovum described as only a blueprint. What of this comparison?

The blueprint of your home is merely the plan for your home. After using this instruction sheet to build your house, you can throw the blueprint away. It has not become the house. The fertilized ovum is not the blueprint, but is, in fact, the house in miniature. It, itself, will grow into the house in time. It is, in toto, the house already. Your home was built piece by piece until it ultimately assumed a shape which could be identified as a house. The tiny human, who you once were, developed into the adult you now are, but you were there *totally* at conception. All you needed to become the adult you now are was nutrition, oxygen, and time.

But it is so small. How can it be human yet?

If the only scientific instruments you use are your own unaided eyes, then a common judgment that you might make would be that "it isn't human until it looks human." We do have microscopes, ultrasonic movies, stethoscopes, and genetic knowledge now, all of which go far beyond the limited knowledge obtained by sight alone. To base your opinion solely on what you see, rather than upon what science is capable of telling you, isn't very rational.

What of a cell from some part of a person's body which can be kept alive in a tissue culture, either separated from his living body or maintained after that person has died. Does this not upset the concept of the fertilized ovum as a human life?

No. Those cells were a part of a complete human body and can only reproduce themselves as a specific type of cell. The fertilized ovum is not a part of another body, but is a whole body him or herself. It (he or she) will not merely reproduce, but is, in totality, a complete human being and will grow into a full adult if given time. Any one of hundreds of millions or billions of these cells in a human's body can die and we do not say that that human has died. When a single fertilized ovum cell dies, however, the entire new human being dies.

The other important difference is that the fertilized ovum, which subdivides and multiplies into many cells, moves immediately in the direction of specialized and differing parts, which are organized as a single unified complex being. Cells from parts of an adult human body in a tissue culture can only reproduce their own kind and cannot go on to develop differing specialized parts.

Wouldn't a successful human clone upset this reasoning?

First, there has never been a human clone. It may well be that man, the highest species, can never be successfully cloned. However, even granting that possibility, the clone, at the first moment of his or her existence, would be an intact and complete human life. He or she would be, in effect, the identical twin of the donor human, but of a different age. Being a total human, this living human would, in justice, be due the same protection of the law as the older donor human.

R. McKinnelly, Professor of Genetics and Cell Biology at the University of Minnesota, who does frog cloning, has said, "I never expect to witness the construction of carbon copy humans. I do not believe that nuclear [the cell nucleus] transplantation for the purpose of producing human beings will ever routinely occur."

R. McKinnelly, *Cloning*,
University of Minnesota Press, 1979, p. 102

Can't we consider the developing embryo a form of plant or animal life which only becomes human at some later state of development?

Definitely not! The fertilized seed or ovum of a plant, or an animal, or of a human, at the time of fertilization and beginning growth, already is — in totality — that plant, animal, or human. Because of our present scientific knowledge of chromosome and gene structure and because of the intricate genetic programming that we are now aware of, we know that a plant can only develop into what it already is — that is, a plant. An animal, a dog, for instance, can only develop into a dog and a specific species of that dog. All this is predetermined and already exists in totality when fertilization occurs. The same is true of a human.

But can you then call an acorn an oak tree?

That is like saying "can you call an infant an adult?" Rather, you must ask "are they both complete oaks?" Yes they are, all the acorn needs to develop into an adult tree is time and nutrition.

What of twins?

Non-identical twins are two separate individuals created by the union of two eggs and two sperm. Identical twins, however, occur when one fertilized ovum or zygote apparently splits into two, after which each of the two divided parts (each now a zygote in itself) grows independently in the very same manner toward full development and maturity as the average single zygote will. This occurs sometime between fertilization and implantation, but never after implantation.

Can we say, then, that one living human being (zygote) can split into two living human beings (identical twins)?

Scientific opinion is far from unanimous about how to consider this. One way of considering it is that the original human zygote, in splitting in half (whatever exactly happens, we don't know), can be considered, in effect, the parent of the new human being. This might be a form of parthenogenesis, or non-sexual reproduction. We know that this does occur in certain forms of plant and animal life. We could postulate this type of process to explain identical twinning in a human.

The other possibility is that the existing human being, in splitting, dies, to give new life to two new identical human beings like himself (herself).

What is crucial to either of these explanations is that, at the time when a total human being exists, he or she should be recognized as such and given all rights due other living human beings.

But the sperm has life. The ovum has life. Why is either of these lives any different than when the two join and become a fertilized ovum?

The sperm has life, but not an independent life; it shares in the life of the body of the father. The sperm is genetically identified as a cell of the father's body. It has reached the endpoint of its maturation. It cannot reproduce itself. It is destined to fertilize an ovum or to die. It is at the end of the line.

The ovum has life, but not an independent life; it shares in the life of the body of the mother. The ovum is genetically identified as a cell of the mother's body. It has reached the endpoint of its maturation. It cannot reproduce itself. Its destiny? To be fertilized or die. It, too, is at the end of the line.

But when sperm and ovum join, there is created at that time a new living being; a being who has never before existed in the history of the world and never again will exist; a being not at the end of the line, but at the dawn of existence; a being completely intact and containing within himself or herself the totality of everything that that being will ever be; a being moving forward in an orderly process of growth and maturation, destined to live inside the mother for almost nine months and for as many as a hundred years outside.

Will you cite some scientific authorities as to human life beginning at fertilization?

In 1981 the U.S. Senate considered Senate Bill #158, the "Human Life Bill." Extensive hearings (eight days, 57 witnesses) were conducted by Senator John East. National and international authorities testified. We quote from the official Senate report, 97th Congress, S-158:

> "Physicians, biologists, and other scientists agree that conception [they defined fertilization and conception to be the same] marks the beginning of the life of a human being — a being that is alive and is a member of the human species. There is overwhelming agreement on this point in countless medical, biological, and scientific writings."
>
> Report, Subcommittee on Separation of Powers to
> Senate Judiciary Committee S-158, 97th Congress,
> 1st Session 1981, p. 7

On pages 7-9, the report lists a "limited sample" of 13 medical textbooks, all of which state categorically that the life of an individual human begins at conception.

Then, on pages 9-10, the report quotes several outstanding authorities who testified personally:

- Professor J. Lejeune, Paris, discoverer of the chromosome pattern of Down's Syndrome: "Each individual has a very neat beginning, at conception."

- Professor W. Bowes, University of Colorado: Beginning of human life? — "at conception."

- Professor H. Gordon, Mayo Clinic: "It is an established fact that human life begins at conception."

- Professor M. Matthews-Roth, Harvard University: "It is scientifically correct to say that individual human life begins at conception."

But Dr. Leon Rosenberg, from Yale University, and others said otherwise!

Dr. Rosenberg did state that he knew of no scientific evidence showing when actual human life begins. But, he then defined human life in a philosophic way, and spoke to a value judgment.

To quote the Senate report (on page 11):

"Those witnesses who testified that science cannot say whether unborn children are human beings were speaking in every instance to the value question rather than the scientific question. No witness raised any evidence to refute the biological fact that from the moment of human conception there exists a distinct individual being who is alive and is of the human species."

Even though Dr. Rosenberg and others used the word, "science," they did not mean biologic science. Rather, they were speaking of their philosophic beliefs such as what Dr. Rosenberg called, "the complex quality of humanness" (Hearings, S-158, 24 April at 25).

This confusion of provable natural biologic science with value judgments based upon non-provable theories and beliefs must be shown at every opportunity to be two entirely different ways of reasoning.

How about other proof?

See the First International Symposium on Abortion, which concluded:

> "The changes occurring between implantation, a six-weeks embryo, a six-months fetus, a one-week-old child, or a mature adult are merely stages of development and maturation.
>
> "The majority of our group could find no point in time between the union of sperm and egg, or at least the blastocyst stage, and the birth of the infant at which point we could say that this was not a human life."

Willke & Willke, *Handbook on Abortion*, (1971, 1975, 1979 Editions), Ch. 3, Cincinnati: Hayes Publishing Co.

But what if a person would still sincerely doubt that this is human life in the womb?

Even if a person did doubt the presence of actual human life in the uterus at a particular time, what would be the fully human way to go? Perhaps a guide would be how we have always treated other human life when there has been a doubt that it exists. Would we not resolve a doubt in favor of life? We do not bury those who are doubtfully dead. We work frantically to help rescue entombed miners, a child lost in the mountains, or a person under a collapsed building. Does a hunter shoot until he knows that it is a deer and not another man? We suggest that the truly human way of thinking would be to give life the benefit of the doubt.

But isn't "conception" different from "fertilization?"

Ever since its discovery 150 years ago, both words were used to mean the union of sperm and ovum. In the 1960s the U.S. Food and Drug Administration and the American College of OB & GYN agreed to attempt to redefine "conception" to mean implantation.

"Conception is the implantation of the blastocyst. It is not synonymous with fertilization."

E. Hughes, ed., *OB & GYN Terminology,*
Philadelphia: F. A. Davis, 1972

This made it possible to call an intrauterine device a "contraceptive" even though it was an abortificient (see chapter 29).

But in 1982, lengthy hearings in the U.S. Senate and the two-volume report of the Human Life Bill defined "conception" and used it exclusively to mean the time of union of sperm and ovum.

Human Life Bill, U.S. Senate Common Judiciary, Subcommittee of
Separation of Powers, 97th Congress, S-158, April-June 1982,
Serial No. J-97-16

Did you "come from" a fertilized ovum? No, you once were a fertilized ovum who grew and developed into the child or adult you are today. Nothing has been added to the fertilized ovum who you once were except nutrition.

CHAPTER 8

Development in the Womb
The Process of Growth

When does implantation occur?
The tiny human implants himself or herself in the nutrient lining of the womb at one week of life.

And then?
At ten days, this tiny living human male or female sends a chemical hormonal message out into the mother's body, which stops her menstrual periods. Later, it is this tiny passenger who causes her breasts to enlarge in preparation for nursing, softens her pelvic bones to prepare for labor, and, without question, sets his or her birthday. The onset of labor is a unilateral fetal decision (see chapter 7, p. 3).

When does the heart begin to beat?
At 18 days, and by 21 days it is pumping, through a closed circulatory system, blood whose type is different from that of the mother.

J. M. Tanner, G. R. Taylor, and the
Editors of Time-Life Books, *Growth*,
New York: Life Science Library, 1965, p. 64

When is the brain functioning?

At 40 days. Brain waves have been recorded at 40 days on the Electroencephalogram (EEG).

H. Hamlin, "Life or Death by EEG,"
JAMA, Oct. 12, 1964, p. 120

Brain function, as measured on the Electroencephalogram, "appears to be reliably present in the fetus at about eight weeks gestation," or six weeks after conception.

J. Goldenring, "Development of the Fetal Brain,"
New England Jour. of Med., Aug. 26, 1982, p. 564

Only several generations ago, doctors used the ending of respiration to measure the end of human life. This is no longer true, for the use of artificial ventilators is common.

Only one generation ago, doctors were using the ending of the heartbeat to measure the end of human life. This is no longer true, for now the heart can be stopped and restarted for different operations. It also may stop during a heart attack and sometimes can be restarted.

Today, the definitive and final measure of the end of human life is brain death. This happens when there is irreversible cessation of total brain function. The final scientific measurement of this is the permanent ending of brain waves.

- Since all authorities accept that the end of an individual's life is measured by the ending of his brain function (as measured by brain waves on the EEG), would it not be logical for them to at least agree that that individual's life began with the onset of that same human brain function as measured by brain waves recorded on that same instrument?

When does the developing baby first move?

"In the sixth to seventh weeks.... If the area of the lips is gently stroked, the child responds by bending the upper body to one side and making a quick backward motion with his arms. This is called a 'total pattern response' because it involves most of the body, rather than a local part."

L. B. Arey, *Developmental Anatomy* (6th ed.),
Philadelphia: W. B. Sanders Co., 1954

At eight weeks, "if we tickle the baby's nose, he will flex his head backwards away from the stimulus."

A. Hellgers, M.D., "Fetal Development, 31,"
Theological Studies, vol. 3, no. 7, 1970, p. 26

But pregnant women don't "feel life" until four or five months!

The inside of the uterus has no feeling. The baby has to be almost a foot long and weigh about one pound (454 gm.) before he or she is large enough to brace a shoulder against one wall and kick hard enough against the opposite wall to dent it outward. Then the mother feels it because the outside of the uterus is covered by a sensitive peritoneal surface.

How many weeks are there in a pregnancy and how do you measure them?

There are 40 weeks. We measure a pregnancy from the time the ovum begins to grow, that is, at the start of a woman's menstrual period. After about two weeks of growth, the egg is released from the ovary. Fertilization can then occur. This is about two weeks before her next period is due. Four of the 40 weeks have already elapsed at the time she misses her first period.

Gestational age dates from the first day of the mother's last menstrual period. Actual age of the baby dates from conception.

When do teeth form?

All 20 milk-teeth buds are present at six and a half weeks.

"Life Before Birth,"
Life Magazine, Apr. 30, 1965, p. 10

But, early on, this is just a simple fish-like creature.

Not so.

"The body of the unborn baby is more complex than ours. The preborn baby has several extra parts to his body which he needs only so long as he lives inside his mother. He has his own space capsule, the amniotic sac. He has his own lifeline, the umbilical cord, and he has his own root system, the placenta. These all belong to the baby himself, not to his mother. They are all developed from his original cell."

Day & Liley, The Secret World of a Baby,
Random House, 1968, p. 13

What is the development at seven to eight weeks?

The baby's stomach secretes gastric juice by eight weeks. Now we can listen to the tiny one's heartbeat on an ultrasonic stethoscope. These are now common in doctors' offices and on hospital wards. They are *never* used in abortion facilities, however, as this information is universally withheld from mothers prior to abortion. Abortionists know that if they tell women there already is a heartbeat — and certainly if they would let her listen to the heartbeat — some mothers would change their minds. The actual sounds of an eight-week-old baby's heartbeat are available on tape from Cincinnati Right to Life, 8228 Winton Rd., Cincinnati, OH 45231 ($3.00).

When are all his body systems present?

By eight weeks (two months).

Hooker & Davenport, The Prenatal Origin of Behavior,
University of Kansas Press, 1952

When can the baby start thumb sucking?

This is often seen on *Realtime* ultrasound movies of babies as early as eight weeks. The most dramatic accounting of movement very early has been recorded as follows:

"Eleven years ago, while giving an anesthetic for a ruptured tubal pregnancy (at two months), I was handed what I believed to be the smallest human being ever seen. The embryo sac was intact and transparent. Within the sac was a tiny (one-third inch) human male swimming extremely vigorously in the amniotic fluid, while attached to the wall by the umbilical cord. This tiny human was perfectly developed with long, tapering fingers, feet and toes. It was almost transparent as regards the skin, and the delicate arteries and veins were prominent to the ends of the fingers.

"The baby was extremely alive and swam about the sac approximately one time per second with a natural swimmers stroke. This tiny human did not look at all like the photos and drawings of 'embryos' which I have seen, nor did it look like the few embryos I have been able to observe since then, obviously because this one was alive.

"When the sac was opened, the tiny human immediately lost its life and took on the appearance of what is accepted as the appearance of an embryo at this stage (blunt extremeties, etc.)."

P. E. Rockwell, M.D., Director of Anesthesiology,
Leonard Hospital, Troy, New York, U.S. Supreme Court.,
Markle vs. Abele, 72-56, 72-730, p. 11

At nine to ten weeks, he squints, swallows, moves his tongue, and if you stroke his palm, will make a tight fist.

By nine weeks he will "bend his fingers round an object in the palm of his hand."

Valman & Pearson, "What the Fetus Feels,"
British Med. Jour., Jan. 26, 1980

When does he start to breathe?

"By 11 to 12 weeks (3 months), he is breathing fluid steadily and continues so until birth. At birth, he will breathe air. He does not drown by breathing fluid within his mother, because he obtains his oxygen from his umbilical cord. This breathing develops the organs of respiration."

"Life Before Birth,"
Life Magazine, Apr. 30, 1965, p. 13

"Maternal cigarette smoking during pregnancy decreases the frequency of fetal breathing by 20%. The 'well documented' higher incidence of prematurity, stillbirth, and slower development of reading skill may be related to this decrease."

F. Manning, "Meeting of Royal College of Physicians & Surgeons," *Family Practice News*, March 15, 1976

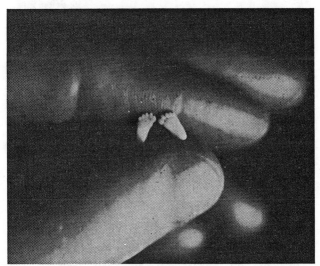

Tiny human feet at 10 weeks development.

"The measurement of fetal breathing movements may soon provide an indication of fetal well being that is at least as useful as the evaluation of the fetal heart rate."

"In the 11th week of gestation fetal breathing is irregular and episodic. As gestation continues, the breathing movements become more vigorous and rapid."

C. Dawes, "Fetal Breathing: Indication of Well Being," *Family Practice News*, Mar. 16, 1976, p. 6

When can he swallow?
At 11 weeks.

Valman & Pearson, *British Med. Jour.*, p. 7

What of detailed development, like fingernails and eyelashes?

Fingernails are present by 11 to 12 weeks; eyelashes by 16 weeks.

At what point are all his body systems working?

By 11 weeks.

"Life Before Birth,"
Life Magazine, Apr. 30, 1965, p. 13

How does the size of the baby increase in weight?

At 12 weeks (three months) she weighs one ounce; at 16 weeks, six ounces; and at 20 weeks (four months), approximately one pound (454 gm.).

When is taste present?

"Taste buds are working between 13 and 15 weeks gestation" (11 to 13 weeks after conception).

Mistretta & Bradley, *Taste in Utero,*
1977, p. 62

How about hearing?

"Auditory sense is present in the infant 24 weeks before birth [14 weeks after conception]. This involves brain functioning and memory patterns."

M. Clemens, "5th International Congress Psychosomatic,"
OB & GYN, Rome: Medical Tribune, Mar. 22, 1978, p. 7

Although the watery environment in which he lives presents small opportunity for crying, which does require air, the unborn knows how to cry, and given a chance to do so, he will. A doctor

... "injected an air bubble into the baby's amniotic sac and then took x-rays. It so happened that the air bubble covered the baby's face. The whole procedure had no doubt given the little fellow quite a bit of jostling about, and the moment that he had air to inhale and exhale they heard the clear sound of a protesting wail emitting from the uterus. Late that same night, the mother awakened her doctor with a telephone call, to report that when she lay down to sleep the air bubble got over the baby's head again, and he was crying so loudly he was keeping both her and her husband awake. The doctor advised her to prop herself upright with pillows so that the air could not reach the baby's head, which was by now in the lower part of the uterus."

Day & Liley, *Modern Motherhood,*
Random House, 1969, pp. 50-51

Did Dr. Liley, the "Father of Fetology," think the tiny being was human?

Dr. Liley, who did the first fetal blood transfusion in the womb, said that seven days after fertilization,

"... the young individual, in command of his environment and destiny with a tenacious purpose, implants in the spongy lining and with a display of physiological power, suppresses his mother's menstrual period. This is his home for the next 270 days and to make it habitable, the embryo develops a placenta and a protective capsule of fluid for himself. He also solves, single-handed, the homograft problem, that dazzling feat by which foetus and mother, although immunological foreigners who could not exchange skin grafts nor safely receive blood from each other, nevertheless tolerate each other in parabiosis for nine months.

"We know that he moves with a delightful easy grace in his buoyant world, that foetal comfort determines foetal position. He is responsive to pain and touch and cold and sound and light. He drinks his amniotic fluid, more if it is artificially sweetened, less it if is given an unpleasant taste. He gets hiccups and sucks his thumb. He wakes and sleeps. He gets bored with repetitive signals but can be taught to be alerted by a first signal for a second different one.

51

And, finally, he determines his birthday, for unquestionably, the onset of labour is a unilateral decision of the foetus.

"This, then, is the foetus we know and, indeed, we each once were. This is the foetus we look after in modern obstetrics, the same baby we are caring for before and after birth, who before birth can be ill and need diagnosis and treatment just like any other patient."

A. Liley, *A Case Against Abortion*, Liberal Studies
Whitcombe & Tombs, Ltd., 1971

What measure would you use to define Human Life?

We would ask:
* Is this being alive?

Yes. He has the characteristics of life. That is, he can reproduce his own cells and develop them into a specific pattern of maturity and function.

* Is this being human?

Yes. This is a unique being, distinguishable totally from any other living organism, completely human in all of his or her characteristics, including the human 46 chromosomal pattern, and can develop only into a fully mature human.

* Is this being complete?

Yes. Nothing new will be added from the time of union of sperm and egg until the death of the old man or woman except growth and development of what is already there at the beginning. All he needs is time to develop and mature.

Does the unborn baby dream?

Using ultrasound techniques, it was first shown that REM (rapid eye movements) which are characteristic of active dream states have been demonstrated at 23 weeks.

J. Birnhaltz, "The Development of Human Fetal Eye Movement Patterns,"
Science, 1981, vol. 213, pp. 679-681

Recently, REM have been recorded 17 weeks after conception.

S. Levi, Brugman University of Brussels,
American Medical Association News, February 1, 1983

Since REM are characteristic of dream states *after* birth, researchers are asking if the unborn child also dreams?

Does he/she think?

In adults, when we contemplate a physical move or action from a resting state, our heart rate accelerates several seconds before the motion. Similarly, the fetal baby's heart rate speeds up six to ten seconds prior to fetal movement. Is this conscious thought and planning?

N. Lauerson & H. Hochberg, "Does the Fetus Think?"
JAMA, vol 247, no. 23, July 18, 1982

"We now know that the unborn child is an aware, reacting human being who from the sixth month on (and perhaps earlier) leads an active emotional life.

"The fetus can, on a primitive level, even learn in utero.

"Whether he ultimately sees himself and, hence, acts as a sad or happy, aggressive or meek, secure or anxiety-ridden person depends, in part, on the messages he gets about himself in the womb."

T. Verney & J. Kelly, *The Secret Life of the Unborn Child*,
Delta Books, 1981, p. 12

"At eight weeks of life a tapping stimulus on the amniotic sac results in arm movements ... the primitive brain receives the stimulus, selects a response and transmits the response as a signal to the arm."

M. Rosen, "Learning Before Birth,"
Harpers Magazine, April, 1978

You mean that the unborn baby's emotions can be affected?

This is probably true.

"We know already that even embryonic nervous tissue is 'open' to maternal communication via brain chemicals called 'neurotransmitters.' This is a finding with enormous implications. It means that the mother's emotional state can affect the unborn almost from conception onward. Even before the baby can hear in the womb, or think consciously, it is capable of sensing discord between its parents. If the mother is in constant turmoil, its own environment will be tainted by the biochemistry of fear and hostility, grief, and anger."

Shettles & Varick, *Rites of Life*,
Grand Rapids: Zondervan, 1983, pp. 87-89

At four and one-half months, a very bright light on a woman's abdomen will cause the baby to slowly move its hand to a position shielding the eyes.

Loud music will cause the baby to cover its ears.

A woman in an unhappy marriage has a 237% greater risk of bearing a child with physical and psychological problems than a woman in a secure relationship.

Verney & J. Kelly, *The Secret Life of the Unborn Child*,
Delta Books, 1981, p. 49

Agreeing with Dr. Liley, Dr. W. Freud (grandson of Sigmund Freud), observed 10,000 ultrasound visualizations and reported, "It looks as if the fetus has a lot of intentionality." He also once saw unborn twins fighting.

1st International Congress, Pre & Peri Natal Psychology,
Toronto, July 8-10, 1983

What is birth?

Birth is the emergence of the infant from the mother's womb, the severing of the umbilical cord, and the beginning of the child's existence physically detached from the mother's body. The only change that occurs at birth is a change in the external life support system of the child. The child is no different before birth than after, except that he has changed his method of feeding and obtaining oxygen. Before birth, nutrition and oxygen were obtained from the mother through the baby's umbilical cord. After birth, oxygen is obtained from his own lungs and nutrition through his own stomach, if he is mature enough to be nourished that way. If he is quite premature, nourishment would continue through our present reasonably sophisticated external life support systems in the form of intravenous feeding, which is similar to the umbilical cord feeding from the mother.

Note: Four-Color Photos of Developing Babies at back of Book

CHAPTER 9

Viability

What is viability?

It is that stage of fetal development when the baby is "potentially able to live outside the mother's womb [that is, can survive], albeit with artificial help."

Roe vs. Wade
U.S. Supreme Court, 1973, p. 45

The U.S. Supreme Court used viability as a measure of humanness. Do you agree with this measure?

No. Their position was completely untenable.

Why was viability at 30 weeks? Why is it now at 20 weeks? Why will it be ten weeks someday? The babies haven't changed. What has changed has been the development of better life support systems around the baby. The doctors and nurses of today have more knowledge, and their equipment is far more advanced.

Viability is a measure of the sophistication of the life support systems around the baby; it does not measure the humanness or aliveness of the baby himself or herself.

But some laws held abortion legal until the baby was "viable." What does this mean?

Most people define viable as "capable of independent

existence." We believe this should be stricken from the law books. By this definition, even a seven-pound baby after birth is not viable. Leave this healthy full-term child alone and she will die in a few days from neglect. She is not capable of independent existence, but depends totally on the life support given her by her mother.

So when *is* a child capable of independent existence?

Certainly not before she's old enough to go to school. And we can make a pretty good case for her not being capable of it much before she's a teenager.

Viability should not determine legal rights?

The frightening aspect of using viability as a dimension of someone's right to life is quickly apparent when we consider that, by this standard, a newborn baby or a child of any age with a handicap is also not "viable." By the above criterion, the senile old person rendered incompetent by a stroke, the completely psychotic individual, or even the quadriplegic war veteran is not "viable," since they are not capable of independent existence. Some of these persons also do not have mental "viability." To make a judgment of an unborn child's right to live or not in our society by his mental or physical competence, rather than merely by the fact that he is human and alive, brings only too close the state's determination of a person's right to continued life as measured by one's mental or physical competence — or whatever the current price tag is.

How do you measure age of survival?

The age of a premature baby at birth is measured by age from first day of last menstrual period (LMP). Weight is also a measure when the dates are uncertain, a 20- to 22-week-old baby has an average weight of 500-600 gm (1 lb., 2 oz. to 1 lb., 5 oz.) with "normals" varying from 400 to 700 gm (14 oz. to 1 lb., 9 oz.). There are also other maturation factors that are used.

With the widespread establishment of premature intensive care units, the age of survival has dropped dramatically. For example, in 1950 it was rare for a baby to survive if born at 30 weeks (A full-term pregnancy is 40 weeks). Today, survivability has occurred in infants born as early as 20 weeks premature. Tomorrow, babies born even more prematurely will survive.

What is the "survival rate?"

Survival rate is a measure of the percentage of chance for survival at a particular age. The younger the baby, the lower the rate. At the University of Pennsylvania, the survival rate in the years 1944-77 was 40% for babies with birth weights between 750 to 1,000 gm (1 lb., 10 oz. to 2 lbs., 2 oz.), with only 6% having major neurologic abnormalities.

Kuma et al., *Pediatrics 66*, vol. 3, Sept. 1980

At Vanderbilt, University of Tennessee, for the years 1978-81, 39% of 500 to 750 gm infants survived and 69% of those weighing 751 to 1,000 gm survived.

Barnett et al., "Effect of Type of Delivery on Neonatal Outcome," *JAMA*, vol. 250, no. 5, Aug. 5, 1983

At the Good Samaritan Hospital Regional Prenatal Center in Cincinnati, the survival rate was:

500-750 gm
  (1 lb, 1-5 oz.-1 lb., 10 oz.) 30%
750-1000 gm
  (1 lb., 10 oz.-2 lb., 3 oz.) 75%
1000-1250 gm
  (2 lb., 3 oz.-2 lb., 12 oz.) 88%
1250-1500 gm
  (2 lb., 12 oz.-3 lb., 5 oz.) 100%

K. Weddig. Personal communication with author. Dec. 1984

Only six percent abnormal?

Extremely low birth-weight infants have "a remarkably favorable outcome," reported Dr. F. Bennett of the University of Washington in Seattle. Of sixteen infants weighing 800 gm (1 lb., 12 oz.) or less at birth, only one turned out to have a handicap "that would interfere with his vocational choice and independence."

F. Bennett, *Family Practice News*, June 1, 1982

"It is reassuring that the proportion of children with congenital abnormalities, or developmental delays of all types of severity combined, decreased and that the gains in reducing mortality have apparently not been at the expense of enlarging the pool of children with such impairments."

Jour. of Pediatrics, vol. 72, 1983, pp. 408-415

"Preterm infants of less than 1,000 gm (2 lbs., 2 oz.) do not appear to have significantly higher incidence of severe developmental abnormalities in the first 18 months of life than do 1,000 to 1,750 gm babies."

M. Hoffman-Williamson, Amer. Academy for Cerebral Palsy and Developmental Med., Chicago, 1983

But is the cost worth it?

The cost is high. Back in 1979, Dr. T. McCarthy in Denver reported that the mean cost for 500 to 999 gm infants was $25,000. The cost for infants born weighing between 2,000 to 2,499 gm was only $5,000.

J. T. McCarthy, et al., "Who Pays the Bill for Neonatal Intensive Care?" *Jour. of Pediatrics*, vol. 95, 1979, p. 755

A Chicago study of infants born before 34 weeks showed that they averaged costs amounting to $10,000, if born in a perinatal center, but $18,000, if transferred in from an outlying hospital.

C. L. Anderson, "An Analysis of Maternal Transport within a Suburban Metropolitan Region," *Amer. Jour. of OB/GYN*, 1981

But what does a coronary bypass cost? How much for a kidney transplant or joint replacements, or extensive cancer treatment? Compare the total cost of these and divide the number of years of life expectancy. Then take the cost of saving the preemie, divide by a normal life expectancy of 80 or more years and, even on a strict cost-benefit analysis, we get a real bargain. If the expense today would be $80,000 for such an infant, that would "cost out" at just $1,000 per year.

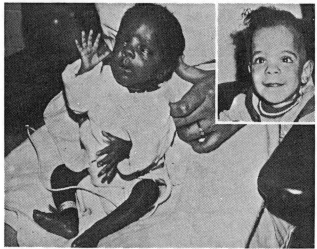

Baby Marcus Richardson, born 1-1-72 at Cincinnati General Hospital exactly 20 weeks (4½ months) from the first day of his mother's last menstrual period. An entirely normal child, he is shown 10 weeks after birth and 10 months after birth.

What about very early survivors?

Since single cases are not usually reported in professional journals, we turn to the daily press for data on these little ones. There were a few very young survivors as early as ten years ago. These included:

Alicia Ponce — 24 weeks — 644 gm — April '74 — (Associated Press)

Tascha Hudson — 23 weeks — 580 gm — March '74 — (Brooke Army Hosp.)

Tracy LaBranch — 22 weeks, 1 day — 538 gm — March '72 — (Battle Creek Enquirer)

Suzanne South — 21 weeks, 2 days — 644 gm —
  July '71 —(Bethesda Hosp., Cincinnati)
Kelly Thorman— 21 weeks — 596 gm — March '71
  — (St. Vincent Hosp. Toledo)
Marcus Richardson — 19 weeks, 6 days — 780 gm
  — Jan. '72 — (University Hosp., Cincinnati)

More recently there have been increasing numbers
reported:

Simmonne Jayette — 23 weeks — 595 gm — April
  '78 — (Montreal Jewish General Hospital)
Melissa Comer — 20 weeks — 450 gm — Dec. '83
  — (Sault Ste. Marie Hosp., Cincinnati Enquirer)
Ernestine Hudgins — 22 weeks — 484 gm — Feb.
  '83 — (San Diego, Washington Post)
Mimi Faulkner — 23 weeks — 484 gm — Nov. '78
  — (San Diego, Boston Herald)
Melissa Murray — 22 weeks — 510 gm — June '83
  — (Victoria, Texas — Houston Post)

At this writing, an inquiry in your authors' city revealed
two preemies in one hospital, both born at 24 weeks,
weighing 580 gm and 608 gm at birth. Both progressed
normally and survived without apparent abnormalities.

H. Falciglia, Prof. of Pediatrics, University of Cinn. College of
Med., Personal communications with authors.
Apr. 1984 and Dec. 1984

The age and weight don't always track together?

There is a variance, just as with children and adults, but
a much narrower one. Dr. L. Lubchenco, University of
Colorado, has been the recognized authority in preparing
most of the charts used. Babies can be small for stated age
or "runts," if malnourished. They can also be large for
stated age, as was baby Marcus Richardson in the list
above, but still fall within the 90 percentile range on the
charts.

How tiny can one presently survive?

Here is a list of some infants born who weighed under one pound (454 gm):

Jamie Baire — 24 weeks — 446 gm — Oct. '83 — (Garfield Hospital, Monterey, CA)

Chaya Snyder — 26 weeks — 420 gm — Oct. '79 — (Albert Einstein Hospital, NYC)

Melissa Comer — 20 weeks — 450 gm — Dec. '83 — (Sault Ste. Marie Hospital, Cincinnati Enquirer)

Russell Williams — 26 weeks — 450 gm — Nov. '79 — (Long Beach, CA Memorial Hospital)

Will the survival age ever drop under 20 weeks?

It's only a question of time and technology. Some day there will be artificial placentas and then who knows how early a preemie will be able to survive?

CHAPTER 10

Fetal Pain

"When the lives of the unborn are snuffed out, they often feel pain, pain that is long and agonizing."
President Ronald Reagan to National Religious
Broadcasters, *New York Times,* Jan. 31, 1984

That statement by President Reagan was denied by some!

Yes, but, then it was confirmed as accurate by a well-documented statement from an auspicious group of professors, including pain specialists and two past presidents of the American College of Obstetrics and Gynecology. The text of their letter follows:

February 13, 1984

President Ronald Reagan
The White House
Washington, DC

Mr. President:

As physicians, we, the undersigned, are pleased to associate ourselves with you in drawing the attention of people across the nation to the humanity and sensitivity of the human unborn.

That the unborn, the prematurely born, and the new-born of the human species is a highly complex, sentient, functioning, individual organism is established scientific fact. That the human unborn and newly born do respond to stimuli is also established beyond any reasonable doubt.

The ability to feel pain and respond to it is clearly not a phenomenon that develops de novo at birth. Indeed, much of enlightened modern obstetrical practice and procedure seeks to minimize sensory deprivation of, and sensory insult to, the fetus during, at, and after birth.

Over the last 18 years, real time ultrasonography, fetoscopy, study of the fetal EKG (electrocardiogram) and fetal EEG (electroencephalogram) have demonstrated the remarkable responsiveness of the human fetus to pain, touch, and sound. That the fetus responds to changes in light intensity within the womb, to heat, to cold, and to taste (by altering the chemical nature of the fluid swallowed by the fetus) has been exquisitely documented in the pioneering work of the late Sir William Liley — the father of fetology.

Observations of the fetal electrocardiogram and the increase in fetal movements in saline abortions indicate that the fetus experiences discomfort as it dies. Indeed, one doctor who, the *New York Times* wrote, "conscientiously performs" saline abortions stated, "When you inject the saline, you often see an increase in fetal movements, it's horrible."

We state categorically that no finding of modern fetology invalidates the remarkable conclusion drawn after a lifetime of research by the late Professor Arnold Gesell of Yale University. In The Embryology of Behavior: The Beginnings of the Human Mind (1945, Harper Bros.), Dr. Gesell wrote, "and so by the close of the first trimester the fetus is a sentient, moving being. We need not speculate as to the nature of his psychic attributes, but we may assert that the organization of his psychosomatic self is well under way."

Mr. President, in drawing attention to the capability of the human fetus to feel pain, you stand on firmly established ground.

Respectfully,

Dr. Richard T. F. Schmidt
Past President, A.C.O.G.
Professor of Ob/Gyn
University of Cincinnati
Cincinnati, OH
Dr. Vincent Collins
Professor of Anesthesiology
Northwestern University
University of Illinois Medical Center
Dr. John G. Masterson
Clinical Professor of Ob/Gyn
Northwestern University
Dr. Bernard Nathanson, F.A.C.O.G.
Clinical Assistant Professor of Ob/Gyn
Cornell University
Dr. Denis Cavanaugh, F.A.C.O.G.
Professor of Ob/Gyn
University of South Florida
Dr. Watson Bowes, F.A.C.O.G.
Professor of Material and Fetal Medicine
University of North Carolina
Dr. Byron Oberst
Assistant Clinical Professor of Pediatrics
University of Nebraska
Dr. Eugene Diamond
Professor of Pediatrics
Strict School of Medicine
Chicago, IL
Dr. Thomas Potter
Associate Clinical Professor of Pediatrics
New Jersey Medical College
Dr. Lawrence Dunegan
Instructor of Clinical Pediatrics
University of Pittsburgh
Dr. Melvin Thornton
Professor of Clinical Pediatrics
University of Texas (San Antonio)
Dr. Norman Vernig
Assistant Professor of Pediatrics
University of Minnesota (St. Paul)
Dr. Jerome Shen
Clinical Professor of Pediatrics
St. Louis University

Dr. Fred Hofmeister
Past President, A.C.O.G.
Professor of Ob/Gyn
University of Wisconsin (Milwaukee)
Dr. Matthew Bulfin, F.A.C.O.G.
Lauderdale by the Sea, FL
Dr. Jay Arena
Professor Emeritus of Pediatrics
Duke University
Dr. Herbert Nakata
Assistant Professor of Clinical Pediatrics
University of Hawaii
Dr. Robert Polley
Clinical Instructor of Pediatrics
University of Washington (Seattle)
Dr. David Foley
Professor of Ob/Gyn
University of Wisconsin (Milwaukee)
Dr. Anne Bannon, F.A.A.P.
Former Chief of Pediatrics
City Hospital (St. Louis)
Dr. John J. Brennan
Professor of Ob/Gyn
Medical College of Wisconsin
(Milwaukee)
Dr. Walter F. Watts
Assistant Professor of Ob/Gyn
Strict School of Medicine
Chicago, IL
Dr. G. C. Tom Nabors
Assistant Clinical Professor of Ob/Gyn
Southwestern Medical College
Dallas, TX
Dr. Konald Prem
Professor of Ob/Gyn
University of Minnesota (Minneapolis)
Dr. Alfred Derby, F.A.C.O.G.
Spokane, WA
Dr. Bernie Pisani, F.A.C.O.G.
President, NY State Medical Society
Professor of Ob/Gyn
New York University

But the unborn baby can't tell us that he or she feels pain.

Pain can be detected when nociceptors (pain receptors) discharge electrical impulses to the spinal cord and brain. These fire impulses outward, telling the muscles and body to react. These can be measured.

Mountcastle, *Medical Physiology*,
St. Louis: C. V. Mosby, pp. 391-427

The first detectable brain activity in response to noxious (pain) stimuli occurs in the thalamus between the
ninth and tenth weeks.

Reinis & Goldman, *The Development of the Brain,*
Thomas Publishers, 1980, pp. 223-235

But isn't pain mostly psychological?

There is also organic, or physiological pain which elic-
its a neurological response to pain.

P. Lubeskind, "Psychology & Physiology of Pain,
Amer. Review Psychology, vol. 28, 1977, p. 42

Some is reflex pain?

Yes. When you stick a baby with a diaper pin, she will
object. Her initial reflex recoil is exactly what happens in
the womb after eight weeks when the same child is pain-
fully stimulated.

Changes in heart rate and fetal movement also suggest
that intrauterine manipulations are painful to the fetus.

Volman & Pearson, "What the Fetus Feels,"
British Med. Jour., Jan. 26, 1980, pp. 233-234.

How have lawmakers reacted to this knowledge?

There have been bills introduced to require abortionists
to anesthetize the unborn baby before killing him or her.

M. Siljander, *Congressional Record,*
E609, Feb. 23, 1984

One early dramatic account was by Dr. R. Selzer of
Yale University. A needle had been inserted through the
mother's abdominal wall and into the four-month-old
baby's bag of waters when, suddenly, he related,

"... the hub of the needle in the woman's belly has
jerked. First to one side. Then to the other side. Once
more it wiggles, is *tugged*, like a fishing line nibbled by a
sunfish. It is the fetus that worries thus."

R. Selzer, "What I Saw in Abortion,"
Esquire, pp. 66-67

Give some more specific quotes.

"... as soon as pain mechanism is present in the fetus — possibly as early as day 45 — the methods used will cause pain. The pain is more substantial and lasts longer the later the abortion is. It is most severe and lasts longest when the method is salt poisoning.... They are undergoing their death agony."

Noonan, "The Experience of Pain," In *New Perspectives on Human Abortion*, Aletheia Books, 1981, p. 213

What of the "Nathanson" movie?

A *Realtime* ultrasound video tape and movie of a 12-week suction abortion is commercially available as, *The Silent Scream*, narrated by Dr. B. Nathanson, a former abortionist. It dramatically, but factually, shows the pre-born baby dodging the suction instrument time after time, while its heartbeat doubles in rate. When finally caught, its body being dismembered, the baby's mouth clearly opens wide — hence, the title (available from American Portrait Films, 1695 W. Crescent Ave., Suite 500, Anaheim, CA 92801). Proabortionists have attempted to discredit this film. A well documented paper refuting their charges is available from National Right to Life, 419 7th St. NW, Washington, DC 20004, $200 pp.

Pain? What of just comfort?

"One of the most uncomfortable ledges that the unborn can encounter is his mother's backbone. If he happens to be lying so that his own backbone is across hers [when the mother lies on her back], the unborn will wiggle around until he can get away from this highly disagreeable position."

M. Liley & B. Day, *Modern Motherhood*, Random House, 1969, p. 42

Give me more testimony verifying fetal pain.

"By 13- weeks, organic response to noxious stimuli occurs at all levels of the nervous system, from the pain receptors to the thalamus. Thus, at that point, the fetal organic response to pain is more than a reflexive response. It is an integrated physiological attempt to avert the noxious stimuli."

Wm. Matviuw, M.D., Diplomate, Amer. College of OB & GYN

"When doctors first began invading the sanctuary of the womb, they did not know that the unborn baby would react to pain in the same fashion as a child would. But they soon learned that he would."

Dr. A. Liley, Prof. of Fetology, University of Aukland, New Zealand

"Lip tactile response may be evoked by the end of the 7th week. At 11 weeks, the face and all parts of the upper and lower extremities are sensitive to touch. By 13.5 to 14 weeks, the entire body surface, except for the back and the top of the head, are sensitive to pain."

S. Reinis & J. Goldman,
The Development of the Brain

"The fetus needs to be heavily sedated. The changes in heart rate and increase in movement suggest that these stimuli are painful for the fetus. Certainly it cannot be comfortable for the fetus to have a scalp electrode implanted on his skin, to have blood taken from the scalp or to suffer the skull compression that may occur even with spontaneous delivery. It is hardly surprising that infants delivered by difficult forceps extraction act as if they have a severe headache."

Valman & Pearson, "What the Fetus Feels"
British Med. Jour., Jan. 26, 1980

"As early as eight to ten weeks gestation, and definitely by thirteen and a half weeks, the human fetus experiences organic pain." (See letter to President Reagan above.)

V. Collins, M.D., Diplomate and Fellow,
Amer. Board of Anesthesiologists

"Dilatation and evacuation, for example, where fetal tissue is progressively punctured, ripped and crushed, and which is done after 13 weeks when the fetus certainly responds to noxious stimuli, would cause organic pain in the fetus. Saline amnioinfusion, where a highly concentrated salt solution burns away the outer skin of the fetus, also qualifies as a noxious stimulus."

T. Sullivan, M.D., FAAP, Amer. Academy of Neurosurgeons

CHAPTER 11

In Vitro

What is In Vitro fertilization?

It involves giving a woman drugs to induce ovulation and then harvesting (collecting) those mature eggs through a laparoscope. The man masturbates to collect the semen. Then, the semen and ova are mixed in a dish, where fertilization may occur. Then the tiny, new embryonic human (humans) are put into the cavity of the woman's uterus with the hope that they will plant and grow.

What does Right to Life think of this?

Since RTL limits its official organizational policy to protecting human life already conceived, it has no official position on the "preliminaries." It does, however, totally object to the destruction of any of these tiny human lives once they exist. It, therefore, condemns the "pick of the litter" practice. This is when certain "concepti" (embryos) are discarded (killed) while others are planted. Since, probably, more living humans die even if implanted than in normal human intercourse and conception, RTL strongly objects to in vitro fertilization.

But these are not really humans yet, are they?

Wrong! The success of in vitro fertilization techniques has only added further proof that each human being is alive, sexed, intact, complete, human, and growing from the single cell stage. This tiny being *is* a complete human body.

To illustrate, let's assume that a new, tiny embryonic male human, from a black mother and father was planted in the womb of a white woman. The baby she would deliver, months later, would be the black son of those black parents. The white woman would have provided only nutrition and a home for the tiny unborn baby to grow and develop.

Human life, total and complete, begins at conception.

What of frozen embryos?

Preliminary thinking poses all kinds of moral objections. Since present technology involves the death of 50% of frozen embryos in the thawing process, it must be condemned.

J. Kennan, *USA Today,* October 25, 1984, p. 7A

The live birth of babies, who had been placed in wombs after they had been frozen and stored as embryos, has happened. The first ones are apparently normal.

What of embryo transplant?

This technique almost inevitably results in the direct killing of some of the live human embryonic male and female humans who are transplanted. One report had only two of twelve (or 16%) survive.

Bustillo et al., "Ovum Transfer in Infertile Women," *JAMA,* vol. 251, no. 9, Mar. 2, 1984

Another had 14% success.

Marshall & Merz, *Stock Breeding Technique Applied to Human Fertility, JAMA,* vol. 250, no. 10, Sept. 9, 1983, p. 1257

What of resultant abnormal humans?

If any of these techniques result in the conception and growth of babies with handicaps, their lives must be respected and protected just as yours and ours. The use of midtrimester amniocentesis or of chorionic villi sampling to detect those who are not perfect (in order to kill them) would be condemned.

What is chorionic villi sampling?

This sampling, or biopsy, is an exam which involves passing a small instrument through the cervix, in early pregnancy, to cut away a very small piece of the edge of the tissue surrounding the baby. Since this tissue is a part of the baby's body, it has the same genetic makeup as the rest of the baby. The same information previously obtained only by amniocentesis will probably be obtained in the future by this newer technique.

Is it safe?

It has its hazards. Early reports indicate that from 3.5% to 12% of the babies so tested are lost in a miscarriage as a result of the sampling. Unless newer developments change this risk of death, we must strongly object to chorionic villi sampling.

One report gave only a 5% loss "in experienced hands," but noted that "the question of potential Rh Iso-immunization, subtle birth defects, prematurity, placental separation, and intrauterine growth retardation — all the-oretical possibilities — will be answered as more infants are delivered."

M. Golbus, "Initial Chorionic Biopsy Problems Being Resolved," *OB-GYN News*, Nov. 15, 1984, p. 4

Why is it done?

To seek out and identify babies with handicaps — so they can be killed. There is no genetic abnormality or disease known to medical science that can be treated in the first six months of pregnancy.

Is living embryo experimentation presently taking place?

Yes, although few centers will admit it. In Britain the government established an official commission to look into this. Their recommendation was that experimentation on living human embryos was all right, but that they must be killed and not allowed to grow beyond 14 days.

The resultant public reaction and also the reaction in the British Parliament has made the acceptance of this recommendation highly unlikely.

> "Warnock" Commission of Inquiry into Human Fertilization and
> Embryology, *New York Times,* Oct. 16, 1984

Give an example of such embryo experimentation.

England's Dr. Robert Edwards, at an international meeting of medical scientists in Norfolk in 1983, spoke of experimenting on some "concepti" and then discarding them. Right to Life has condemned this.

> *Human Reproduction and Extracorporeal Fertilization with*
> *Embryo Transfer,* Norfolk, VA, Sept. 12, 1983

At the Norfolk meeting, Dr. Edwards suggested one experiment which would use micro-surgery to cut, exactly in half, a two, four, or eight cell living human embryo. If both halves continued to live and grow, there would be identical twins. Dr. Edwards would plant one back into the mother's womb. The other would be artificially grown larger, and then he or she would be killed and a chromosome exam done. If this baby proved to be abnormal, the twin would also be killed (by very early abortion).

AMERICAN WAR CASUALTIES

The war casualties represent all American combat-related deaths.
Each cross-mark represents 50,000 killed.

*REVOLUTIONARY WAR	25,324	†
*CIVIL WAR	498,332	††††††††††
*WORLD WAR I	116,708	†††
*WORLD WAR II	407,316	††††††††
*KOREAN WAR	54,246	†·
*VIETNAM WAR	58,655	††

WAR ON THE UNBORN   15,000,000
since abortion was legalized in 1973

††††††††††
††††††††††
††††††††††
††††††††††
†††
†††
†††
†††
†††
†††
†††

*Statistics from 1982 World Book

CHAPTER 12

Abortions

How Many? When? Where?

How many abortions are there?

In 1982, 1,573,920 abortions were done in the U.S. (Alan Guttmacher Institute's figure). When the unreported abortions are added (income tax evasion, cover-up for privacy, etc.), a figure of 1,800,000 is probably more realistic. Live births have hovered around the 3,600,000 figure for several years. Therefore: *Almost every third baby conceived in America is killed by abortion.*

In Canada, in 1982, there were 66,319 abortions, which is 17.5% of their birth rate, or just half of that of their southern neighbors.

This is the same in all areas?

No. There are more abortions in some regions and always more in cities than in small towns or rural areas. Some cities have more abortions than births. For example, in 1978 the cities of Atlanta, Atlantic City, Charlotte, Columbia (SC), Gainesville, Harrisburg, Iowa City, Madison, Miami, Raleigh, Reno, Richmond (VA), San Francisco, Seattle, Toronto and Washington, DC had more abortions than live births.

How far along in pregnancy were they?

"Abortion after 20 weeks, according to U.S. Department of Health and Human Services, Center for Disease Control, probably occurs 30,000 times per year in the U.S. Probably 4,000 of these are in the third trimester. Less than 5% of that number have induced abortion because of a known defect in the fetus."

U.S. Surgeon General, to Congressman C. Smith
Doc. no. 1, Feb. 24, 1984

Are any infants born alive after abortion?

Yes. In Atlanta, GA, there were ten babies born alive in 1980; in Madison, WI, four in 1982; in New York City, 27 in 1970; in upstate New York, 38 in 1970-72; in Wilmington, DE, 2 in 1979; the list is even longer.

"About once a day, somewhere in the U.S., something goes wrong and an abortion results in a live baby." Forty-five of the 607 midtrimester abortions done at Mount Sinai Hospital in Hartford, CT, between 1974 and 1976 resulted in live births."

"Avoiding Tough Abortion Complication, A Live Birth,"
Medical World News, Nov. 14, 1977, p. 83

"Not many are officially reported. Dr. Willard Cates, the aggressively pro-abortion former Chief of Abortion Surveillance for the Center for Disease Control, said that reporting abortion live births "is like turning yourself in to the IRS for an income tax audit. What is there to gain?"

L. Jeffries & R. Edmonds, "The Dreaded Complication,"
Philadelphia Inquirer, Aug. 2, 1981

Do these babies survive?

Almost all die, usually because the abortionist neglects them or actively kills them. Some have survived to be adopted and are normal. In one case, an unborn baby had her left arm amputated at the shoulder by the abortionist and also had deep scalp lacerations. Healing occurred and the baby was later delivered alive. A medical journal later carried her photo, which was taken by Dr. R. Thomsen of Walla Walla, WA.

Are twins ever aborted?

Yes! In early pregnancy, abortion usually kills them both. But, in England, after a ten-week abortion and sterilization, a woman "stayed pregnant" and later delivered the dead baby's twin.

The Sun, London, July 11, 1974

In later pregnancy the survival of a twin can be unintended, as at New York Cornell Medical Center, when the abortionist, Dr. F. Fuchs, in an attempted abortion, injected salt into only one of a set of twin's amniotic sacks without knowing there were twins. That baby was killed and was aborted. Its twin was later delivered alive, but was too tiny to survive.

New York Daily News, Sept. 11, 1970

Finally, the ultimate in technologically sophisticated killing occurred when one of a set of twins was selectively killed. Tests had shown one to have Down's Syndrome, the other to be normal. At 20 weeks, a needle was passed into the body and heart of the tiny handicapped boy and the blood sucked out, killing him instantly. Later, the mother delivered the normal baby, and the tiny, shrunken dead body of his little brother.

Kerenyi & Chitkara, "Selective Birth in Twin Pregnancy with Discordancy for Down's Syndrome," *New England Jour. of Medicine*, vol. 304, no. 25, 1981, p. 1525

What about repeat abortions?

The longer a nation has legal abortion, the higher the percent of repeaters. In 1970 only 0.6% of New York City abortions were repeats. By 1974 it was 21%; and by 1975, it was 38%. Nationwide in the U.S., in 1978, it was 30%.

A. Guttmacher Institute, *Issues in Brief*, vol. 1, no. 9, Oct., 1981

What about Informed Consent?

This is one of the most tragic abuses associated with the abortion industry. In any other type of surgery, the doctor is required to explain in detail what the procedure is, its possible complications, etc. Only then does the patient give "informed" consent.

Abortion is unique in that, while it is surgery that is potentially dangerous to the mother, it also destroys the being within her. To be fully informed, she should be given full factual information on the surgery, its possible complications (immediate and long-term), and, also, full details about "what she carries."

What is done? Very little factual information is given at all, and what is given is often false. The complications are ignored, glossed over, or given on a paper in fine print. Her passenger is referred to as "pregnancy tissue," "not alive yet," "not a baby yet," "just a bunch of cells," "only a glob." These descriptions are given at a stage of development when the baby already sucks her thumb and feels pain, and when we can listen to her tiny heartbeat on an office ultrasonic stethoscope.

Such deception of the mother and planned railroading of her into an abortion is never more evident than when the so-called "counselor" asks her, "Do you want your menstrual period re-established? If so, just sign up for this procedure." Abortion is not mentioned, nor anything about the baby.

There is no better example of the exploitation of women than this continuing, commercialized, and almost universal deception.

And it is legal till birth?

"Thus, the [Judiciary] Committee observes that no significant legal barriers of any kind whatsoever exist today in the United States for a woman to obtain an abortion for any reason during any stage of her pregnancy."

Report of the Senate Judiciary Committee on the Human Life Federalism
Amendment, June 8, 1982, p. 3

How else are abortions different?

Abortions are unique among all types of surgery.

	ABORTION	ETHICAL SURGERY
Payment	Cash at door	Pay later
Pathologic exam	Seldom	Routine
Advertising	Routine	Rare
Counseling	Usually a farce	Done if needed
Second opinion	Never	If needed
Informed consent	Legally not required	Always
Kickbacks	Sometimes	Never
Record Keeping	Sketchy	In detail
Pre-op. exam	Often not done until she is on the table	Mandatory and detailed
Follow-up exam	None	Mandatory and detailed
Correct Diagnosis	10-15% done on non-pregnant women	Surgeon is disciplined if he does many wrong operations
Husband's consent	Not needed	Expected
Husband informed	Not necessary	Always
Consent of parents of minor	Not needed	Legally required
Parents informed	Seldom	Legally required
Tissue disposal	In garbage	In humane and dignified manner
Burial	In garbage	Yes, if large enough
Surgical training	Not required	Absolutely required
Non-medical reasons	99%	About 1%

Is abortion done for sex selection?

Yes. And the girls are almost always the ones killed.

"Of a series of 100 pregnant women recently tested and told the sex of their unborn children, a female fetus was detected in 46. Twenty-nine of these mothers elected to abort. Of 53 found to be carrying males, only one woman chose to terminate her pregnancy."

Med. World News, Dec. 1, 1945, p. 45

How about race?

Based on a percentage of total population, since legalization there have been two minority race babies killed by abortion for every one white baby. This stands in stark contrast to the fact that all polls have consistently shown a higher percentage of minority race people opposing abortion than white people.

Why? Michael Novak, in an article in the *Washington Star*, pointed to the loss of 1.3% of the total population of black people annually in the U.S. through abortion and expressed his surprise "that black leaders so easily go along with the abortion rate among black women."

M. Novak, "How Placidly They Accept Aborting So Many Black Babies," *Washington Star*, Nov. 14, 1976

For the actual statistics of white and non-white abortions for the years 1978-80, see below.

ABORTION RATE PER 1,000 WOMEN AGED 15-44

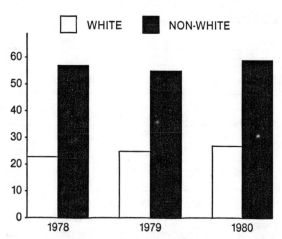

from ABORTION SERVICES IN THE UNITED STATES, EACH STATE AND METROPOLITAN AREA, 1979-1980, The Alan Guttmacher Institute

Abortion statistics from the state of Michigan also show this. In 1982, 67% of Medicaid abortions were performed on black women, while only 35% of blacks of all ages were receiving Medicaid.

But black leaders often support legal abortion.

"Black leaders react in traditional, knee-jerk liberal fashion to issues across the board, even though, in general, black Americans are decidedly conservative on a number of issues. The Black Caucus, for example, advocates a 'right' to abort, whereas 62% of blacks oppose abortion (National Opinion Research Center, 1984)."

J. Perkins, "Are Black Leaders Listening to Black America?"
Wall Street Journal, Oct. 16, 1984, p. 28

What percentage of those who get abortions are teenagers?

About one-third. Another one-third are in the 20-24 age group, while slightly more than the remaining one-third are age 25 and older.

Three-fourths of the women getting abortions are unmarried.

Planned Parenthood claims that one million teenagers get pregnant each year. Is this true?

This is a classic half-truth. The inference is that all of them are unmarried and young. In fact, 280,000 teenagers who get pregnant are married, and an additional 100,000 marry when the pregnancy is confirmed, so only 620,000 are unmarried. That is less than two-thirds the number Planned Parenthood claims.

As for the actual ages of these one million teenage pregnancies claimed by Planned Parenthood, fewer than 250,000 were under 18 years old and unmarried. There were 9,632 births in the 14-year-old and under group.

New York Times, (AP Washington), Nov. 7, 1984

No one should be proud of these figures, but they are sharply less than those claimed by Planned Parenthood. Further, there has been no increase in the percentage of teenagers becoming pregnant in recent years. The National Center for Health Statistics reports that the births among under 20-year-old women in 1981 were 537,024, which amounted to 18% fewer births than in 1970, when far fewer teenagers gave birth to 656,460 babies.

PART IV
Abortion

CHAPTER 13

Abortions — How They Are Done

Induced abortions are of three general types:

• Those that invade the uterus from below.

• Those that use drugs which kill the unborn child
and then empty the uterus through subsequent labor
and delivery.

• Those that invade the uterus from above.

What is a miscarriage?
   A miscarriage or "spontaneous abortion" happens
when the uterus, for natural reasons, goes into labor early
in pregnancy.

Why does this happen?

We don't always know. Usually, the growing baby has died because of abnormalities within itself or its placenta, and after this has occurred, the mother has the miscarriage.

Is this dangerous?

Most miscarriages could quite safely occur at home. There is sometimes excessive bleeding, however, or incomplete emptying of the uterus requiring hospitalization, during which the surgeon must gently tease the rotting remnants of the placenta (afterbirth) from the inside walls of the womb with a blunt instrument. Even when this procedure (called a D&C) is needed, there is rarely damage to the mother because the cervix (womb opening) is already softened and partly opened. Infection is rare. Baby parts are seldom found.

What of abortion "from below?"

There are several types:

- **Menstrual extraction:** This is a very early suction abortion, often done before the pregnancy test is positive.

- **Suction-aspiration:** In this method, the abortionist must first paralyze the cervical muscle ring (womb opening) and then stretch it open. This is difficult because it is hard or "green" and not ready to open. He then inserts a hollow plastic tube, which has a knife-like edge on the tip, into the uterus. The suction tears the baby's body into pieces. He then cuts the deeply rooted placenta from the inner wall of the uterus. The scraps are sucked out into a bottle (see color plate). The suction is 29 times more powerful than a home vacuum cleaner.

- **Dilitation & Curettage (D&C):** This is similar to the suction procedure except that the abortionist inserts a curette, a loop-shaped steel knife, up into the uterus. With this, he cuts the placenta and baby into pieces and scrapes them out into a basin. Bleeding is usually profuse.

- **Dilitation & Evacuation (D&E):** This is done after 12 weeks. A pliers-like instrument is needed because the baby's bones are calcified, as is the skull. There is no anesthetic for the baby. The abortionist inserts the instrument up into the uterus, seizes a leg or other part of the body and, with a twisting motion, tears it from the baby's body. This is repeated again and again. The spine must be snapped, and the skull crushed to remove them. The nurse's job is to reassemble the body parts to be sure that all are removed.

Isn't this as dangerous as it is barbaric?

It is both. Even though it is dangerous, a report from the Center for Disease Control, Dept. HEW, stated that it is still safer for the mother than the salt-poisoning or Prostgalandin method.

"Comparative Risks of Three Methods of Midtrimester Abortion,"
Morbidity and Mortality Weekly Report,
Center for Disease Control, HEW, Nov. 26, 1976

What of the "Drug" abortions?

The first one widely used was Salt Poisoning (saline amiocentesis): This is done after the 16th week. A large needle is inserted through the abdominal wall of the mother and into the baby's amniotic sac. A concentrated salt solution is injected into the amniotic fluid. The baby breathes and swallows it, is poisoned, struggles, and sometimes convulses. It takes over an hour to kill the baby. When successful, the mother goes into labor about one day later and delivers a dead baby.

Is it actually poisoning?

Yes. The mechanism of death is acute hypernatremia or acute salt poisoning, with development of widespread vasodilitation, edema, congestion, hemorrhage, shock, and death.

Galen et al., "Fetal Pathology and Mechanism of Death in Saline Abortion, *Amer. Jour. of OB & GYN*, 1974, vol. 120, pp. 347-355

Some people refer to salt-poisoned babies as "candy apple babies." Why is this?

The corrosive effect of the concentrated salt often burns and strips away the outer layer of the baby's skin. This exposes the raw, red, glazed-looking subcutaneous layer of tissue. The baby's head sometimes looks like a candy apple.

Some have also likened this method to the effect of napalm on innocent war victims. It is probably every bit as painful.

Are there other "Drug" abortions?

Yes. The other widely used method is Prostaglandin Abortion: The first form of this human hormone marketed was Prostin F2a, which was for injection into the baby's bag of waters. Its first approved use (by the U.S. Food and Drug Administration) was for "the induction of mid-trimester abortion." Since then, its manufacturer, the Upjohn Company, has marketed a vaginal suppository form, Prostin E2, and an intramuscular shot form, Prostin 15M. The action of this hormone is to produce violent labor and delivery of whatever size baby the mother carries. If the baby is old enough to survive the trauma of labor, she may be born alive, but is usually too small to survive.

In one article, among the complications listed was "live birth."

Upjohn is the first major drug company that has abandoned the ethic of producing only drugs which will save lives and is now making one whose specific purpose is to kill. For this reason, many pro-life people have stopped using its products, since they do not want to support such a company. (See chapter 34, Boycotts.)

Are the Prostaglandins safe for the mother?

"... a large complication rate (42.6%) is associated with its use. Few risks in obstetrics are more certain than that which occurs to a pregnant woman undergoing abortion after the 14th week of pregnancy."

Duenhoelter & Grant, "Complications Following Prostaglandin F-2 Alpha Induced Mid-trimester Abortion," *Jour. of OB & GYN*, Sept. 1975

What of abortions "from above?"

The most common of these is Hysterotomy: This is an early Caesarian section. The mother's abdomen is surgically opened, as is her uterus. The baby is then lifted out, and, with the placenta, discarded. This method is usually used late in pregnancy.

One abortionist who used this method removed a tiny baby who breathed, tried to cry, and was moving his arms and legs — so he threw the placenta on top of the baby and smothered him. Another solution abortionists use to snuff out the baby's life is to plunge the little one into a bucket of water. Still others cut the cord while the baby is still inside the uterus. This deprives the baby of oxygen. Then, after waiting five minutes or so — after the baby has died of suffocation — the abortionist takes out the "product of pregnancy" (as they call the tiny boy or girl).

What about abortion to save the mother's life?

These are almost nonexistent in today's sophisticated medical climate. Such an abortion would be a true "therapeutic" abortion.

If the mother's actual life were threatened, a conscientious doctor would try to save both. In the rare, rare case where such a decision is really needed, the problem would be that of balancing one human life against another (note that all other reasons given for abortion are reasons less than human life itself).

In such a case, it would be proper to give to the local family and local medical and ethical authorities the right to make whatever decision they believed right. An ethical physician would certainly try to save both, but might have to make a choice. The proposed Human Life Amendments allow this exception.

Is surgery on an ectopic pregnancy an abortion?

Some do define this as an abortion. By the time most ectopic surgery is done, the developing baby is dead and often destroyed by the hemorrhage. In any case, such surgery is done primarily to prevent the death of the mother. This is good medical practice because there is no chance for the baby to survive.

Even if a yet-alive, tiny baby were removed from the tube, the Right to Life movement would allow this, for without the procedure, both would die. The baby has a zero chance of survival. The surgery will save the mother's life.

If medical technology were advanced enough to allow transplanting the baby from its pathological location, and placing it into the uterus, then most ethicists would say that this should be done. Since this is not possible with present technology, the tiny new baby's life will be lost.

How about removal or treatment of a cancerous or of a traumatized pregnant uterus, or of some other organ while the mother is pregnant?

The same applies. Surgery is done or treatment is given to prevent the death of the mother. The death of the baby, if it occurs, would be an unfortunate and undesired secondary effect. If at all possible, the baby should also be saved.

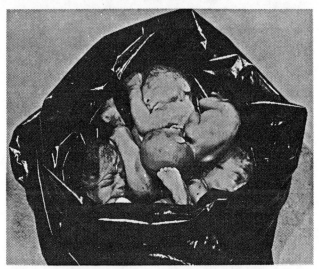

This was the result of one morning's work in a Canadian teaching hospital. These babies had attained fetal ages of 18-24 weeks (4-5 months) before being killed by abortion.

Note: Four-color photos of aborted babies in back of book.

CHAPTER 14

*Immediate Physical Complications and
Under-Reporting*

> *The major immediate complications of
> abortion are infection, bleeding, and perfora-
> tion of the uterus.*

What about infection?

How often do women get infections as a consequence of
induced abortion? A study from one of the most pres-
tigious medical centers in the world, John Hopkins University, reported: "Occurrence of genital tract infection
following elective abortion is a well-known complication." This institution reports rates up to 5.2% for first
trimester abortions and up to 18.5% in midtrimester.

Burkman et al., "Culture and Treatment Results in Endometritis
Following Elective Abortion," *Amer. Jour. OB/GYN,*
vol. 128, no. 5, 1977, pp. 556-559.

For the local freestanding abortion facility in your community, with far inferior quality of care, the number of
such infections will be at least double that of such a medical center.

"One sequel to abortion can be a killer. This is
pelvic abscess, almost always from a perforation of

the uterus and sometimes also of the bowel," said two professors from U.C.L.A., in reporting on four such cases.

C. Gassner & C. Ballard, *Amer. Jour. OB/GYN*, vol. 48, p. 716
(as reported in *Emerg. Med. After Abortion-Abscess*,
vol. 19, no. 4, Apr. 1977

Infection causes damage?

Infection in the womb and tubes often does permanent damage. The Fallopian tube is a fragile organ, a very tiny bore tube. If infection injures it, it often seals shut. The typical infection involving these organs is pelvic inflammatory disease or PID.

Patients with Chlamydia Trachomatis infection of the cervix (13% in this series) who get induced abortion "run a 23% risk of developing PID."

E. Quigstad et al., *British Jour. of Venereal Disease*, June 1982, p. 182

"Pelvic Inflammatory Disease (PID) is difficult to manage and often leads to infertility, even with prompt treatment.... Approximately 10% of women will develop tubal adhesions leading to infertility after one episode of PID, 30% after two episodes, and more than 60% after three episodes."

M. Spence, "PID: Detection & Treatment," *Sexually Transmitted Disease Bulletin*, John Hopkins Univ., vol. 3, no. 1, Feb. 1983

"Acute inflammatory conditions occur in 5% of the cases, whereas permanent complications such as chronic inflammatory conditions of the female organs, sterility, and ectopic [tubal] pregnancies are registered in 20-30% of all women ... these are definitely higher in primagravidas [aborted for first pregnancy]."

A. Kodasek, "Artificial Termination of Pregnancy in Czechoslovakia," *Internatl. Jour. GYN/OB*, vol. 9, no. 3, 1971

Venereal disease, usually Gonorrhea or Chlamydia, causes PID. This, if present, vastly complicates an induced abortion.

"Chlamydia trachomatis was cultured from the cervix in 70 of 557 women admitted for therapeutic abortion. Among the 70, 22 developed acute PID postoperatively (4% of the total)."

E. Quigstad et al., "PID Associated with C. Trachomatis Infection, A Prospective Study," *British Jour. of Venereal Disease,* vol. 59, no. 3, 1982, pp. 189-192

In a classic English study at a university hospital which reported on four years' experience, "there was a 27% complication rate from infection."

J.A. Stallworthy et al., "Legal Abortion: A Critical Assessment of its Risks," *The Lancet,* Dec. 4, 1971

What of bleeding?
Bleeding is common. Most get by, but some need blood transfusions. The Stallworthy study (above) reported that 9.5% needed transfusions. Most recent studies are reporting smaller percentages.

Are blood transfusions a cause of death in abortions?
Yes, and these deaths are never associated directly nor reported as statistics related to abortions. Here's how this works:

First, we must know how many women need blood transfusions after getting induced abortions. These figures are hard to come by. The only controlled studies are from university medical centers, which do only a small fraction of all abortions. Over 90% of abortions are done in free-standing abortion chambers where the medical care is only a faint shadow of the competence of those medical centers. Women who hemmorrhage from these abortions are sent to "real" hospitals for transfusions and surgery. The percent who need transfusions then must remain an estimate, for these commerical establishments would never report. How many then? Let's be conservative and say that one in every hundred needs a blood transfusion. If there are 1,600,000 abortions annually in the United States, that means that 1% or 16,000 women were transfused.

Viral hepatitis is transmitted in up to 10% of patients transfused.

Amer. Assn. Blood Banks and Amer. Red Cross,
Circular Information, 1984, p. 6

One percent of 16,000 is 1,600 women. With a mortality rate of 1%, there are 16 women who die annually in the U.S., and 99 x 16 or 1,600 more who become very ill from this direct aftermath of induced abortion. If these cases were included, this would double the mortality rate reported for women dying from abortions annually in the United States.

J. Mosley, "Transfusion-Transmitted Viral Hepatitis,"
Clinics in Lab. Med., vol. 2, no. 1, March 1982, pp. 239-240

If, instead of "gestimating" that only one woman in a hundred is transfused, we accept a figure of two or three per hundred who need transfusions, then we multiply the number of deaths from hepatitis by two or three.

AIDS is another threat. A very small number of those who get transfusions contract Acquired Immune Deficiency (AIDS) Syndrome (1% of AIDS is acquired by blood transfusion).

Are blood clots ever a problem?

Blood clots are one of the causes of death to mothers who deliver babies normally. They are also a cause of death in healthy young women who have abortions performed.

Embolism (floating objects in the blood that go to the lungs) is another problem. Childbirth is a normal process, and the body is well prepared for the birth of the child and the separation and expulsion of the placenta. Surgical abortion is an abnormal process, and slices the unripe placenta from the wall of the uterus into which its roots have grown. This sometimes causes the fluid around the baby, or other pieces of tissue or blood clots, to be forced into the mother's circulation. These then travel to her lungs, causing damage and occasional death. This is also a major cause of maternal deaths from the salt poisoning method of abortion.

For instance, pulmonary thromboembolism (blood clots to the lungs) was the cause of eight mothers dying, as reported to the U.S. Center for Disease Control.

W. Cates et al., *Amer. Jour. OB/GYN*, vol. 132, p. 169

And this can occur in those as young as 14 years old.

Pediatrics, vol. 68, no. 4, Oct. 1971

Also, amniotic fluid embolism has "emerged as an important cause of death from legally induced abortion." Of 15 cases, the risk seems to be greater after three months. Treatment is ineffective."

R. Guidotti et al., *Amer. Jour. OB/GYN*, vol. 41, 1981, p. 257

There are other blood-related problems?
The most feared is Disseminated Intravascular Coagulation. This is a sudden drop in blood clotting ability which causes extensive internal bleeding and, sometimes, death. The classic paper was on hypertonic saline (salt poisoning) abortions (see reference below).

H. Glueck et al., "Hypertonic Saline Abortion, Correlation with D.I.C.," *JAMA*, vol. 225, no. 1, July 2, 1973, pp. 28-29

"Saline-induced abortion is now the first or second most common cause of obstetric hypofibrinogenemia."

L. Talbert, Univ. of NC, "DIC More Common Threat with Use of Saline Abortion," *Family Practice News,* vol. 5, no. 19, Oct. 1975

Since then, it has also been caused by D&E and Prostaglandin abortions.

White et al., "D.I.C. Following Three Mid-Trimester Abortions," *Anaesthesiology*, vol. 58, 1983, pp. 99-100

What causes perforation of the uterus?

It can be caused by suction, D&C, or D&E. Salt poisoning and Prostaglandin-type abortions also cause perforations, but it is then more accurately described as a rupture or blow-out of the uterus.

How often does perforation occur?

For early abortions, it is plus or minus 1%. In the later ones, it is more frequent.

I've heard that Prostaglandin abortions are safer than the Salt Poisoning type.

This is certainly true for the baby, as more are born alive with this method (see chapter 13).

It is probably also true for the mother. Nevertheless, complications include uterine rupture, cervical laceration, sepsis, mild to severe Disseminated Intravascular Coagulation, hemorrhage, sudden death, convulsions, cardio-respiratory arrest, vomiting and aspiration, stroke, acute kidney failure, amniotic fluid embolus, and blood clots to the lung.

A major study from the University of Texas, Dallas, concluded:

> "... a large complication rate (42.6%) is associated with its [Prostaglandin] use. Few risks in obstetrics are more certain than that which occurs to the gravida [pregnant woman] undergoing abortion after the 14th week of pregnancy."
>
> Duenhoelter & Grant, "Complications Following
> Prostaglandin F-2A Induced Midtrimester Abortion,"
> *Amer. Jour. OB/GYN*, vol. 46, no. 3, Sept. 1975, pp. 247-250

Why don't we hear more about such complications?

A busy chief of an OB department in Ft. Lauderdale reported, "An unusually large number of complications are being seen by private physicians. Because many of these adolescent patients, in whom complications develop, do not return to the physician who did the abortion, accurate data on complications are difficult to obtain."

He then discussed 54 teenage patients seen in his private practice (he does not do abortions) in a six-year period. He also noted that, of the young women, "none felt they had been given any meaningful information as to the potential dangers of abortion."

M. Bulfin, "A New Problem in Adolescent Gynecology,"
Southern Med. Jour., vol. 72, no. 8, Aug. 1979

"There has been almost a conspiracy of silence in declaring its risks. Unfortunately, because of emotional reactions to legal abortion, well-documented evidence from countries with a vast experience of it receives little attention in either the medical or lay press. This is medically indefensible when patients suffer as a result.

"It is significant that some of the more serious complications occurred with the most senior and experienced operators.

"[These complications] are seldom mentioned by those who claim that abortion is safe ..."

J.A. Stallworthy et al., "Legal Abortion:
A Critical Assessment of its Risks," *The Lancet,* Dec. 4, 1971

Do the statisticians admit their figures are inaccurate?

They seldom do, and that is incredible. Ask a health officer what the Gonorrhea incidence is in his or her county and you will be given the number officially reported. But ask again, "How many cases *are* there actually?" The answer will likely be, "Oh, we know that only a small percent are actually reported. If you want the true incidence, multiply by three or five or more."

Since the reason to cover up an abortion is far more compelling than the reason to cover up a case of VD, it should be obvious, as indicated above, that most abortion deaths and injuries are not reported, or are reported as something else.

Reported cases of Gonorrhea increased from 600,000 to 1 million in a five-year period, and "it is estimated that only one-third are reported."

S. Gabbe, *OB-GYN News*, Oct. 1, 1983, p. 15

I thought that reporting an abortion was required by law.

In many states, reporting is not required. For example, almost five years after legalization of abortion nationwide, the Department of Health of the State of Ohio stated, "The reporting on this statistic has been very minimal. At the present time, there is no information available as to complications of the abortion procedure."

K. Bajo, Asst. Adm., Ohio Dept. of Health
Report to Ohio Right to Life, May 3, 1977

But there are studies from universities that report much better safety records.

Some reports are correct. Some of the questionable reports, however, are written by well-known abortionists who are profiting from this grisly business. There are *no* well-funded, comparably-sized studies done by pro-life physicians.

Also, the standard of care at a university teaching hospital is far better than that at your local abortion mill. The so-called "freestanding clinics," which do over 90% of all abortions in the U.S., are often little better than back-alley operations that have been legalized, and their follow-up care (and ability to report accurately) is usually nonexistent.

The claim that relevant statistics can be collected from the place where the abortion was performed "is little short of science fiction."

"Complications following abortions performed in free-standing clinics is one of the most frequent gynecologic emergencies ... encountered. Even life-endangering complications rarely come to the attention of the physician who performed the abortion unless the incident entails litigation. The statistics presented by Cates represent substantial under-reporting and disregard women's reluctance to return to a clinic, where, in their mind, they received inadequate treatment."

L. Iffy, "Second Trimester Abortions,"
JAMA, vol. 249, no. 5, Feb. 4, 1983, p. 588.

But, at least deaths are reported accurately?

All deaths, of course, are reported, but not all abortion deaths are reported as abortion related. If nondisclosure (and, therefore, nonreporting) of venereal disease is the rule, not the exception, how much more pressure is there on the doctor to not disclose that this complication and/or death was related to an induced abortion? Your authors' *HANDBOOK ON ABORTION* detailed many specific instances of such cover-up during the 1970s.

Willke & Willke, "Mothers Die from Abortions."
In *Handbook on Abortion,* Cincinnati: Hayes Pub. Co.,
1971, 1975, 1979 Editions

- Consider the mother who hemorrhaged, was transfused, got hepatitis, and died months later. Official cause of death? Hepatitis. Actual cause? Abortion.

- A perforated uterus leads to pelvic abscess, sepsis (blood poisoning), and death. The official report of the cause of death may list pelvic abscess and septicemia. Abortion will not be listed.

- Abortion causes tubal pathology. She has an ectopic pregnancy years later and dies. The cause listed will be ectopic pregnancy. The actual cause? Abortion.

- Deep depression and guilt following an abortion leads to suicide. The cause listed? Suicide! Actual cause? Abortion.

- The abortionist does follow a patient who dies from his abortion. But he doesn't want the reputation of being a butcher, so he lists another cause.

- A new doctor sees a patient who dies from the damage done from an abortion, but she and her family hotly deny the abortion. The abortion connection cannot be absolutely proven, and the new doctor fears a suit for malpractice or for defamation of character, and so he lists another cause.

- The kindhearted surgeon, unable to save the life of an abortion victim, feels that she and her family have been punished enough. He doesn't want to ruin her and her family's reputation in the community — so he forgets to mention abortion on the death certificate.

How about specific cases? Recently?

One abortion chamber, Woman's Care Center, Biscayne Blvd., Miami, FL, "killed" four mothers: R. Montero (August 7, 1979), M. Morales (May 8, 1981), M. Baptise (December 18, 1982), and S. Payne (January 4, 1983).

The pro-abortion *Chicago Sun Times* ran a multi-issue exposé in 1978. They discovered 12 mothers who had died from abortions, who had previously been unreported. They also reported abortions being done on non-pregnant women as well as some by incompetent medical persons in unsterile conditions.

> "What the Supreme Court legalized in some clinics in Chicago is the highly profitable and very dangerous back-room abortion."
>
> Special Reprint, *Chicago Sun Times*, Field Enterprises, 1978

That sounds like only a fraction of maternal abortion deaths are actually reported as such!

Most active pro-life people are convinced of this.

But I read that abortion is safer than childbirth!

The most professional analysis of this was by Professor T. Hilgers. He shows that it depends upon the statistics that you use.

T. Hilgers, "Abortion Related Maternal Mortality."
In *New Perspectives on Human Abortion*,
Univ. Pub. of Amer., 1981, pp. 69-92

But which is safer?

Safety probably isn't a factor. Women don't have babies or choose abortion because of safety. Maternal mortality in childbirth is only ten deaths per 100,000 deliveries.

Another interesting consideration is that pro-abortion people always compare reported figures of all maternal deaths (10/100,000) to mortality figures for only first trimester abortions (1-2/100,000), conveniently omitting the deaths from second and third trimester abortions (40-50/100,000). If the pro-lifers were to play the same statistical game, they should speak only of deaths from vaginal deliveries (1.1/100,000) and omit those from C-section deliveries (100/100,000).

Lanska et al., "Mortality from Abortion & Childbirth,"
JAMA, vol. 250, no. 3, July 15, 1983, pp. 361-362.

Even so, the situation today is better than the "8,000 to 10,000 women who died annually from back-alley abortions," isn't it?

These figures, often cited by pro-abortionists, are simply false. During the debate on the floor of the U.S. Senate on the Hatch-Eagleton Pro-Life Amendment in 1983, the U.S. Bureau of Vital Statistics provided the data on such deaths.

Its reports showed that you must go back to the pre-Penicillin era to find more than 1,000 maternal deaths per year from illegal and legal abortions combined. The precipitous drop in maternal deaths in the 1950s and '60s occurred while abortions were still illegal. When the first state legalized abortions in 1967, the total deaths were down to 167 per year. By 1973, when the Supreme Court legalized abortion in all 50 states, it was down to 45 per year in the entire U.S. Since legalization, the slow decline has continued, so that now the only difference is that more mothers are dying from legal, rather than illegal abortions.

U.S. BUREAU OF VITAL STATISTICS
CENTER FOR DISEASE CONTROL

YEAR	Reported Maternal Deaths from Abortion in U.S. Illegal and Legal
1940	1,679
1950	316
1960	289
1967	160 (First State Legalized)
1970	128
1973	45 (U.S. Supreme Court Decision)
1977	21
1981	8

Taken from U.S. Senate graph Chapter 21.

Commenting on the fact that the decline of maternal abortion deaths was faster for the years 1961-68 than after legalization of abortion in the years 1968-1973, Dr. Dennis Cavanaugh stated that, since abortion has been legalized,

"... there has been no major impact on the number of women dying from abortion in the U.S.... After all, it really makes no difference whether a woman dies from legal or illegal abortion, she is dead nonetheless. I find no comfort in the fact that legal abortion is now the leading cause of abortion-related maternal deaths in the U.S."

D. Cavanaugh, "Effect of Liberalized Abortion on
Maternal Mortality Rates," *Amer. Jour. OB/GYN*,
Feb. 1, 1978, p. 375

What, then, is the bottom line?

Most women have abortions without significant physical injury, but a disturbing number do sustain damage, and some die.

Many women end up with real emotional and guilt after-effects.

**Abortions May Be Legal
But
They Are Not Always Safe**

CHAPTER 15

Late Physical Complications

The Mother

Sterility?
Forty-five percent of America's 27 million couples are unable to have children or have difficulty conceiving. Of these, 10% wanted children but have been sterilized for medical reasons, 19% were voluntarily sterilized, and 15% just could not conceive.

New York Times, Feb. 10, 1983, p. C9.

Reasons include the tripling of cases of Gonorrhea in the past decade, the sixfold increase in women using I.U.D. birth control devices, the sharp rise in Chalmydia infections, and the major increase in induced abortions.

Please cite some studies.
OK. "The relative risk of secondary infertility among women with at least one induced abortion and no spontaneous miscarriages was 3-4 times that among non-aborted women."

D. Trichopoulos et al., "Induced Abortion & Secondary Infertility," British Jour. OB/GYN, vol. 83, Aug. 1976, pp. 645-650

In 1974 Dr. Bohumil Stipal, Czechoslovakia's Deputy Minister of Health, stated: "Roughly 25% of the women who interrupt their first pregnancy have remained permanently childless."

Also, see chapter 14 regarding PID and sterility.

If the abortionist's curette scrapes or cuts too deeply across the opening of the tubes, there is scar formation and often, blockage. If total, the woman is sterile. But when partial blockage is a result of this procedure, the microscopic sperm can still travel through the tube to fertilize the ovum as it breaks out of the ovary. After fertilization, this new human life, many hundred times larger than the sperm, may not be able to get back through the tube if it has been partly scarred closed. Then, the tiny baby nests in the tube, and the mother has an ectopic pregnancy.

What is the incidence of ectopic pregnancies?

There has been a 300% increase in ectopic (or tubal) pregnancies in the U.S. since abortion was legalized. In 1970 the incidence was 4.8 per 1,000 live births. By 1980 it was 14.5 per 1,000 births.

U.S. Dept. H.H.S., *Morbidity & Mortality Weekly Report,*
vol. 33, no. 15, April 20, 1984

Is this bad?

Yes. The thin-walled tube cannot support this life, and it soon ruptures, causing internal bleeding and requiring emergency surgery. Sometimes these women die. (In the U.S. 437 deaths in the past nine years.)

Medical Tribune, Jan. 26, 1983

Nine of these deaths were *after* induced abortions. The mothers had their wombs emptied by "abortion," when, in reality, the tiny baby was lodged in the tube. Later, the tube ruptured and the women died.

Rubin et al., "Fatal Ectopic Pregnancy After
Attempted Induced Abortion," *JAMA,*
vol. 244, no. 15, Oct. 10, 1980

"Especially striking is an increased incidence in ectopic pregnancies."

A. Kodasek, "Artificial Termination of Pregnancy in Czechoslovakia," *Internatl. Jour. of GYN & OB,* vol. 9, no. 3, 1971

Why is this?

"The increased incidence of PID — especially Chlamydia — and induced abortion appear to play leading roles in the dramatic rise in ectopic pregnancies."

H. Barber, "Ectopic Pregnancy, a Diagnostic Challenge," *The Female Patient,* vol. 9, Sept. 1984, pp. 10-18

Do menstrual symptoms change after abortion?

"Women with prior abortions consistently reported an excess of symptoms in all age groups."

L. Roth et al., "Increased Menstrual Symptoms Among Women Who Used Induced Abortion," *Amer. Jour. OB/GYN,* vol. 127, Feb. 15, 1977, p. 356

What about synechia?

"The frequency of uterine adhesions [synechia] is especially high among patients who have had two or more curettages.... Dr. J. G. Asherman, for whom the syndrome is named, has reported intrauterine adhesions in 44 of 65 women who had two or more curettages."

"Abortion Risks: Getting the Picture," *Medical World News,* Oct. 20, 1972

Do miscarriages occur more frequently after induced abortions?

A Boston study by a group who have aggressively done abortions denied any increase after one abortion, but, after two or more abortions, they did find a "two- to three-fold increase in risk of first trimester spontaneous abortions," as well as "losses up to 28 weeks gestation."

Levin et al., "Association of Induced Abortion with Subsequent Pregnancy Loss," *JAMA,* vol. 243, no. 24, June 27, 1980, pp. 2495-2499

Of a group of 52 women who had induced abortions 10-15 years previously and who were followed very closely for that length of time, it was found that one-half (27) had no problem with subsequent pregnancies. There was one ectopic pregnancy, eight subsequent — but long-delayed — conceptions, and three women with permanently blocked tubes. Of the remaining 11 women, there were 33 pregnancies with 14 early and 3 midtrimester losses, 6 premature deliveries, and only 10 full-term births.

Hilgers et al., "Fertility Problems Following an Aborted First Pregnancy." In *New Perspectives on Human Abortion,* edited by S. Lembrych. University Publications of America, 1981, pp. 128-134

A high incidence of cervical incompetence resultant from abortion has raised the incidence of spontaneous abortions (miscarriage) to 30-40%.

ibid, Kodasek

Women who had one induced abortion had a 17.5% miscarriage rate in subsequent pregnancies, as compared to a 7.5% rate in a non-aborted group.

Richardson & Dickson, "Effects of Legal Termination on Subsequent Pregnancy," *British Med. Jour.,* vol. 1, 1976, pp. 1303-4

What about second trimester losses?

There was a doubled incidence of midtrimester spontaneous losses.

Herlap, *New England Jour. of Med.,* no. 301, 1979, pp. 677-681

"In a series of 520 patients who had previously been aborted, 8.1% suffered a mid-trimester loss (compared to 2.4% controls)."

G. Ratter et al., "Effect of Abortion on Maturity of Subsequent Pregnancy," *Med. Jour. of Australia,* June 1979, pp. 479-480

"There was a tenfold increase in the number of second trimester miscarriages in pregnancies which followed a vaginal abortion."

Wright et al., "Second Trimester Abortion after Vaginal Termination of Pregnancy," *The Lancet,* June 10, 1972

What of placenta previa?

Placenta previa is when the afterbirth (placenta) covers part or all of the cervix, the womb's opening into the birth canal. It can be very serious and usually requires a Cesarean section, sometimes with loss of the baby.

Doctor Barrett and others did a study at Vanderbilt University in which they evaluated over 5,000 deliveries and found that those who had prior induced abortions in the first trimester had a "seven to fifteen fold increased prevalence of placenta previa." They linked it to scaring of the lining of the womb from the curretage or suction aspiration "predisposing to the abnormal site of placental implantation and an increased placental surface area." They also found that the changes occurred with the first induced abortion and *were* permanent. Neither the time elapsed nor the number of induced abortions changed this.

Barret et al., "Induced Abortion, A Risk Factor for
Placenta Previa," *Amer. Jour. OB/GYN,*
Dec. 1981, pp. 769-772

"We rather often observe complications such as rigidity of the cervical os, placenta adherens, placenta accreta, and atony of the uterus."

A. Kodasek, "Artificial Termination of Pregnancy in
Czechoslovakia," *Internatl. Jour. of GYN & OB,*
vol. 9, no. 3, 1971

"We cannot exclude the possibility that the large number of induced abortions plays a role in the remarkable increase in cases of placenta previa."

Z. Bognar, "Mortality and Morbidity Associated with
Legal Abortions in Hungary, 1961-1973"
Amer. Jour. Public Health, 1976, pp. 568-575

What of uterine ruptures?

This condition occurs during labor in almost 1% of cases when women have had earlier first trimester abortions.

D. Nemec et al., "Medical Abortion Complications,"
OB & GYN, vol. 51, no. 4, April 1978, pp. 433-436

Six percent of women who become pregnant after hysterotomy abortions suffered rupture of their uterus. Substantial risk of rupture was demonstrated in 26% of these cases. Babies who were born subsequently were small for their due date.

Clow & Crompton, "The Wounded Uterus: Pregnancy after Hysterotomy," *British Med. Jour.*, Feb. 10, 1973, p. 321

Uterine rupture (1%) is also one of the feared and sometimes fatal complications from prostaglandin abortions.

Duenhalter & Gant, "Complications Following Prostaglandin Mid-Trimester Abortion," *OB & GYN*, vol. 46, no. 3, Sept. 1975, pp. 247-250

What about endometriosis?

This can develop along the needle or catheter tract from the midtrimester puncture.

Ferrare et al., "Abdominal Wall Endometriosis Following Saline Abortion," *JAMA*, vol. 238, no. 1, July 4, 1977, pp. 56-57

Do abortions affect Rh sensitization?

"Even in very early suction abortions done prior to eight weeks, fetal-maternal hemorrhage can occur, thereby sensitizing Rh-negative women."

M. Leong, "Rh Therapy Recommended in Very Early Abortion," *OB-GYN Observer*, June 1978

This means that in later pregnancies, babies of these mothers will have Rh problems, need transfusions, and occasionally be born dead or die after birth. This can be tested for prior to the abortion and largely prevented by giving the mother a very expensive medication called RhoGAM. If not done, the number who become sensitized varies from "3% to 17%." Unfortunately, many abortion chambers do not take this expensive precaution.

J. Queenan, Cornell University *Medical World News*, April 30, 1971, p. 36G

What about teenage abortions? Are they different?

After years of legalized abortion experience, a pro-abortion professor of OB/GYN at the University of New-castle-on-Tyne reported on his follow-up, ranging from two to twelve years, of 50 teenage mothers who had been aborted by him. He noted that "the cervix of the young teenager, pregnant for the first time, is invariably small and tightly closed and especially liable to damage on dilatation." He reported on the "rather dismal" results of their 53 subsequent pregnancies:

Six had another induced abortion.
Nineteen had spontaneous miscarriages.
One delivered a stillborn baby at 6 months.
Six babies died between birth and 2 years.
Twenty-one babies survived.

J. Russell, "Sexual Activity and Its Consequences in the Teenager," *Clinics in OB, GYN,* vol. 1, no. 3, Dec. 1974, pp. 683-698

"Physical and emotional damage from abortion is greater in a young girl. Adolescent abortion candidates differ from their sexually mature counterparts, and these differences contribute to high morbidity." They have immature cervixes and "run the risk of a difficult, potentially traumatic dilatation." The use of lamanaria "in no way mitigates our present concern over the problems of abortion."

C. Cowell, *Problems of Adolescent Abortion,* Ortho Panel 14, Toronto General Hospital

"The younger the patient, the greater the gestation (age of the unborn), the higher the complication rate.... Some of the most catastrophic complications occur in teenagers."

"Eighty-seven percent (87%) of 486 obstetricians and gynecologists had to hospitalize at least one patient this year due to complications of legal abortions."

M. Bulfin, M.D., *OB-GYN Observer,* Oct.-Nov. 1975

But pregnancy for teenagers has higher risks, too!
That is incorrect. Earlier opinion had taught this. In

recent years, however, it has been shown that teenage mothers have no more risks during pregnancy and labor, and their babies fare just as well as their more mature sisters' babies, *if* they have had good prenatal care.

"We have found that teenage mothers, given proper care, have the least complications in child-birth. The younger the mother, the better the birth. [If there are more problems,] society makes it so, not biology."

B. Sutton-Smith, *Jour. of Youth and Adolescence*.
As reported in the *New York Times*, April 24, 1979

Pregnancy in a very young teenager (12 to 16 years) does not appear to be inherently high risk.

J. Dwyer, Roosevelt Hospital, New York
Family Practice News, May 1, 1978

Dr. Jerome Johnson of John Hopkins University, and Dr. Felix Heald, Professor of Pediatrics, University of Maryland, agree that the fact that teenage mothers often have low birth weight babies is not due to "a pregnant teen-ager's biologic destiny." They pointed to the fact that the cause for this almost invariably is due to the lack of adequate prenatal care. "With optimal care, the outcome of an adolescent pregnancy can be as successful as the outcome of a non-adolescent pregnancy."

Family Practice News, Dec. 15, 1975

"The overall incidence of pregnancy complications among adolescents 16 years and younger is similar to that reported for older women."

E. Hopkins, "Pregnancy Complications Not Higher in Teens,"
OB-GYN News, vol. 15, no. 10, May 1980

"Obstetric and neonatal risks for teenagers over 15 are no greater than for women in their twenties, provided they receive adequate care."

There is evidence that in 15- to 17-year-old women, pregnancy may even be healthier than in older ages.

E. McAnarney, "Pregnancy May Be Safer,"
OB-GYN News, Jan. 1978

Pediatrics, vol. 6, no. 2, Feb. 1978, pp. 199-205

Abortions May Be Legal
But
They Are Not Always Safe

CHAPTER 16

Late Physical Complications

The Baby

Premature births have increased?

In the early years of legalized wide-open abortion, there was ample evidence of the fact that induced abortion caused a sharp increase of premature births and their unfortunate aftermaths. Some of the major original studies included:

- After one legal abortion, premature births increase by 14%; after two abortions, it is 18%, after three, it increases to 24%.

  Klinger, "Demographic Consequences of the Legalization of Abortion in Eastern Europe," *Internatl. Jour. GYN & OB*, vol. 8, Sept. 1971, p. 691

- Non-aborted women have a premature birth rate of 5%, aborted women have a rate of 14%.

  R. Slumsky, "Course of Delivery of Women Following Interruption of Pregnancy," *Czechoslovakia Gyn.*, vol. 29, no. 97, 1964

- Women who have had abortions have twice the chance of delivering a premature baby later.

G. Papaevangelou, U. Hospital, Athens, Greece,
Jour. OB-GYN British Commonwealth,
vol. 80, 1973, pp. 418-422

- In Czechoslovakia, premature births resulting from abortions are so frequent that a woman who has had several abortions and who becomes pregnant is examined, and:

"If the physicians can see scar tissue, they will sew the cervix closed in the 12th or 13th week of pregnancy. The patient stays in the hospital as long as necessary, which, in some cases, means many months."

"Czechs Tighten Reins on Abortion,"
Medical World News, 106J, 1973

Among others, Dr. Zedowsky reported a higher percent of brain injuries at birth. His report cited "a growing number of children requiring special education because of mental deficits related to prematurity."

ibid, above

Why this increase in prematurity?

During an abortion procedure, the cervical muscle must be stretched open to allow the surgeon to enter the uterus. There is no harm to the muscle in a D&C performed because of a spontaneous miscarriage, as the cervix is usually soft and often open. Also, there is rarely any damage caused by a D&C done on a woman for excessive menstruation, etc. When, however, a normal, well-rooted placenta and growing baby are scraped out of a firmly closed uterus, protected by a long, "green" cervical muscle, the task of dilating this muscle is more difficult. Attempts have been made to lessen this damage to the woman's future childbearing ability by using laminaria.

What is a laminaria?

This is a small bit of dehydrated material which is inserted into the cervix one day before the abortion. It absorbs water and swells up to many times its size and, in the process, dilates the cervix. When used, it may reduce the damage to the cervical muscle that would be caused by instrumental dilatation before the abortion.

How does cervical dilatation relate to later complications?

Perhaps you've been present for, or experienced first-hand, a woman's first labor and delivery. Twelve to twenty hours is not unusual. The nurse, as she checks the mother's progress, uses the terms "two fingers" (or cm) — "four fingers" — then "complete." These terms refer to measuring the slow dilatation of the cervix. Only when it is wide open ("complete") can the baby begin the journey through the birth canal.

Before birth, nature opens this "door" very slowly. In a miscarriage, all those cramps do the same thing. After emptying the uterus, this strong donut-like muscle closes tight again.

When an abortion is done, for example, on an 18-year-old's first pregnancy at two months, the abortionist must dilate (or stretch open), an elongated, firm, unripe cervix. This is commonly accomplished in 30 to 60 seconds. This forceful stretching often tears enough of the muscle fibers to permanently weaken the cervix.

The lowest part of a woman's uterus is the cervix, and, when a woman is pregnant and stands upright, the baby's head rests on it — in effect, bouncing up and down on the "door" throughout the pregnancy. The muscle must be intact and strong in order to keep the cervix closed. If it is weak, or "incompetent," it may not stay closed and may result in premature opening and miscarriage, or premature birth.

The most damage is done to the primiparous (first pregnancy) cervix. In Eastern Europe pro-abortion policy has slowly changed and now strongly discourages aborting the first pregnancy. In America all authorities, even the strongest pro-abortion propangandists, agree on this complication. Laminaria, incidentally, have not been used in most freestanding abortion chambers because it means two visits, smaller volume, and smaller cash flow.

There have been studies recently at several teaching hospitals that reported fewer complications than earlier studies. Some of these are seriously suspect since the grants of research money were given only to vocal and aggressive abortionists. (No comparable grants were given to pro-life researchers.)

One writer frequently heard from is Dr. Willard Cates, who published an article suggesting that the charge for abortions be on a graduated scale — determined by measuring the size of the fetal foot.

W. Cates, "For a Graduated Scale of Fees for Abortion,"
Family Planning Perspectives, vol. 12, no. 4, July 1980

In another paper, Cates reported that Gonorrhea was the most common sexually transmitted disease, but that the second most common "disease" transmitted sexually was pregnancy. He then compared the two as to "incidence," "incubation time," "familial predisposition," and "recurrence rate" by correlating age groups, seasonal variations, the amount of time missed from work, the type of "treatment" (abortion), complications of "treatment," the relative cost of "treatment," etc., and concluded:

"If legal abortion were viewed as a justifiable treatment for a sexually transmitted condition, it would not be considered an elective or preventive procedure which is usually ineligible for insurance programs. Rather, it would be a curative treatment, making it eligible for remuneration from federal and private third party insurance plans."

Cates et al., "Abortion as a Treatment of Unwanted Pregnancies:
The Number Two Sexually Transmitted 'Disease.'"
Paper presented at the 14th Annual Meeting,
Planned Parenthood Physicians, Miami, Nov. 1976

Do more recent studies still report the same complications?

"The main risk of induced abortion is ... permanent cervical incompetence."

L. Iffy, "Second-Trimester Abortions,"
JAMA, vol. 249, no. 5, Feb. 4, 1983, p. 588

Second trimester miscarriage and premature birth frequently follow induced abortions.

A. Arvay et al., "Relation of Abortion to Premature Birth,"
Review French GYN-OB,
vol. 62, no. 81, 1967

Levin et al.,
JAMA, vol. 243, 1982, p. 2495

A. Jakobovits & L. Iffy, "Perinatal Implications of
Therapeutic Abortion." In *Principals and
Practice of OB & Perinatalogy,*
New York: J. Wiley & Sons: 1981, p. 603

C. Madore et al., "Effects of Induce Abortion on
Subsequent Pregnancy Outcome," *Amer. Jour. OB/GYN,*
vol. 139, 1981, pp. 516-521

The use of laminaria reduces, but does not eliminate, cervical incompetence.

S. Harlap et al., "Spontaneous Fetal Losses After
Induced Abortions," *New England Jour. Med.,*
vol. 301, 1979, pp. 677-681

"In a series of 520 patients who had previously been aborted, 8.6% had premature labor compared to 4.4% of [non-aborted] controls."

G. Ratten et al., "Effect of Abortion on Maturity of
Subsequent Pregnancy," *Med. Jour. of Australia,*
June 1979, pp. 479-480

"The induced abortion group had the highest incidence of late spontaneous abortion and premature delivery."

O. Kaller et al., "Late Sequellae of Induced Abortion
in Primigravidae," *Acta OB GYN Scandinavia,*
vol. 56, 1977, pp. 311-317

Do some of these premature babies die?

A study of 26,000 consecutive deliveries at U.C.L.A. was done to determine if previous abortions (and premature births) had increased the number of stillborn babies and neonatal (after birth) deaths. The findings were that the death rate "increased more than threefold."

S. Funderburk et al., "Suboptimal Pregnancy Outcome
with Prior Abortions and Premature Births,"
Amer. Jour. OB/GYN, Sept. 1, 1976, pp. 55-60

Will having an abortion affect women who marry after the abortion?

The bluntest statement yet was made by an impeccable source, Dr. Margaret Wynn, co-author of the landmark Wynn Report. Because of the physical problems and occasional sterility resultant from abortion, she stated that a young man has the right to know that a young woman has had an abortion because, "A single girl who has had one or more abortions is made less eligible for motherhood and, therefore, for marriage."

Wynn & Wynn, "Some Consequences of
Induced Abortion to Children Born Subsequently,"
British Med. Jour., Mar. 3, 1973, p. 506

Are there any comprehensive studies on premature births?

In New York State a major prospective study was done between 1975 and 1979 which compared over 40,000 women; half of whom had an abortion and half of whom had a live birth. V. Logrillo et al. analyzed the subsequent reproductive history of these women and found a definite pattern of increased complications for those who had abortions. (See chart below.)

V. Logrillo et al., "Effect of Induced Abortion on
Subsequent Reproductive Function,"
N.Y. State Dept. of Health,
Contract #1-HD-6-2802, 1975-78

	Study Group	Control Group	Difference
	had an abortion	had a live birth	
Spontaneous fetal deaths All subsequent pregnancies	8.7%	5.3%	1.65 times more
Spontaneous fetal deaths First subsequent pregnancy	8.7%	4.7%	1.85 times more
Low Birthweight (-2500 gm) white non-white	7.0% 13.4%	4.7% 8.4%	1.5 times more 1.6 times more
Premature Birth (-33 weeks)	2.3%	1.3%	1.8 times more
Labor Complications	13.0%	4.3%	3.0 times more
Congenital Malformations	----------	----- same ----	------------
Newborn deaths	1.36%	0.98%	1.4 times more

CHAPTER 17

Mental Health

There is serious question whether mental health, viewed as a psychiatric illness, can ever be a reason to induce abortion.

The term "mental health," as commonly used, is synonymous with the United Nations' definition of "health," which means social, emotional, and economic well-being, as judged by the person him/herself. This is a broad, sweeping definition which soars far beyond and cannot be equated with "mental health," as medically defined.

As early as 1971, Dr. Louis Hellman, Deputy Assistant Secretary of the Department of Health, Education, and Welfare (HEW), who was strongly pro-abortion, said (at Columbia Women's Hospital, Washington, DC), that the requirement of a psychiatrist's permission for abortion was a "gross sham."

Washington Post, Nov. 25, 1971

This reference was made in spite of (or because of), the fact that, of a total 63,672 hospital abortions performed during 1970 in California, 98.2% were for mental health purposes.

In the same year (1970), in New York, where the law did not require such a subterfuge, only 2% of the total abortions were reported as being done for "mental health" reasons. Every state or nation that has legalized abortion for "health" has abortion-on-demand.

There used to be only physical health reasons?

Yes. But prior to legalization, these reasons had all but vanished. Already in 1951, Dr. R. J. Heffernan, of Tufts University, said:

> "Anyone who performs a therapeutic abortion (for physical disease) is either ignorant of modern methods of treating the complications of pregnancy, or is unwilling to take time to use them."
>
> Congress of American College of Surgeons, 1951

Aren't there *any* valid psychiatric reasons for abortion?

Dr. R. Sloan, who was pro-abortion, said:

> "There are no unequivocable psychiatric indications for abortion."
>
> R. Sloan, *New England Jour. Med.*, May 29, 1969

Later, Frank Ayd, M.D., medical editor and nationally known psychiatrist, said:

> "True psychiatric reasons for abortion have become practically non-existent. Modern psychiatric therapy has made it possible to carry a mentally ill woman to term."
>
> F. Ayd, *Medical Moral Newsletter*

Are you saying that "mental illness" is usually just an excuse for an abortion?

We are saying exactly that.

What of the woman in poor mental health? If the abortion won't help her, will it harm her?

This has been a rather well-kept secret. In an otherwise strongly pro-abortion paper, it was stated that "women with a history of psychiatric disturbance were three times as likely to have some psychiatric disturbance" after an abortion as others who had no such history.

E. Greenglass, "Abortion & Psychiatric Disturbance," *Canadian Psych. Assn. Jour.,* vol. 21, no. 7, Nov. 1976, pp. 453-459

Dr. Charles Ford and his associates at U.C.L.A. reported the same finding.

"The more serious the psychiatric diagnosis, the less beneficial was the abortion."

C. Ford et al., "Abortion, Is It a Therapeutic Procedure in Psychiatry?" *JAMA,* vol. 218, no. 8, Nov. 22, 1971, pp. 1173-1178

"The more severely ill the psychiatric patient, the worse is her post-abortion psychiatric state."

E. Sandberg, "Psychology of Abortion." In *Comprehensive Handbook of Psychiatry,* 3rd ed. Kaplan & Friedman Publishers, 1980

All of these support the original official statement of the World Health Organization in 1970:

"Serious mental disorders arise more often in women with previous mental problems. Thus, the very women for whom legal abortion is considered justified on psychiatric grounds are the ones who have the highest risk of post-abortion psychiatric disorders."

What of bad effects if a woman is in good mental health?

"The trauma of abortion may have significant emotional sequelae [aftermath].... Few medical subjects are as fraught with strong sociological, political, cultural, and moral implications as abortion."

C. Hall & S. Zisook, "Psychological Distress Following
Therapeutic Abortion," *The Female Patient*,
vol. 8, Mar. 1983, pp. 34/47-34/48

"When patients present with emotional problems, and there is a history of abortion, then the emotional sequelae of the abortion should be considered the major offending life event until proven otherwise. Patients usually never make this association because the offending conflicts are predominantly lodged in the unconscious mind."

R. Maddock & R. Sexton, "The Rising Cost of Abortion,"
Medical Hypnoanalysis, Spring 1980, pp. 62-67

But most polls show few emotional problems — only a sense of relief!

Yes, but "What women really feel at the deepest level about abortion is very different from what they say in reply to questionnaires." A Canadian study took a group of women, questioned them, and then subjected a randomly chosen one-half the study group to in-depth psychotherapy, even though they denied problems.

"What emerged from psychotherapy was in sharp contrast [to the questionnaires], even when the woman had rationally considered abortion to be inevitable, the only course of action." It was demonstrated that the conscious, rationalized decision for an abortion can coexist with profound rejection of it at the deepest level. Despite surface appearances, abortion leaves behind deeper feelings "invariably of intense pain, involving bereavement and a sense of identification with the foetus."

I. Kent et al., "Emotional Sequelae of Elective Abortion,"
British College of Med. Jour., vol. 20, no. 4, April 1978

I. Kent, "Abortion Has Profound Impact,"
Family Practice News, June 1980, p. 80

Does it ever lead to suicide?

Suicide is rare among pregnant women, but much more common after induced abortion. It is never reported under maternal mortality from abortion, of course, even though it is causative.

Rare while pregnant? I thought it was common in women who were refused abortion.

This is an oft-repeated fallacy. Suicide among pregnant women is extremely rare. Several well-controlled studies have shown this conclusively. The State of Ohio had only two maternal suicide deaths between the years 1955-1963.

"Maternal Deaths Involving Suicide,"
Ohio State Med. Jour., Dec. 1966, p. 1294

Between 1938 and 1958, over 13,500 Swedish women were refused abortions. Only three committed suicide.

J. Ottosson, "Legal Abortion in Sweden,"
Jour. Biosocial Sciences, vol. 3, 1971, p. 173

In Brisbane, Australia, no pregnant woman has ever committed suicide.

F. Whitlock & J. Edwards, "Pregnancy & Attempted Suicide,"
Comp. Psychiatry, vol. 9, no. 1, 1968

In Birmingham, England, in seven years, 119 women under 50 committed suicide. None were pregnant.

M. Sim, "Abortion & the Psychiatrist,"
British Med. Jour., vol. 2, 1963, p. 145

In a detailed report of the Minnesota experience from 1950-65 entitled, *Criminal Abortion Deaths, Illegitimate Pregnancy Deaths, and Suicides in Pregnancy,* the following facts are reported:

• There were only 14 maternal suicides in the state of Minnesota in 15 years, or one for every 93,000 live births. Four were first pregnancies. None were illegitimately pregnant.

- Ten of these women committed suicide after delivery, only four while pregnant, leading to the author's comment, "The fetus in utero must be a protective mechanism. Perhaps women are reluctant to take another life with them when they do this."

- Twelve of the 14 suicides were psychotic depressions. Two were schizophrenics. Only four had seen a psychiatrist.

- Male suicide during these years averaged 16 per 100,000 population. Non-pregnant female suicides averaged 3.5 per 100,000, and pregnant female suicides 0.6 per 100,000.

- The authors concluded that therapeutic abortion for psychiatric reasons "seems a most nebulous, non-objective, non-scientific approach to medicine. It would seem that psychiatrists would accomplish more by using the available modalities of their speciality in the treatment or rehabilitation of the patient instead of recommending the destruction of another one."

Minnesota Maternal Mortality Committee,
Dept. of OB & GYN, Univ. of Minn.,
Amer. Jour. of OB/GYN, vol 6, no. 1, 1967

What of post-abortion suicide?

In one report, two teenaged mothers, following induced abortion, attempted suicide on the very dates their babies would have been born.

C. Tishler, "Adolescent Suicide Attempt: Anniversary Reaction,"
Pediatrics, vol. 68, 1981, pp. 670-671

Post-abortion suicide is slowly growing into a rather frightening phenomenon. Suiciders Anonymous is a national fellowship patterned after Alcoholics Anonymous. It tries to help those who have attempted suicide.

Suiciders Anonymous, in a 35-month period in the Cincinnati, Ohio area, reported counseling 5,620 members. These people were described as, "those suffering in-depth, deep depression, anxiety, stress, and fears they cannot overcome, those who have attempted suicide, often several times, and failed, and those who are considering taking that final desperate step." Of these 5,620 people:

- 4,000 were women

- 1,800 had abortions, of whom

- 1,400 were between 15-24 years old.

M. Uchtman, Ohio Director of Suiciders Anonymous
Report to the Cincinnati City Council, Sept. 1, 1981

What are the psychodynamics of post-abortion suicide?

In her report, M. Uchtman (Suiciders Anonymous), said it in a way which makes it clearly understandable:

"After years of listening to their [would-be suicides'] stories, we know there are thousands more out there being brave. By holding a tight reign on their emotions, they tuck all that unexpressed emotion and unshared experience deep down inside themselves, where it keeps growing, like a pressured tumor of pain.

"Of all the emotions they experience during the abortion crisis, none brings more pain and distress than the one they now know and identify five to ten times more than any other feelings. These women always tell us the same thing. 'Oh, my God, I am evil. I have to be evil to have done this thing. I feel so alone, so forsaken.'

"Panic and distress grips them after an abortion, because the feelings are allowed to remain shadowy, ominous, ghost-like. They are shapes dancing around the edges of their consciousness. They commonly postpone the moment of truth as long as possible. But when the subconscious throws it forward, they go through mental hell! Even at age 87, the critical moment comes when the chilling reality overwhelms them and cold reality numbs their spirit and casts them into those dark 'pits' of despair and pain!

"They fantasize that the 'cancer' will disappear. But it cannot! So feelings cannot be denied and repressed without doing violence to every other area of their living. And of all those they touch! It is vital that parents are prepared!

"Here are the two questions they always ask us:

- 'Will this pain never die?'

- 'How many years does it take to get over this pain?'

"Margaret Wold writes: 'This pain remains as a counterpoint to the rest of their lives, even though time mutes its sharpness. Women who have had abortions and made the decision on their own are too often faced with intentionally hurting others. Each woman actually does unintentionally hurt others immediately after abortion. Why? Because they are seeking forgiveness. Under any circumstances! Sad, isn't it?'

"Many women purposely keep the pain alive by never forgiving the spouse or mate after the decision. He rejects her, leaving her to live in the pits alone, in the depths and in deep depression!

"They become more and more depersonalized, superficial, and artificial. Suicide is now more desirable for them than a lifetime of false pretense and hopelessness."

ibid, Uchtman

Does Suiciders Anonymous support Parental Notification Laws?

Yes. "It is an act of cruelty to remove parental duties and rights during the abortion crisis."

ibid, Uchtman

But few teenagers want to tell their parents!

We believe the following article, written by one of your authors after the U.S. Supreme Court decision, provides an alternative path for many of those young women Meta Uchtman described above.

Your Daughter — Pregnant?

And under 18 years? What does she think of you, her parents? Should she tell you? Sadly, few girls want to. They think you'll explode, condemn, reject, feel ashamed. She doesn't want to hurt you. But she is alone, frightened, defiant, worried. Yes, but still a young girl who desperately needs your love and help.

The Supreme Court ruling assures her that she can have her baby killed, can internalize all of the psychic trauma, the loneliness, the bitterness, and never know that...

If she had told you — Yes, you might have "exploded" initially. But then, with rare exceptions, you would have shared your tears and given her the help, support, and love she so desperately needed. To her surprise, you would not condemn, but offer all the love, help, and understanding you could in this time of trial.

In my 25 years of counseling, I have found that when a girl does come to her parents, and receives the help they can offer, it becomes the occasion of a real growth in maturity, self-confidence, and ability to love by the girl. She faces her responsibility and stands tall. The family bond is strengthened by the sharing of the burden.

But no, now the tragic Supreme Court decision can guarantee that she'll never know that you really love her and would have helped her. Thanks to them, she can have her baby killed in secret and become disillusioned, embittered, hardened.

May God have mercy on those judges for what they have done.

J. Willke, *Cincinnati RTL Newsletter,*
July 1976, p. 3

What if a woman has a psychosis, is pregnant, and needs shock treatment? Shouldn't she be aborted?

Pregnancy does not rule out the use of almost any known psychiatric therapy, including electric shock.

But don't some women have psychotic breakdowns after delivering a baby?

Yes. Postpartum psychosis is relatively common following childbirth. It, however, is almost entirely unpredictable. It does not bear any particular relationship to whether or not a woman had mental trouble during her pregnancy. It frequently occurs in a woman who was entirely mentally stable during her pregnancy. Furthermore, these "after the baby blues" are rarely permanent and seldom have relapses. Also, drug treatment today usually clears the problem promptly and usually without relapse.

Are there post-abortion psychoses?

Yes. And compared to post-delivery disturbances, they are much more serious, last longer, and are more likely to recur. They are more often the "hard" cases. This had been the experience before abortion legalization.

M. Sim, "Abortion and the Psychiatrist,"
British Med. Jour., vol. 2, 1963, pp. 145-148

After legalization, a repeat investigation in a larger series of the same problem gave the same result. Of 199 postpartum depressive psychoses, "with two exceptions the prognosis was good." Of 34 post-abortive psychoses, "16 had an adverse prognosis."

M. Sim, *Instability Associated with Pregnancy,*
Univ. of Birmingham Press

"The patients clearly functioned well before the abortion and later experienced psychoses precipitated by guilt over the abortion."

J. Spaulding & J. Cavernar, "Psychosis Following
Therapeutic Abortion," *Amer. Jour. Psychiatry,*
vol. 135, no. 3, March 1978, p. 364

Does having a baby help the mental problems?

It is certainly better than not having children, but just having children later, in and of itself, doesn't heal the wound in her mind and heart.

It is interesting that early in the next pregnancy, "Eight of 21 women who had obtained a past abortion were found to be clinically depressed and anxious. In contrast, only 8 of 98 who had not had abortions were depressed."

The women with prior abortions expressed fear for their baby's health because "punishment was due."

R. Kumar & K. Robson, *Psychol. Med.,* vol. 8, 1978, pp. 711-715

How is her guilt problem resolved?

Through God's forgiveness and by restitution.   A confirmed alcoholic can usually only be cured through spiritual help. This is the cornerstone of the success of Alcoholics Anonymous. Just so, peace of mind and heart after an abortion is rarely achieved except through an acceptance of the fact that God has forgiven her. Equally as important is that she forgive herself. Finally, many only feel at peace if they make restitution. This often brings them into the RTL movement as activists. The most spontaneous evidence of this is the organization Women Exploited by Abortion (see chapter 36).

How about an example from a non-Christian culture?

In Japan, where abortion has been legal and accepted for 35 years, a rapidly growing custom is to conduct Mizuyo Kuyo services in honor of the god Jizo. This god has been made the patron saint of infants who died of starvation, abortion, or infanticide. Small baby statues, in his honor, are bought and dressed. Then, in a Buddhist Temple, rites of sorrow and reconciliation are carried out.

Also, Mother Theresa's visits there and her pleas to protect the unborn have been met with an extraordinary response.

These guilt feelings don't come from religious beliefs then?

Certainly there are guilt feelings related to religious beliefs, but most guilt feelings after abortion have little to do with religious belief. Abortion violates something very basic in a woman's nature. She normally is the giver of life. Most women who are pregnant are quite aware of the fact that they have a baby growing within them. Most women who have an abortion have the feeling that "I have killed my baby."

What of the unwanted pregnancy?

This is not a psychiatric indication (see chapter 18). In any case, it is crucial to understand that how a woman feels early in her pregnancy and how she will feel after delivery are often completely different. If all upset women with unwanted pregnancies had been aborted in years past, at least one-third of our readers would not be living today.

How long after an abortion can psychological problems occur?

There is no time limit. An example can often tell more than many scientific papers. Your author will never forget a 44-year-old lady who had been childless during her marriage. A Christian woman with a Jewish husband, they had been unable to adopt a child because of their mixed religion. She longed for a child but was sterile, as several tests had shown her tubes to be blocked. Theirs was an excellent marriage, and both had given of themselves to many community and charitable efforts. On this day, after a routine exam, I told her that, because of a continuing fibroid enlargement, her uterus would have to be removed.

She gasped as if hit by a pole, and collapsed in a hysterical heap, completely out of control in her grief and crying.

After considerable time, sedatives, and support, I was able to again talk with her and the story tumbled out. She related how she had become pregnant while in college and had had an abortion "by an excellent surgeon." Throughout her subsequent marriage, she had hoped against hope that, somehow, she would still conceive. Now I had just told her that her womb must be removed and her last, faint hope for a baby was forever gone.

Through tear-reddened eyes and with a pathos that still brings a lump into my throat, she quietly said, "I killed the only baby I ever bore."

It is Easier to Scrape the Baby Out of the Mother's Womb than to Scrape the Memory of the Baby Out of Her Mind

PART V
Social Questions

CHAPTER 18

Unwanted Pregnancies

*Since when does anyone's right to live
depend upon
someone else wanting them?*

Shouldn't every child be wanted?

At first glance, yes! "Every Child a Wanted Child" is the famous Planned Parenthood slogan, and who can argue? That isn't the disagreement. It is how to achieve such a goal.

We agree that every child should be wanted. A world with only wanted children would be an idyllic place in which to live. No one could quarrel with that a an idealistic goal. Wouldn't it also be a wonderful world if there were no unwanted wives by husbands, no aging parents unwanted by their children, no unwanted Jews, blacks, Catholics, Chicanos, or ever again a person who, at one time or place, finds himself or herself unwanted or persecuted. Let's all try to achieve this, but also remember that people have clay feet and, sadly, the unwanted will probably always be with us.

A second thought. Women resent that the value of a woman is sometimes determined by whether a man wants her. Yet radical feminists insist that the value of an unborn man (or woman) is to be determined by whether a woman wants him (or her).

To use being wanted by someone as a measure of whether a human life is allowed to live is a frightening concept. Its converse logically awaits us — that the unwanted can be eliminated. Don't forget, Hitler's Germany was ideal for wanted Aryans.

Since when does anyone's right to live depend upon someone else wanting them?

"Every Child a Wanted Child" should be completed with "and if not wanted, kill!" for that is exactly what that Planned Parenthood slogan means. To thus complete the sentence removes the mask from this misleading slogan and reveals it for the monstrous evil that it is.

That certainly makes it sound different!

Yes, and it is of crucial importance that every time we hear that phrase, we should add Planned Parenthood's solution... "and if not wanted, kill!"

Do parents kill teenagers when they are not wanted, or Uncle Joe after his stroke, or Mom, now that she is such a burden? You say no?

Do we give the mother the legal right to kill the two-year-old daughter who is a burden to her? No! Then why and how can we give her the legal right to kill the two-month-old daughter living inside her who is a burden to her?

The U.S. Supreme Court and Parliaments in many other nations have, for the first time in modern history, granted to one citizen (the mother) the absolute legal right to kill another, if that first person does not want them!

Think of the logic of the inevitable extension of such a freedom to kill. We could solve poverty by killing unwanted poor people, or religious or political groups, or those too old, too burdensome, and on and on...

OK, the ethic is horrible, but unwanted pregnancies do result in unwanted children, don't they?

No, not in any greater percentage than wanted pregnancies.

Think of your own pregnancies. Was each planned, or was this or that one a surprise? Were you really happy each time, in the first month or two? Be honest. In the first few weeks or months, were all of your pregnancies really "wanted?"

But now look at your children. Are you glad you have them? Would you give any back — have any of them killed?

You've changed your mind, haven't you? For almost all of you, a pregnancy that was truly unwanted has resulted in a dearly loved and wanted son or daughter.

Now, what makes you think that the same change of mind can't occur to most pregnant women today who initially judge their pregnancy to be unwanted?

That sounds right by a mother's judgment, but is that your experience as a doctor?

After more than 34 years of medical practice, your author personally can say without hesitancy that he has seen many unwanted pregnancies, but has yet to see the first unwanted newborn child. If we permit abortion for an unwanted pregnancy, we will be destroying vast numbers of children who, by the time of their birth and through their childhood, would have been very dearly wanted and deeply loved children indeed. If the judgment of being wanted at an early stage of pregnancy were a final judgment, and abortions were permitted freely, a high percentage of everyone reading this book would never have been born.

Are there any scientific studies?

Dr. Ferriera found no relationship between unplanned pregnancies and newborn deviant behavior. In fact, there were more deviant babies of mothers who had planned their pregnancy than those who had not.

A. J. Ferriera, "The Pregnant Woman's Emotional Attitude and Its Reflection in the Newborn," *Amer. Jour. Orthopsychiatry,* vol. 30, 1960, p. 553

"There is a contention that unwanted conceptions tend to have undesirable effects ... the direct evidence for such a relationship is almost completely lacking, except for a few fragments of retrospective evidence. It was the hope of this article to find more convincing systematic research evidence and to give some idea of the amount of relationship between unwanted conception and undesired effect on children. This hope has been disappointed."

E. Pohlman, "Unwanted Conception, Research on Undesirable Consequences," *Eugenics Quarterly,* vol. 14, 1967, p. 143

"It is clear that mothers who initially believed their pregnancy to be 'the worst thing that ever happened to them' came to feel about the same degree of affection for their children as the mothers who were initially 'ecstatic' about the pregnancy.

"Most women who were most regretful of the pregnancy now claim they would have the child again if given the opportunity [whereas] one of every six mothers who were initially pleased with pregnancy would choose not to have the child again.

"[They conclude] ... initial feelings about pregnancy are predictive of how a mother will eventually feel about her child to only a very limited degree."

P. Cameron et al., "How Much do Mothers Love Their Children," *Rocky Mt. Psychological Assn.,* May 12, 1972

Others have conclusively demonstrated a spontaneous change from prepartum rejection to postpartum acceptance of their children by a group of mothers.

M. Zemlich & R. Watson, "Attitudes of Acceptance and Rejection During and After Pregnancy," *Amer. Jour. Orthopsychiatry,* vol. 23, 1953, p. 570

What of other countries?

- Japan has had abortion-on-demand for over 35 years. It is used there as a method of birth control, but "cases of infanticide have been increasing so much that social workers have made appeals to Japanese mothers in newspapers and on television not to kill their babies."

  The Sunday Times, June 23, 1974

- When Rumania reversed its law on abortion in 1966, doctors stated that not only had they *not* overcome the problem of unwanted children — but that one of the factors which had caused some of them to urge for changes in the law was that there had been such an increase in the number of psychiatric cases among lonely only children and children of neurotic mothers.

- In England the Working Party of the Royal College of Obstetricians and Gynecologists stated that the vast majority of unplanned pregnancies become wanted children.

- Aberdeen, Scotland, is a unique city because, through an unusual law, it has had open abortion for 20 years in a nation that has had legal abortion only one-third as long. If the availability of abortion did reduce unwanted children, it should have the best record in Britain. In fact, it has the worst record, with 10.2 per 1,000 abandoned, abused, and uncared for children being supported by public agencies — compared with the national average of 6.6.

  Annual Report, Chief Medical Health Officer,
  Aberdeen, Scotland, 1972

Don't some studies prove the opposite?

No! In the entire world literature on this subject, there are only two studies that attempt to show that there is a negative effect on the children who had been "unwanted pregnancies." Both have been conclusively shown to be invalid.

The first study, from Sweden, concluded that such a child "runs a risk of having to surmount greater mental and social handicaps than its peers..."

Forssman & Thuwe, "One Hundred and Twenty Children Born after Application for Therapeutic Abortion Refused," *Acta Psychiatrica Scandinavica,* vol. 42, 1977, pp. 71-88

Professor Paul Cameron has clearly shown that an evaluation of the mothers in this study showed sufficient differences with the control group so that the authors' conclusions were a "mis-analysis," invalid, and could have been predicted from these differences alone, whether the pregnancy was wanted or not. There were, incidentally, little differences anyway between the children in the study and the control.

P. Cameron, "The Swedish 'Children Born to Women Denied Abortion' Study: A Radical Criticism," *Psychological Reports,* vol. 39, 1976, pp. 391-394

The second study concluded that "Compulsory childbearing has varied and sometimes unfavorable consequences for the subsequent life of the child."

Dytrych et al., "Children Born to Women Denied Abortion," *Family Planning Perspectives,* vol. 7, no. 4, July-Aug. 1975

Professor Samuel Nigro, child psychiatrist at Case Western Reserve University, has published a scathing commentary on this study. He points to the fact that the data found and published in the article "renders the conclusions untenable." He details the "striking differences in the families of the two groups of children," (the study group having more unstable mothers and fathers than the control group), as the obvious cause for the differences in the children.

"The conclusions appear to be contrived by an abuse of scientific method deplorable to the point of discrediting the researchers, of discrediting the

Institute which sponsored the research, and of questioning the use of public funds for a publication which takes such license with scientific data."

S. Nigro, University Hospitals of Cleveland, Open Letter to
Family Planning Perspectives, March 10, 1976

But don't many unwanted pregnancies become battered children?

• Not so. The landmark study on this was done at the University of Southern California. Professor Edward Lenowski studied 674 consecutive battered children who were brought to the in- and out-patient departments of that medical center. He was the first to go to the parents and study to what extent they wanted and planned the pregnancy. To his surprise, he found that 91% were planned and wanted, compared to 63% for the control groups nationally. Further, the mothers had began wearing, on the average, pregnancy clothes at 114 days compared to 171 days in the control, and the fathers named the boys after themselves 24% of the time compared to 4% for the control groups.

E. Lenowski, *Heartbeat*, vol. 3, no. 4, Dec. 1980

• Both parents (or parent figures) lived in 80% of the homes. Two-thirds of the mothers were "housewives" and presumably were at home. Almost all mothers were in the 20-30 age group, and fathers were in the 20-35 age bracket. No special social, racial, or economic class predominated.

Francis, "Child Abuse, A Nationwide Study,"
Amer. Humane Assn. & Child Welfare League, 1963

• The parents commonly "... grew up in a hostile environment, and were abused themselves. When the children fail to satisfy their [unrealistic, neurotic expectations of perfection] emotional needs, the parents react with the same violence they experienced as children."

Not much has changed since these earlier investigations. There is much that we still do not know about the sick psychology that leads to child abuse. One thing does stand out, however: *prenatally, these were not unwanted pregnancies, they were super-wanted pregnancies.*

I've been told that aborting unwanted babies would leave more wanted ones and, therefore, there would be less child abuse.

Exactly the opposite has happened. In New York City, during the 1960s, the number of abused children had averaged about 5,000 cases a year. Abortion was legalized in 1970. By 1975, over 25,000 cases were reported.

Ontario's statistics show the same:

YEAR	ABORTIONS	CHILD ABUSE
1971	16,172	422
1975	24,921	769
1978	38,782	1,762

Child Welfare Branch, Ministry of Human Resource, Ontario, Canada

Child abuse cases in 1973, in the U.S., were estimated to be 167,000 cases (A. Jackson, Natl. Center of Child Abuse and Neglect, U.S. Dept. of Health and Human Services).

By 1979, the figure was 711,142 (Natl. Analysis of Official Child Abuse and Neglect Reporting, 1978-1979), while, in 1982, the total was 929,000 (ibid, Jackson).

DATE	TOTAL NUMBER	% INCREASE
1973	167,000	
1979	711,142	325%
1982	929,000	500%

Dr. Phillip Ney, Professor of Psychiatry at the University of Christ Church, New Zealand, while still at the University of British Columbia, published a widely read study of this. His analysis clearly pointed to the fact that abortion (and its acceptance of the violence of killing the unborn) lowered a parent's psychic resistance to violence and abuse of the born.

P. Ney, "Relationship Between Abortion & Child Abuse," *Canada Jour. Psychiatry,* vol. 24, 1979, pp. 610-620

What if a mother really doesn't want the baby?

There are millions of outstretched arms aching to adopt and love a baby. Her answer is to place the baby in a secure, loving, adoptive home.

What of fetal abuse?

Under the present legal situation, nothing can be done while the baby is still in the womb. A recent study has explored the possibility of a born child suing his mother for abuse from her chronic alcoholism while pregnant with him.

Machenzie et al., "A Case of Fetal Abuse," *Amer. Jour. Orthopsychiatry,* vol. 52, no. 4, Oct. 1982, pp. 699-703

Well, if she is refused abortion in one place, or if welfare won't pay for it, then she will get it anyway, won't she, either legally or illegally? The studies show otherwise. Of a total of 6,298 women in six different studies, only 13.2% went elsewhere for an abortion. The studies showed no disadvantage or problems with the balance of the pregnancy and delivery and "good acceptance of the baby and minimal to moderate psychosocial disadvantages for the child."

What does the Bible say?

It is doubtful whether the Lord would smile upon such fatal selectivity as abortion for unwanted pregnancy or even upon those who would think that sperm from Nobel Prize winners would be the "best." God did not judge from "his appearance or his lofty stature." No, "The Lord has not chosen any one of these," said He, as Jesse lined up his handsome sons. Samuel asked if any were missing. "Yes, the youngest," David, who was tending the sheep. "Send for him," Samuel said, and when he came the Lord said, "there — annoint him, for this is he."

Samuel, 16/1, 6-7, 10-13 (31)

Clearly, God judges not from intelligence or beauty or ability, but rather from what each person is in their mind and heart and what each has done with the gifts that he or she has been given.

The Rev. Charles Carroll, Protestant chaplain of the University of California at Berkeley, student of International Law at Yale, Harvard, and the University of Berlin during the Hitler period, and officer of the United States military government in Germany at the trial of the Nazi doctors at Nuremberg, has stated:

"As I would reject the law of paterfamilias of ancient Rome, so I would also reject the law of materfamilias in present-day America. As I would not sympathize with the grant by the state of the power of life and death of his offspring to the Roman father, so I cannot sympathize with the grant by any state of the power of life and death over her offspring to the American mother. Surely, I would hope our legislators would be as humane as the Emperor Hadrian, who abolished that article of the Roman Law."

A nation and its people will ultimately be judged not by the fact that there are unwanted ones among them, but by what is done for them.

Are They Cared For?
or
Are They Killed?

**"Amen, I say to you
what you have done to these,
the least of my brethren,
you have done to me."**

CHAPTER 19

Assault Rape, Incest

The bruised, upset, crying woman, just victimized by a rapist, goes to the emergency room of the nearby hospital. She is cared for and treated and does not become pregnant.

Another woman, ashamed or too frightened, goes home and cries in her pillow. She does not report in for treatment. On rare occasions she does become pregnant. Much more frequently, she gets V.D.

The V.D. can be treated, but the pregnancy? Should this innocent woman be forced to carry the rapist's child? What if it were your daughter? Shouldn't we allow abortion at least for this reason?

Is pregnancy from rape common?
No. It is very rare.

Why?
There are a number of reasons:

- The woman may be on the pill.

- It may be during the non-fertile days of her cycle.

- She or he may be sterile, naturally or through disease or surgery.

- She may be too young or too old to conceive.

- There can be disruption of the ovulation cycle due to the extreme emotional trauma.

  A. Helligers, U.S.C.C. Ab. Conference,
  Washington, DC, Oct. 1967

- One study shows that there is often no sperm deposited in the vagina.

  Groth & Burgess,
  New England Jour. Med., vol. 297, 1977, pp. 764-766

- Another study shows there is 58% "sexual dysfunction" (no penetration or retarded or premature ejaculation).

  Sexual Medicine Today, Jan. 1978, p. 16

Can you prove that pregnancy is rare?

A study of 1,000 rape victims, who were treated medically right after the rape, reported no pregnancies.

L. Kuchera, "Postcoital Contraception with Diethylstilbesterol,"
JAMA, October 25, 1971

In another study, medical treatment on more than 1,000 women, was "100% effective," according to Dr. B. Craver at the Wilson Foundation.

B. Craver, "Morning After Pill Prevents Pregnancy in Victims of Rape,"
Family Practice News, Mar. 1972

What if the rape victim is not treated?

If it is limited to true assault rape, the pregnancy rate will still be extremely small. If all "reported" rapes, including statutory rape (under 18-years-old, but sometimes with consent given), when drunk (with questionable consent), etc., it is higher. There are two such large, across-the-board studies of all reported rapes (with no reported attempt to validate them), in Washington, DC for the years 1965-1969 and 1969-1970. These reported on rape victims seen by private doctors, clinics, and hospitals, with no details as to treatment, if any. Of the 2,190 women in the first study and the 1,223 women in the second, a total of 23 and of 21 pregnancies occurred, or rates of 6 and 17 per 1,000. If these had been limited to true assaults and the women had been given hormone treatment, the pregnancy rate would have been much lower, perhaps zero.

Hayman & Lanza, "Sexual Assault on Women and Girls,"
Amer. Jour. OB/GYN, vol. 109, no. 3, Feb. 1971, pp. 480-486

Hayman et al., "Rape in the District of Columbia,"
Amer. Jour. OB/GYN, vol. 113, no. 1, May 1972, pp. 91,97

In another series of 117 assault rape victims, of whom only 17 were given hormone treatment after the attack, none became pregnant.

Everett & Jimerson, "The Rape Victim,"
OB & GYN, vol. 50, no. 1, July 1977, pp. 88-90

In still another series of 126 assault rape victims, only half of those at risk of pregnancy were treated, but none became pregnant.

Evrard & Gold, "Epidemiology and Management of Sexual Assault Victims," *OB & GYN*, vol. 53, no. 3, Mar. 1979, pp. 381-387

Dr. Alfred Kinsey reported that of 2,094 single females who had voluntary intercourse 460,000 times, the pregnancy rate was 1 per 1,000 exposures. Many of these women had used contraception, many had not, but it is also true that some assaulted women have I.U.D.s or/and are on the pill.

A. Kinsey, *Sexual Behavior of the Human Female*,
N. Saunders Publishers, 1953, p. 327

And in other countries?

In Czechoslovakia, out of 86,000 consecutive induced abortions, only 22 were done for rape.

In England, in 1938, Dr. Aleck Bourne had a 14-year-old girl brought to him who had been raped. She became pregnant. He did the abortion, and then gave himself up to the police. He was tried and finally acquitted on the grounds that he had performed the operation in order to save the girl's sanity. It was on the findings of this trial that British law was based until all abortion was legalized in that country in 1967. For many years it was very conservatively interpreted to provide protection for doctors to use their medical judgment in the "hard cases." Ultimately, however, it opened the door to abortion-on-demand.

It is significant to point out that the same Aleck Bourne, "appalled" by the way in which the results of his case ultimately opened to door to abortion-on-demand and all of its abuses, became a founding member of the Society for the Protection of Unborn Children in 1967.

How many assault rape pregnancies are there?

In 1981, in the U.S., there were 99,000 rapes reported. There are about 100,000,000 females old enough to be at risk. This means that 1 in 1,000 is raped each year.

If we use the figure of 1 rape/1,000 women/year and calculate on the basis of 1 pregnancy for every 500 rapes, we find 200 pregnancies. If we use the more reasonable 1 per 1,000, we find only 100 pregnancies per year in the entire United States, or only 1 pregnancy per year in a state of 2 million people.

If we assume that only half of all assault rapes are reported and that there are 200,000 rapes/year, and then calculate a pregnancy rate of 1/500 and 1/1,000, we get 400 and 200 pregnancies per year.

If we use the figure of 1 rape/1,500 women/year, we have 60,000 victims and 120 or 60 pregnancies. This would agree with one reliable report listing a total figure of 63,020 rapes per year.

F.B.I., U.S. Dept. of Justice
Uniform Crime Reports, 1977, pp. 15-18

Again, using the 1 rape/1,000/year, even if we use the

146

totally unrealistic pregnancy rate of 1 pregnancy/100 assaults, there would still be only 1,000 pregnancies/year in the entire U.S. resulting from rape.

Since only half of those who become pregnant will want abortions, the final figure could be somewhere between 30 and 500 rape pregnancy abortions per year, with a more likely figure between 50 and 100.

That isn't many!

No! Using a figure of 1,600,000 abortions/year in the U.S., that means there will be about 25,000 elective abortions done in the U.S. for other reasons for every one abortion performed because of rape.

What of legal proof for rape?

If the woman goes directly to the hospital, her word is accepted. But, sadly, through fright or ignorance, she may not report it and quietly nurse her fears. She misses her period and hopes against hope that it isn't what she thinks it is. Another month, another month, and finally, in tears, she reports to her mother, her physician, or some other counselor or confidante. To prove rape then is impossible. The only proof of rape then is to have a reliable witness corroborate the story, and such a witness almost never exists.

What of a law that would allow abortion only for assault rape or incest?

Such a law would affect only a few women. If she does go immediately to the hospital and is treated, the rape victim almost certainly will not get pregnant. If she doesn't go and does become pregnant, she cannot prove it was due to rape.

Responsible lawmakers have always agreed that "hard cases make bad laws." This means that laws must speak to the general norm. Judges have always allowed certain exceptions to laws or to punishment out of mercy for a "hard" or tragic case. The Bourne Case was a good example, until some judges and countries (like Jamaica) stretched its meaning to allow abortion-on-demand.

147

The plea to legalize abortion here and abroad leaned heavily on the tragedy of hard cases such as rape. Once abortion became legal, it was quickly apparent that 99% of abortions were done for social and economic reasons and less than 1% were performed for rape and incest, for physical health problems, and for severe fetal handicap.

But, even if rare, some girls are forcibly raped and some do get pregnant. Should they be forced to carry an unwanted child?

Unquestionably, many would return the violence of killing an innocent baby for the violence of rape. But, before making this decision, remember that most of the trauma has already occurred. She has been raped. That trauma will live with her all her life. Furthermore, this girl did not report for help, but kept this to herself. For several weeks or months, she has thought of little else. Now, she has finally asked for help, has shared her upset, and should be in a supportive situation.

The utilitarian question from the mother's standpoint is whether or not it would now be better to kill the developing baby within her. But will abortion now be best for her, or will it bring her more harm yet? What has happened and its damage has already occurred. She's old enough to know and have an opinion as to whether she carries a "baby" or a "blob of protoplasm."

Will she be able to live comfortably with the memory that she *"killed her developing baby"*? Or would she ultimately be more mature and more at peace with herself if she could remember that, even though she became pregnant unwillingly, she nevertheless solved her problem by being unselfish, by giving of herself and of her love to an innocent baby, who had not asked to be created, to deliver, perhaps to place for adoption, if she decides that is what is best for her baby.

Compare this memory with the woman who can only look back and say, *"I killed my baby."*

But carry the rapist's child?

True, it is half his. But remember, half of the baby is also the mother's flesh and blood.

I don't see how she could!

"Interestingly, the pregnant rape victim's chief complaint is not that she is unwillingly pregnant, as bad as the experience is. The critical moment is fleeting in this area. It frequently pulls families together like never before. When women are impregnated through rape, their condition is treated in accordance, as are their families.

"We found this experience is forgotten, replaced by remembering the abortion, because it is what *they* did."

M. Uchtman, Director, Suiciders Anonymous,
Report to Cincinnati City Council, Sept. 1, 1981

"In the majority of these cases, the pregnant victim's problems stem more from the trauma of rape than from the pregnancy itself."

Mahkorn & Dolan, "Sexual Assault & Pregnancy."
In *New Perspectives on Human Abortion*,
University Publishers of Amer., 1981, pp. 182-199

As to what factors make it most difficult to continue her pregnancy, the opinions, attitudes, and beliefs of others were most frequently cited; in other words, how her loved ones treated her.

Mahkorn, "Pregnancy & Sexual Assault." In *Psychological Aspects of Abortion*, University Publishers of Amer., 1979, pp. 53-72

But wouldn't it be safer physically to abort a young girl than to let her deliver?

Quite the contrary! Teenage abortions have more complications than those done on older women. Teenage deliveries are as safe as, and perhaps safer, than deliveries done on older women. For detailed studies, see chapters 15 & 17.

The "treatment" for rape, isn't it abortive?

This is best illustrated by giving two theoretical case histories. Woman "A" is raped at midnight on Saturday and is treated in a hospital emergency room with a female hormone medication at 3:00 a.m. Sunday morning. In this case, the woman's body was scheduled to ovulate two days later, on Monday. If that were to have occurred, and if the assailant's sperm were still alive in her body, she might have been fertilized two days after the assault and might have become pregnant at that time. There is a substantial body of medical opinion that believes that the dose of medication given would prevent that ovulation, and she would therefore not get pregnant. This mechanism of action would be one of temporary sterilization, or, in more commonly used (however technically inaccurate) terms, the action would be contraceptive.

Woman "B" presents a different case. She had ovulated at 9:00 p.m. on Saturday, was raped at midnight, and also received treatment at 3:00 a.m. To her own observation, this lady also does not "get pregnant." In fact, something entirely different happened inside her body. Let us assume that she was one of those very rare cases where fertilization did occur, and had, in fact, occurred prior to the giving of the medication. The life of a tiny new little boy or girl had begun. The cells of this tiny body begin to divide and divide again, but at one week of life, when implantation within the nutrient lining of the mother's womb should occur, this tiny new human being could not implant and died. The mechanism of action of the drug, in this case, had been to "harden" the lining of the womb in order to prevent implantation. This effect was one of a micro-abortion, at one week of life.

Would a Human Life Amendment prevent such treatment?

Most legal opinion is quite positive about the fact that, since these drugs would never be removed from the market because they have a multiplicity of other beneficial and therapeutic effects, and since the affect they would have in some (most?) cases, such as the above, would be a legally permissible one (that is, temporary sterilization), that even with a strong Human Life Amendment in place, the use of such drugs after rape could not be forbidden. Therefore, the choice now available to a woman after an assault rape, to use or not use such treatment, would still be available after a Human Life Amendment.

But in a rape pregnancy, everyone loses!

In her beautiful autobiography, *His Eye Is on the Sparrow,* Ethel Waters reveals that she was conceived following the rape of her 13-year-old mother, at a time when rape treatment was unavailable. Her mother's love and Ethel Water's value to society were not diminished by the circumstances surrounding her conception.

In our own experience, once, after answering questions on rape on a radio show, one of your authors was called to the phone after the program. A woman's voice said,

> "You were talking about me. You see, I am the product of rape. An intruder forced his way into my parents' house, tied up my father and, with him watching, raped my mother. I was conceived that night. Everyone advised an abortion. The local doctors and hospital were willing. My father, however, said, 'Even though not mine, that is a child and I will not allow it to be killed!' I don't know how many times that, as I lay secure in the loving arms of my husband, I have thanked God for my wonderful Christian father."

What of incest?

Incest is intercourse by a father with his daughter, uncle with niece, etc. It usually involves a sick man, often a sick woman (she frequently knows it's happening, even if not consciously admitting it), and an exploited child. Fortunately, pregnancy is not very common. When incest does occur, however, it is seldom reported and, when reported, is hard to prove.

Pregnancy is not common?

Correct. "Considering the prevalence of teenage pregnancies in general, incest treatment programs marvel at the low incidence of pregnancy from incest." Several reports agree at 1% or less.

G. Maloof, "The Consequences of Incest," *The Psychological Aspects of Abortion*, University Publications of Amer., 1979, p. 74

When pregnancy does occur, it is often an attempt to end the relationship. In a twisted sort of way, however, the father is a love object. In one study, only 3 of 13 child-mothers had any negative feelings toward him.

H. Maisch, *Incest*,
New York: Stein & Day Publishers, 1972

How does the incest victim feel about being pregnant?

For her, it is a way to stop the incest; a way to unite mother and daughter; a way to get out of the house. Most incestuous pregnancies, if not pressured, will not get abortions.

"As socially inappropriate as incest and incestuous pregnancies are, their harmful effects depend largely upon reaction of others."

ibid, Maloof, p. 100

The answer?

Even strongly pro-abortion people, if they approach an incest case professionally, must be absolutely convinced before advising abortion, for it not only is an assault on the young mother, who may well be pregnant with a "love object," but it may completely fail to solve the original problem.

It is also unusual for wisdom to dictate anything but adoptive placement of the baby.

**Finally,
Isn't it a Twisted Logic
that would Kill an Innocent Unborn Baby
for the Crime of His Father?**

CHAPTER 20

Western Civilization is Dying

Dying? When there is overpopulation?

There isn't overpopulation at all. The problem is too low a birth rate and an aging population.

POPULATION IN MILLIONS – 1980

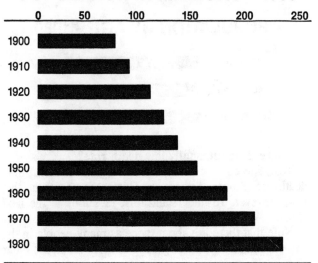

In which countries?

Almost all of Western Europe, Canada, and the United States, Japan, Australia, and New Zealand.

But the population of the U.S. is still growing.

That is correct. The total number of people living in the U.S. (and Canada) is still increasing. The 1982 figure was 237 million. The rate of growth is slowing markedly, however, as is evident from the 1980 Census below.

But this continued growth is not due to an adequate birth rate, for the birth rate is much too low. It is due to two other reasons:

- Immigration; this accounts for half of the growth.

  J. Passel, Census Bureau, U.S.A.
  Today, Nov. 18, 1982

- The longer life span of the elderly. Many, who in years past would have already died, are still alive. The average life expectancy has been dramatically lengthened in recent years.

POPULATION BY AGE – 1980

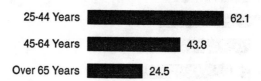

25-44 Years	62.1
45-64 Years	43.8
Over 65 Years	24.5

So there is an unusually low death rate?

Yes. The current death rate in the U.S. is about nine deaths per thousand per year. This cannot continue this low, however. To understand this, let's look at the next chart.

Note that there are about twice as many people in the two younger 20-year age groups as there are in the older one.

- Not many people die in the 25-45 age group.

- Some people die in the 45-65 age group.

- Everyone dies in the 65-and-older group.

Today, there are 9/1,000/year persons dying (almost all in the 65-and-older group). Tomorrow, there will be twice as many people in the "dying" age group. Therefore, there will be twice as many people dying.

- Today, we are burying 9/1,000/year.

- Tomorrow, we will by burying 15-20/1,000/year.

What about the birth rate?

Ah, there's the rub! The only factor that ultimately determines population growth or decline is the birth rate. In order for a population to just replace itself — to have ZPG (zero population growth) — the average woman, in her reproductive years, must have 2.1 to 2.2 children. If the average is higher, the nation grows. If the average is lower, the nation ages and slowly dies.

The U.S. has been at, or below, 1.8 since 1972. Only three of the 50 states have rates over 2.5: Wyoming, 2.4; Idaho, 2.5; and Utah, 3.2; whereas Rhode Island, North Carolina, and Massachusetts have the lowest birth rate at 1.5.

"Drop in Fertility Rate," *USA Today,* Oct. 10, 1984, p. 5A

POPULATION REPLACEMENT

Needed 2.1 – 2.2 Babies/Woman

Actual Is 1.8 Babies/Woman

We Are An Aging, Dying Nation

What will this lead to?

Today, more persons are born than we are burying.

Tomorrow, we will be burying more people than are born.

The clear and inevitable result will be a nation with more and more elderly and fewer and fewer young people. Then, given time alone, the population will crest and begin to drop. For example, comparing 1980 with 1970, there were 6,500,000 fewer school-age children and 9,000 public elementary schools had to close.

Newsweek, Mar. 30, 1981

What can prevent this?

It could be prevented by continuing heavy immigration. Both the U.S. and Canada are host to large numbers of immigrants. At the current birth and immigration rates, the indigenous Anglo race (white, European ancestry) in the U.S. will be a minority by the middle of the next century. If immigration is heavy enough and the new immigrants have enough babies, the population could even grow, but the ethnic composition will be far different from today.

The second possibility would require a dramatic increase in the birth rate in the near future within our present population. There is no sign of this happening. Furthermore, the increase would have to happen soon if it is to replenish the indigenous population. If too many years pass before another "baby boom," even if all women had twice as many babies as they are having today, they would not be able to "catch up," for there would be too few women of childbearing age.

What is the current situation in Europe?

Other Western nations are slightly above or below this. West Germany, at 1.2, is the most rapidly dying nation in the world. In Canada the rate is 1.8. In all of Western Europe, only one country is well above replacement level — Ireland.

"The European Parliament is seriously disturbed by statistics showing a rapid decline in the birth rate on the European Economic Community, which fell from 2.79 in 1964 to 1.68 in 1982."

In 1950 the ten European nations accounted for 8.8% of the world's population. At the present rate, it will drop to 4.5% by the year 2000 and to 2.3% by the year 2030.

European Parliament News, no. 53, April/May 1984

As mentioned, Germany is dying faster than any other nation, with only 1.2 children per family. With 57 million people, it has about 500,000 abortions per year. If the birth trend continues, Germany's "population is expected to fall to 38 million in 50 years."

W. Drozdiak, "West German Birthrate Dropping," *Washington Post,* Jan. 10, 1984

And the Third World?

Most of it still has a growing population, but the rate of growth is progressively declining.

A number of things must be said about this.

Overall, there has been, and continues to be, a steady decline in the fertility rate of Third World countries. "For the first time in history, the growth rate of the world's population has peaked and is now falling," said the World Bank. The population should level off at 11 billion people in the year 2150.

J. Walte, *USA Today,* July 11, 1984, p. 4A

The U.S. policy paper presented to the 1984 United Nations Population Conference in Mexico City was very clear. It noted that economic growth and a rising standard of living is associated with a falling birth rate. It also stated that the U.S. AID program will not fund family planning programs if they include abortion.

The UN Population Conference adopted a recommendation, without dissent, that abortion "in no way should be promoted" as a family planning method.

Even John D. Rockefeller, Jr., the most zealous population control advocate of all, finally admitted, after the 1974 UN Population Conference in Bucharest, that the outside imposition of any type of family planning (abortion, sterilization, contraception) on an underdeveloped nation or subgroup within a nation has never been effective. People just won't cooperate. The only measures that have worked have been to raise that group's standard of living, to reduce infant and childhood mortality, and to raise expectation of (and provide opportunity for) education. If these changes are accomplished, people will then *voluntarily* limit the number of their children for two reasons: a) they want more for each child, and b) they can reasonably expect their children to survive to adulthood and be alive to care for them in their old age.

Each country is its own case. Just because there is overpopulation in one country doesn't mean that a more developed one should commit national suicide.

What's Russia's birth rate?

Russia is a special case. Along with all of the Eastern European Iron-Curtain countries, White Russia (the western part) has a birth rate well below replacement level. Eastern Russia and its large Moslem areas have high birth rates. The West speaks Russian and is better educated. East and Southeast Russians do not speak Russian and are less well educated. White Russians will soon comprise less than 50% of the population, and Russia has no immigration to speak of. It seems many people want out, but few want in.

What are the effects of an aging population?

The effects are far reaching. Fewer children become fewer adolescents and fewer young people, and fewer taxpaying workers. By 2025 the world (not just the U.S.) will have twice as many grandparents as babies.

U.N. Conference, Vienna
Washington Times, July 24, 1982

The Western world, in the past half-century, has become very socially conscious and has supported its senior and disabled citizens with tax funds on a scale previously unknown. But, unless there are enough taxpaying younger workers, there will be no way that such retirement and medical benefits can continue. The U.S. Social Security Program is a classic example, as shown below.

	RETIRED	WORKERS SUPPORTING
1980	1	3.5
2000	1	3.0
2020	1	2.
2040	1	1.5

But doesn't the U.S. use up a high percentage of the world's natural resources?

It is a fact that there are more such resources available today than there were a decade or two ago. In America one farmer feeds 99 other people. In some countries, one farmer cannot even feed his own family. What is our solution? Should we encourage American farmers and industrial workers to kill their own preborn children or should we stay strong, have children, and help to teach those other farmers and workers to be more productive?

Aren't we having a mini baby boom now?

In 1957 the average woman, during her reproductive years, had 3.7 children. There were 4,300,000 children born that year. (Keep in mind that replacement level is 2.1 children per woman.) Through the 1970s this rate dropped to only 1.8 children born per woman. But, with many more women of childbearing age (as a result of previous higher replacement rates), the total births were about 3,500,000 babies per year. The baby boom women born in the 1950s-60s are now in their prime childbearing years. If they had maintained the fertility rate of their mothers, the U.S. would be having over 7,000,000 births per year. Just to maintain a ZPG replacement rate, we would need 4,200,000 births per year. In reality, we have only inched up to 3,600,000 from the low of 3,200,000 in 1975. Because of this drastic shrinkage of young people in our population, the number of taxpayers supporting each retired person will continue to be fewer. At current birth rates, note the chart below.

LIVE BIRTHS & ABORTIONS IN THE UNITED STATES

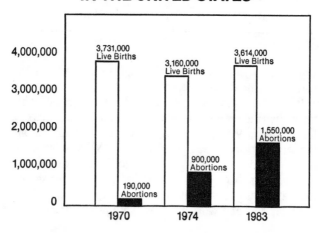

Only one and one-half taxpayers to support every retired person? That's an impossible situation! What will happen?
Euthanasia!
Yes, that will be the answer. Today's "Every Child a

Wanted Child" will become tomorrow's "Every Grandparent a Wanted Grandparent."

Doctor Gallop said it well; we should listen.

"Once you permit the killing of the unborn child, there will be no stopping. There will be no age limit. You are setting off a chain reaction that will eventually make you the victim.

"Your children will kill you because you permitted the killing of their brothers and sisters. Your children will kill you because they will not want to support you in your old age. Your children will kill you for your homes and estates.

"If a doctor will take money for killing the innocent in the womb, he will kill you with a needle when paid by your children. This is the terrible nightmare you are creating for the future."

Dr. R. A. Gallop

That is frightening. Is there no other answer?

Only the obvious one. Canadians are killing one out of six babies conceived. Americans are killing almost one of three. Some European countries have even worse statistics.

Why Not Quit Killing Preborn Babies?
It just Might be Worth Our Own Lives

CHAPTER 21

Illegal Abortions and Abortion Funding

> *The "coat hanger" and the "back alley"
> abortions were moving arguments which orig-
> inally convinced many to work for legalized
> abortion.*

**If abortion was again forbidden, wouldn't we have a
return to these "back alley" abortions, resulting in
thousands of women dying?**

Before we answer that, we must first ask, "How many
women used to die from illegal abortions?"

Why?

Because anyone who gives you a figure on the total number of illegal abortions is guessing. There are no records. By
definition, illegal abortions are not recorded. The only way
to estimate the number of illegal abortions is to first find out
how many women died from abortions. Their deaths were
reported. Then we must guess what percent of such abortions ended in a maternal death and figure backwards to the
total number of abortions there were.

How many women did die?

Mortality figures from the U.S. Bureau of Vital Statistics
were gathered and presented during the U.S. Senate debate

on the Hatch-Eagleton Amendment in June 1983 (see chapter 6). The chart used in that debate (see chart below) included all reported deaths from illegal and legal abortions.

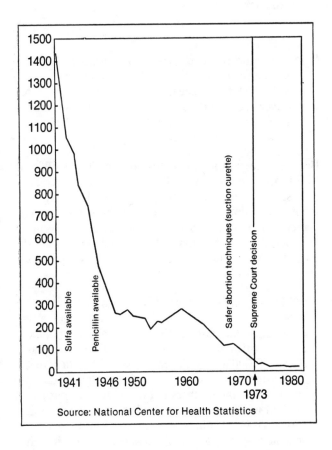

Source: National Center for Health Statistics

One must go back to the pre-Penicillin era to find a year during which more than 1,000 women died from abortions in the U.S. There was a precipitous drop in deaths in the late 1940s and early 1950s which was clearly due to improved medical care.

By the time the first state legalized abortions in 1967, only 160 mothers were dying annually as a result of abortions. In 1973, when the Supreme Court decision was rendered, only 45 women died.

U.S. Dept. HHS, Center for Disease Control,
Abortion Surveillance, Nov. 1980

Once abortion was legal, then fewer women died?

The legality of abortion had no effect on reported deaths. The slowly decreasing line on the chart didn't even waver. It continued on its previous downward course. The figure for 1977 was 21 deaths (17 legal, 4 illegal), for 1981, it was 9 deaths (8 legal, 1 illegal).

But I've heard time and again that between 5,000 and 10,000 women died annually from illegal abortions.

Yes, those were the figures publicized. The only comment about them is the statement from Dr. Bernard Nathanson, a cofounder of the National Association for the Repeal of Abortion Laws (N.A.R.A.L.) — a man who once ran the largest abortion facility in the Western world and is now pro-life. He stated:

> "How many deaths were we talking about when abortion was illegal? In N.A.R.A.L., we generally emphasized the frame of the individual case, not the mass statistics, but when we spoke of the latter it was always '5,000 to 10,000 deaths a year.' I confess that I knew the figures were *totally false,* [italics added] and I suppose the others did too if they stopped to think of it. But in the 'morality' of our revolution, it was a *useful* [Nathanson's italics] figure, widely accepted, so why go out of our way to correct it with honest statistics? The overriding concern was to get the laws eliminated, and anything within reason that had to be done was permissible."

B. Nathanson, *Aborting America,*
Doubleday: 1979, p. 193

So there obviously weren't nearly as many illegal abortions as many claim?

That's right. The often-quoted figure of one million a year in the U.S. is obviously ridiculous.

Then, actually how many illegal abortions were there?

One study quoted in the U.S. Senate debate was authored by Dr. T. Hilgers from Creighton University, who estimated the figure probably was at or somewhere near 100,000 abortions annually in the U.S. prior to legalization.

Are there any other studies?

There have not been many in recent years. Most were done comparing the time before and right after legalization in other countries. In the earlier editions of *HANDBOOK ON ABORTION*, we listed studies done in England (*Brit. Med. Jour.*, May 1970, 1972, and *Lancet*, Mar. 1968); Japan (*Asahi Jour.*, Oct. 16, 1966); Hungary (*Internatl. Jour. of OB/GYN*, May 1971); and the U.S. (*Amer. Jour. of Public Health*, No. 1967). All these studies showed that illegal abortions had not decreased significantly after legalization.

B. Willke & J. Willke, "Reduce Illegal Abortions."
HANDBOOK ON ABORTION, Hayes Publishing, Cinn. 1979: p. 10

So what are we to think?

It is clear that there always were and always will be some illegal abortions, but either the actual numbers were only a small fraction of what the pro-abortionists have claimed, or the illegal abortionists of years past were remarkably skillful.

In fact, it is clear that legal abortions have skyrocketed and today are 10 to 20 times more numerous than illegal ones were.

But, if we do outlaw abortions again, won't some women die?

Today, legal abortion deaths of mothers have replaced

the illegal ones. If abortion were outlawed, we would see a 90% reduction in abortions performed and probably a similar reduction in abortion deaths.

Further, we'll never return to the "coat hanger" abortions.

Never return to the "coat hanger?" Who says?
Dr. Nathanson, the man who helped start it all and then became convinced that he "had in fact presided over 60,000 deaths."

B. Nathanson, "Deeper Into Abortion,"
New England Jour. Med., Nov. 28, 1974, pp. 1189-1190

What did he say?
There are thousands of abortionists who are skilled now. Dr. Nathanson has detailed how much safer the abortion technique is than in years past.

Dr. Nathanson further stated,

> "One can expect that if abortion is ever driven underground again, even non-physicians will be able to perform this procedure with remarkable safety. No woman need die if she chooses to abort during the first twelve weeks of pregnancy."

B. Nathanson, *Aborting America,*
Doubleday: 1979, p. 193

Prior to legalization, Dr. Kinsey's study showed that in 1958, 84% to 87% of illegal abortions were done by "reputable physicians in good standing in their local medical associations." Dr. Mary Calderone, president of Planned Parenthood in 1960, stated that "90% of all illegal abortions are presently done by physicians."

M. Calderone, "Illegal Abortion as a Public Health Problem,"
Amer. Jour. of Health, vol. 50, July 1960, p. 949

Then there is a difference between illegal abortions and "back alley" abortions?
Yes! Doctors who did illegal abortions would let a

woman in the back door, take her money, and do the abortion. Today, the same abortionist lets her in the front door, takes her money, and does the abortion in the same way. There were self-induced abortions (and still are), but abortions from untrained "butchers" were increasingly rare and would be in the future.

I've heard of large numbers of women dying from illegal abortions in other countries.

In Portugal the claimed figure was 2,000 deaths. The actual number of all female deaths in the nation between the ages of 15-46 was 2,106 from all natural causes, accidents and illness. There were only 97 listed in the "complications of pregnancy" of which 12 were due to abortion, including spontaneous and induced, legal and illegal.

Portuguese Anuario Estatistico, Tables 11, 16, 111

In Italy, the claimed figure before their abortion referendum was 20,000 . In the age group 15-45, there were actually only 11,500 female deaths from all causes.

Primum Non Nocere, vol. IV, no. 1, 1983

In Germany the claim was that 15,000 women died annually. In fact, only 13,000 women of reproductive age die annually in West Germany, and less than 100 die of complications of abortion, legal and illegal.

Kurchoff, *Deutches Arzteblatt,* vol. 69, no. 27, Oct. 26, 1972

Isn't it cheaper to abort poor women than raise their children on welfare?

Dr. Louis Hellman, from the U.S. Department of HEW, said: "An abortion costs only about $350 at most, while prenatal care through the first year of a baby's life costs $2,200. It is estimated to cost $35,000 to raise a child to 18 years." In response, the strongly pro-abortion *Washington Post* said, "This is a terrible argument. Its implications are monstrous."

Washington Post, June 2, 1977

Incidentally, the average time a family stays on welfare is 27 months, not 18 years. When we peel away the outer layer of the rhetoric, what we expose is a callous cost-benefit analysis of solving poverty by killing the unborn children of the poor.

This continues to happen. In 1982, in Michigan, for instance, only 14.7% of pregnancies of non-welfare mothers ended in abortion, while 59.3% of welfare mothers were aborted. This clearly suggests compulsion when we realize that the minority classes who make up a large share of the welfare people are more against abortion than are the white middle and upper classes.

What if public funding of abortions is cut off?

There has been an excellent example. In 1977 the federal government of the U.S. paid for 295,000 welfare abortions. In 1978 it only paid for 2,000 abortions because the Hyde Amendment had cut off the funding.

The U.S. government's chief pro-abortion biostatistician, Dr. Willard Cates, predicted "a total of 77 excess deaths to women" who would turn to illegal abortions, plus five additional deaths due to delay of abortions into the later weeks of pregnancy.

Petitti & Cates, "Restricting Medicaid Funds: Projection of Excess Mortality," *Amer. Jour. Public Health,* vol 67, no. 9, Sept. 1977, pp. 860-862

In fact, his projection proved to be completely unfounded. A later article by the same department, which later surveyed ten states, revealed, "No increase in abortion related complications was observed.... No abortion deaths related to either legal or illegal abortions were detected, [and there was] no difference between institutions in funded and non-funded states."

*Morbitity and Mortality Weekly Report,*CDC, U.S. Dept. HEW, vol. 28, no. 4, Feb. 2, 1979

A later attempt to link three deaths as "abortion funding related" was shown not to be related to the funding cutoff at all. Total maternal abortion deaths were actually lower than before the cutoff in 1976.

"Health Effects of Restricting Funds for Abortions,"
*Morbitity and Mortality Weekly Report,*CDC,
U.S. Dept. HEW, vol. 28, no. 4, Feb. 2, 1979, p. 1

But, since you cannot stop illegal abortions, why not legalize them?

Did you know that more than 1,000,000 cars were stolen in the U.S. last year? Surely, this can't be stopped. Therefore, why not make it legal to steal cars? How many banks were robbed? That is a dangerous occupation. People get killed stealing cars and robbing banks. We'll never be able to stop all car stealing and bank robberies, true? Then, let's legalize car stealing and bank robbing to save those lives.

Since when is it possible to eliminate evil by legalizing it?

What do polls show on abortions paid for by tax money?

No poll with unbiased wording has ever shown a majority of citizens favoring government funding of abortions. In 1984 the strongly pro-abortion University of North Carolina polled its state to find that only 32% favored tax funding. An important finding was that 43% of the college educated favored such government "assistance," while only 17% of those with less than a high school education concurred. Also, 36% of men favored assistance, but only 28% of women.

So, those who would receive the "benefit" of tax-funded abortions wanted them the least. One might conclude that the elitist social planners see this as a way of reducing poverty — killing the unborn children of the poor.

**It isn't the poor who want abortions.
It's the rich who want abortions
for the poor**

CHAPTER 22

Impose Morality?

> *"The old law permitted abortion to save one life when two would otherwise die. The new law permits abortion to take one life when two would otherwise live."*
>
> *Herbert Ratner, M.D.*

Abortion was known and practiced in the world of Greece and Rome into which Christianity came. Judaism, having developed a high respect for the family, for women, and for individual life, had condemned abortion but found certain exceptions to it. The Christian message brought a further dignity to the concept of the individual person and the value of life. The idea of an individual, animate, immortal soul given by God to every human person, and hopefully, returning to him for eternity, was a powerful concept which transformed the Roman Empire within two centuries. The value of the unborn person became associated closely with a similar value granted to the born person, and as Christian beliefs crystallized in writing and tradition, condemnation of abortion came to be "an almost absolute value," as Professor John T. Noonan of the University of California at Berkley says in his book.

J. Noonan, *The Morality of Abortion,*
Harvard University Press: 1970, ch.1

What, specifically, was the Christian teaching?

The Gospel taught that Jesus was conceived in Mary's womb by the Holy Spirit. What grew in her womb from conception was not a blob of protoplasm but the person of the God-man Jesus. Also clearly taught was that the infant John (the Baptist) "leaped" in the womb of Elizabeth. These specific references to the living personhood of the human embryo were reinforced by the teachings of the Fathers of the Church. The Didache said, "You shall not slay the child by abortion." Clement of Alexandria condemned abortion, as did Athenagoras: "Those who use abortifacients are homicides." Tertullian said, "The mold in the womb may not be destroyed." The Council of Ancyra in 314 denounced women who "slay what is generated." Another Council in 305 at Alvira excommunicated women committing abortion after adultery and would not even readmit them to the Church at the point of death. While Sts. Jerome and Augustine questioned when the rational soul was given by God, this did not affect their complete moral condemnation of abortion. In the late fourth century, St. Basil wrote, "The hairsplitting difference between formed and unformed makes no difference to us. Whoever deliberately commits abortion is subject to the penalty for homicide."

The early Christians saw their attitudes about women, children, and the structure of the family as distinctive and revolutionary. The second century Epistle to Dionysius proclaims that Christians "marry like everyone else, and they beget children, but they do not cast out their offspring."

By the time the curtain of the barbarian invasions rang down on the glory of Rome, the Christian teaching had codified itself into an extremely firm and certain moral opinion. Abortion was condemned. There was no question about Christian belief.

What was Thomas Aquinas' opinion 700 years later?

Thomas totally condemned abortion for any and all reasons.

Aquinas did question when the soul was created. He spoke of the then-current scientific conviction that a male child was not fully enough developed to be judged human (and therefore to have a soul) until forty days, and that the female fetus could not be judged fully human until eighty days. This obviously says something about scientific knowledge of that age. Aquinas was reflecting a theological and scientific judgment that mirrored the most accurate scientific information of this time. When, to the most exact instrument available, the unaided human eye, the unborn child looked like a child and the individual's sex could be determined, it (he or she) was deemed dignified and developed enough to be the possessor of an immortal soul, and so Aquinas made his conclusions.

Since that time we have progressed to electron microscopes, ultrasonic stethoscopes and *Realtime* ultrasonic movies, and increasingly sophisticated knowledge of chromosomes and genes. We now must make judgments in the light of our new and more accurate biological knowledge. Aquinas' conclusions were the best that could be expected in his day. While not applicable today, they are of historical significance. Had men of his time had today's knowledge of embryonic and fetal development, their conclusions would have been different.

They didn't think that there was life until the soul was created?

Correct, but they still totally forbad abortion, and the penances for the sin of abortion were severe. For the first eleven hundred years, the laws punished fetal destruction, whatever the stage of formation or animation.

D. Granfield, *The Abortion Decision,*
Garden City, NY: Doubleday, 1969, p. 72

The Church's teaching changed then!

The moral prohibition against killing after conception did not change. After the 12th century, there was some legal acceptance that a soul may not be present until the fetus was "formed." However, Canon law still condemned induced abortion. The change was only that the killing of a formed fetus was classified as homicide.

ibid, p. 72

In the penitentia's of *Canones Hibernensus* (A.D. 675), the penance for the sin of abortion was seven years of exclusion from the Sacraments as well as public penance on bread and water for the destruction of "the embryo of a child in the mother's womb."

J. Connery, "Abortion, the Development of the
Roman Catholic Perspective." In *Private Penance*,
Loyola Univ. Press: 1977, p. 68

The Council of Ancyra imposed 10 years of penance.

Anglo-Saxon penitentials proscribed more severe penances after the soul was infused (presumably at 40 days), a practice followed on the continent.

The Council of Elvera made the exclusion from the sacraments permanent (for life).

ibid, pp. 65, 72, 65

When did changes in the earlier absolute Christian position begin to occur?

In the centuries before and after the Protestant Reformation, Christian thinkers came to debate and, in some cases, to justify the use of therapeutic abortion for the purpose of saving the life of the mother. Later, other reasons were added, such as the removal of an ectopic (tubal) pregnancy or of a cancerous pregnant womb. Both of these killed the growing unborn child if still alive, but were not direct assaults upon the child's life for the primary purpose of destroying it. Rather, they had another, more primary effect, that of saving the mother's life. No major religious bodies came to endorse abortion for less serious reasons until the middle of this century.

I've heard that the Catholic Church only forbad abortion after 1869.

In 1869 Pope Pius IX removed the formed-unformed

fetus distinction from Canon law. Instead of a less stringent punishment for early abortions and a more stringent punishment for later abortions, he again made the punishment for all abortions the same. This punishment was excommunication, a penalty which has been continuously reaffirmed since then.

ibid, Connery, p. 212

What needs repeating is that, while the Canon law punishment for the sin of abortion varied, the Church's teaching was constant. Abortion was always condemned.

"Some have thought that the Catholic teaching on the morality of abortion has altered with each change in Canon law. This is altogether mistaken. The Canon law always has assumed that all abortion is a serious sin. From this assumption it has proceeded variously in different periods to try to discourage Catholics from committing this sin."

Grisez, *Abortion, the Myths, the Realities, and the Arguments*,
New York: Corpus Books: 1970, pp. 180-181

But this entire concept of soul is only a belief. It cannot be proven!
That is correct. It is a faith belief. One person may believe the soul is created at conception, another at three months, another at birth, and yet another does not believe in the presence of a soul at all. Each of us has the right to believe what we wish.

If the pro-life forces triumph and abortion is again condemned, it may well be that other family preserving values will be strengthened. But if we fail, few other family life values or interpersonal moral values can endure if the one person ordained by nature and by God to protect this helpless innocent little one is allowed to kill her own flesh and blood to "solve" her own personal, social, or economic problem.

Some think that the nuclear war issue is a more important moral concern than abortion.
Sincere pro-lifers have taken positions on both sides of

the nuclear issue, and we should respect both. As to importance and gravity, there are differences of opinion.

- The nuclear holocaust is still but a threat. Since the U.S.S.R. matched the U.S.'s atom bomb 35 years ago, no one has died in a nuclear war. The abortion holocaust is happening now. Over 1½ million deaths occur annually in the U.S. alone.

- A war is an activity of the state, and any citizen of the nation involved may or may not agree. They do share responsibility but in a distanced, indirect, and corporate way.
    Abortion is an immediate, personal, one-on-one, voluntary decision over which each participating person has direct control.

- A war, if a just one, that is, a defensive one, defends from another's attack. Abortion is direct aggression which kills an innocent baby. In war we defend our lives. In abortion, we aggressively kill others.

How does religious belief influence the abortion issue then?
Belief in God, in our creation by Him, in His authorship of life, of His Commandments and His justice, and in our brotherhood and sisterhood with the unborn is a powerful motivation leading believers to work for the protection of the unborn. The bottom line is that our religious faith *motivates* us. It can never be the sole legal justification for seeking laws to protect the unborn, the handicapped, and the elderly.

What right has any religious body to impose its morality upon a woman?
If this were a sectarian religious belief, there would be justice to such a complaint. In fact, this is not a religious question except in the broad sense of equal rights, dignity, and justice for all.

If any religious philosophy has been imposed upon a nation, it is Secular Humanism. The U.S. Supreme Court has defined Humanism as a religion. The officer corps of the pro-abortion movement is almost entirely made up of secular humanists who have imposed their beliefs upon our nation.

I have the right to swing my fist, but that right stops at your nose. A woman has certain (not total) rights to her own body, but not over another living human's body just because he or she still happens to live inside her.

The Ten Commandments forbad murder and stealing. So do the laws of every civilized nation. Do those laws impose religious morality? Hardly!

This is a civil rights issue. It is a question of whether an entire class of living humans shall be deprived of their basic right to life on the basis of age and place of residence.

Perhaps the question should be turned around:

What Right Does a Mother and Her Abortionist Have to Impose Their Morality Upon Her Unborn Child ... Fatally?

CHAPTER 23

Capital Punishment, War, and Nuclear Arms

> *Charge: Pro-life people are inconsistent.*
> *They are all for stopping the killing of the*
> *unborn, but they all favor the killing resulting*
> *from capital punishment and war.*

Are all pro-lifers for capital punishment?

Certainly not! Your authors, along with a probable majority of pro-life leaders, oppose capital punishment. Two-thirds or more of the general public favor it, as do some very sincere pro-lifers. Some who favor capital punishment are Christians who are convinced that there is Biblical justification for it.

What is the position of pro-abortion advocates?

They are the ones who are inconsistent. With few exceptions, pro-abortion leaders oppose capital punishment. They would spare the guilty, but kill the innocent.

Do women who have had abortions have less regard for human life than non-aborters?

Dr. Paul Cameron has answered this in a study which determined how women perceive capital punishment. The chart below shows the results.

CAPITAL PUNISHMENT	NON-ABORTERS	ABORTERS
Should never be used	26%	6%
OK as option for a heinous crime	54%	83%
Would serve as executioner	8%	22%

His conclusion was:

"Our society has been flirting with many different ways to rid itself of people. Capital punishment fits that pattern. It is reasonable that those who have taken human life would have less regard for its value. More and more people have had a hand in taking human life both in war and on the abortion table. It's a vicious cycle. As you take human life, you justify your action by holding life less dear. Then you are led to take even more life and consequently hold it in even lower regard."

P. Cameron, "Lethal Trend in the U.S., Abortion and Capital Punishment," *Psychology Today,* Nov. 1977, pp. 44-46

But they both kill, don't they?
Yes. But there are clear differences. Let's list them.

CAPITAL PUNISHMENT	ABORTION
To rational adult	To preborn baby
Punishment for a capital crime	Not punishment, no crime
Judged guilty by due process of law	Not guilty, no due process
Killed by the state	Killed by a private citizen

Incidentally, the U.S. Congress, in reinstituting capital punishment for certain high federal crimes, voted unanimously to spare a pregnant woman's life until after delivery because the child was innocent of the crime of his mother. This is directly contradictory to the Supreme Court decision which ruled that this "fetus" was not a person and had no rights prior to birth.

U.S. Senate Bill 1401, 93rd Congress, 1973-74

War kills too. What about that?
If there is a clear-cut justified war, it would be a war of self-defense. Let's list the differences.

WAR	ABORTION
Self-defense	aggression
Not wanted, unplanned	Wanted and planned
Done by the state	By a private citizen
Against another nation	Against a private individual

Is there really any difference between one dead baby whose skin has been burned off by napalm and another dead baby whose skin has been burned off by a salt-poisoning abortion?

Cardinal Joseph Bernardin sees opposition to abortion and nuclear war as a "seamless garment." What is the Right to Life position?
The Board of the National Right to Life Committee (which represents the 50 state RTL organizations and all of their local chapters), has set clear policy on this. It does not agree nor disagree with such linkage. The Board simply does not, and will not, take a stand on nuclear issues. Nor will it take a stand on contraception, economic issues, sex education, fluoride in your water, etc. The RTL movement limits itself to the equal protection, under the law, of innocent individual human life from its beginning at fertilization until natural death.

Some have said that by emphasizing the anti-nuclear issue, Cardinal Bernardin weakens the anti-abortion issue.

The Cardinal did not insist that pro-life people support a nuclear freeze, oppose cruise missiles, or cut the defense budget. He merely invited us to apply our pro-life convictions to these and other issues. An article by M. Schwartz illustrates one view of the Cardinal's statement:

> "[The Cardinal's critics] seem to have read him backwards. They interpret him to say that opposition to abortion is illegitimate if not joined to opposition to nuclear arms. What he really said was just the reverse: those who oppose the arms race are kicking away their most basic premise if they tolerate the willful destruction of life by abortion."
>
> M. Schwartz, "Defending Bernadin,"
> *Catholic Register,* April 8, 1984

Another judgment of his position was made by Joseph Sobran in the "Catholic Eye" in an issue entitled "the Bishops and Abortion" In his view...

> "The linking, however illogically, of abortion, capital punishment, and nuclear weapons is not aimed at taunting anti-nukes or opponents of capital punishment for their inconsistency in not picketing abortion mills. Far from it. The effect of this link-up is to ease the pressure on the abortionists by confusing Catholics with a muddled charge of inconsistency.
>
> Editorial, *Catholicism in Crisis,*
> R. McInerng, Mar. 19, 1985

Which do you think takes first priority, abortion or the anti-nuclear issue?

If a person were to oppose both, they must in logic and justice give the abortion issue first priority. Abortion is here and now, in the U.S., killing 1½ million innocents a year. Nuclear holocaust is a potential threat. The reality of abortion must be faced first.

But abortion is always evil. War and capital punishment may not be!

True, killing in war, if truly in self-defense, may be justified. What if David had not killed Goliath? Also, tens of millions of deeply convinced Christians believe that the Bible advocates capital punishment. The burden of proof, that a defensive war and capital punishment may be wrong, clearly rests with those who teach this interpretation. However, abortion is always and absolutely evil, except when one life is balanced against another.

What of capital punishment for a pregnant woman?

The following states defer capital punishment until after delivery in order to spare the innocent child: Alabama, Arizona, California, Florida, Georgia, Idaho, Kansas, Kentucky, Maryland, Massachusetts, Mississippi, Missouri, Nevada, New Mexico, New York, Oklahoma, South Carolina, South Dakota, Utah, Wyoming. Is your home state listed here? If not, why not?

CHAPTER 24

Doctors and Nurses

Why do doctors do abortions?
Rarely, a doctor will do an abortion because he believes it is necessary to save a mother's life.

But other than that?
If, tomorrow, a law were passed mandating that thenceforth all abortions were to be done for free, at least 98% of the doctors doing them would quit.

Is doing abortion that lucrative?

Yes. See above. An abortionist, working only 20 or 30 hours a week, with no overhead, can earn from 3 to 10 times as much as an ethical surgeon. The above ad was run in the *Dallas Morning News* on June 24, 1974. Guess why they were willing to pay four times the starting salary for regular obstetric practice?

Don't some doctors do them for humanitarian reasons?

There are some. Most of these become disillusioned, however. Dr. Bernard Nathanson is an example of one who quit. Another told his story in the March 4, 1985 issue of *Medical Economics*.

Some do them for mental health?

There is no know psychiatric disease that is helped by an abortion. Further, it is well known that mentally stable women can tolerate the psychic stress of abortion better than unstable ones (see chapter 17).

Don't doctors take the Hippocratic Oath?

All doctors used to. By doing so, they promised to only cure, not to kill, by abortion or any other way. In recent years, however, the abortion part has been quietly dropped. It had said:

> "I will give no deadly medicine to anyone if asked, nor suggest such counsel, and in like manner, I will not give to a woman a pessary to produce abortion."
>
> The Oath of Hippocrates

Today, the abortion portion has been removed and replaced by "I will do nothing that is illegal." We might note that the new oath would have fit well in Nazi Germany, where the doctors who helped to kill Jews were doing nothing that was illegal.

Hippocrates, the father of medical ethics, defined the practitioner of medicine as only a healer and thus, began a new era. Previously, the medicine man's role had combined both healing and killing. Today, turning the clock back several millennia, some doctors are again assuming that dual role.

Are there any other famous pledges?
Yes, as follows:

> "Thou has appointed me to watch over the life and death of thy creatures."
>
> Oath of Maimonides (12th Century A.D.)

The American Convention on Human Rights in San Jose, November 22, 1969 stated:

> "Every person has the right to have his life respected, this right shall be protected by law and, in general, from the moment of conception. No one shall be arbitrarily deprived of his life."

Here is another oath familiar to many:

> "I will not give my patients any poisonous drug, if they ask first, nor will I advise them thus, nor aid in a miscarriage."
>
> Oath of the Arabian Physician

The most modern pledge is:

> "I solemnly pledge myself to consecrate my life to the service of humanity. I will give to my teachers the respect and gratitude which is their due; I will practice my profession with conscience and dignity; the health of my patient will be my first consideration; I will respect the secrets which are confided in me; I will maintain by all means in my power the honour

and noble traditions of the medical profession; my colleagues will be my brothers; I will not permit considerations of religion, nationality, race, party politics, or social standing to intervene between my duty and my patient; I will maintain the utmost respect for human life, from the time of conception; even under threat, I will not use my medical knowledge contrary to the laws of humanity. I make these promises solemnly, freely, and upon my honour."

Declaration of Geneva,
The World Medical Association, Sept. 1948

What is the policy of the American Medical Association?

The AMA policy maintains that if killing of the unborn is legal, then it is also ethical.

Does making something legal, also make it right?

"In 1944 a physician in Germany could participate in genocide with legal sanction. In America he would have been a murderer. In 1977, in America, a physician could perform an abortion with legal sanction. In Germany, he would have been a murderer. We have come 360 degrees on the moral compass."

M. Baten & W. Enos, "Questions of Authenticity and Situational Ethics," *Cancer Bulletin,* vol. 29, no. 4, 1978

Wow!

Yes, that is a total change from the policy that the AMA had always held sacred. The contrast from 100 years ago also makes a chilling comparison.

The American Medical Association on Abortion: An Anatomy of Contrasting Policy Statements

When Does Human Life Begin?	
1871 — "No other doctrine appears to be consonant with reason or physiology but that which admits the embryo to possess vitality from the very moment of conception."	The AMA abortion policy statements of 1967 and 1970 include no references to the scientific fact that human life begins at conception.

What is Abortion:	
1859 — "The slaughter of countless children; such unwarrantable destruction of human life." 1871 — "The work of destruction; the wholesale destruction of unborn infants."	1967 — "The interruption of pregnancy; the induced termination of pregnancy." 1970 — "A medical procedure."

What Should the Ethics of Abortion Be?	
1871 — "Thou shalt not kill. This commandment is given to all without exception...it matters not at what stage of development his victim may have arrived."	1967 — "This is a personal and moral consideration which in all cases must be faced according to the dictates of the conscience of the patient and her physician."

Who Should Perform Abortions?	
1871 — "It will be unlawful and unprofessional for any physician to induce abortion."	1970 — "Abortion should be performed only by a duly licensed physician."

Who Are Physician-Abortionists?	
1871 — "Men who cling to a noble profession only to dishonor it; false brethren; educated assassins; modern Herods; the executioners."	1967 — "Conscientious practitioners; conscientious physicians."

What Should Be Done to Physician-Abortionists?	
1871 — "These men should be marked as Cain was marked; they should be made the outcasts of society."	1970 — They should be permitted to perform abortions as long as they take place "in an accredited hospital."

W. Brennan, *The Abortion Holocaust,*
Landmark Press, 1983, p. 191

How did the AMA deal with physician abortionists back then?

In 1871 the AMA recommended dealing with medical abortionists in the following manner:

"These men should be marked as Cain was marked; they should be made the outcasts of society...respectable men should cease to consult with them, should cease to speak to them, should cease to notice them except with contempt... Resolved, That we repudiate and denounce the conduct of abortionists, and that we will hold no intercourse with them professionally or otherwise, and that we will, whenever an opportunity presents, guard and protect the public against the machinations of these characters by pointing out the physical and moral ruin which follows in their wake."

ibid, Brennan, p. 189

You draw a parallel between today's abortionists and the Nazi doctors?

Yes! There is a direct parallel between the two holocausts, neither of which could have happened without doctors.

THEN	TODAY
"A doctor may interrupt a pregnancy when it 'threatens the life or health of the mother [and] an unborn child that is likely to present hereditary and transmissible defects may be destroyed.'" (German Penal Code and Hamburg Eugenics Court, 1933)	"A licensed physician is justified in terminating a pregnancy if he believes that pregnancy would gravely impair the physical or mental health of the mother or that the child would be born with grave physical or mental defects." (American Law Institute Model Penal Code, 1962)
"Only persons of 'German or related blood' can be citizens; this does not include Jews." (Reich Citizenship Law, 1935)	"The word 'person' as used in the fourteenth Amendment, does not include the unborn." (U.S. Supreme Court, Roe vs. Wade, 1973)
"The authority of physicians is enlarged to include the responsibility for according a 'mercy death [to] incurables.'" (Hitler's Euthanasia Order, Sept. 1939)	"The abortion decision in all its aspects is inherently and primarily a medical decision and basic responsibility for it must rest with the physician." (U.S. Supreme Court, Roe vs. Wade, 1973)

Obedience to Authority

"The accused did not act wrongly because they were covered by law [and] were carrying out the laws of the land." (Hadamar Euthanasia Hospital Trial, 1945)

"I did nothing which was illegal, immoral or bad medicine. Everything I did was in accordance with law." (Dr. Kenneth C. Edelin, 1975)

"The physician is merely an instrument as in the case of an officer who receives an order." (Dr. Karl Brandt, Doctors' Trial, 1947)

"The physician is only the instrument of her decision." (Dr. Bernard N. Nathanson, 1974)

Subhumanity of the Victims

"The Jewish-Bolshevik Commissars personify a repulsive yet characteristic subhumanity." (Dr. August Hirt, 1942)

"For the first four and one-half months the fetus is subhuman and relatively close to a piece of tissue." (Amital Etzionl, Ph.D., 1976)

"It had nothing to do with humanity — it was a mass. I rarely saw them as individuals. It was always a huge mass." (Franz Stangl, former commandant of Treblinka, 1971)

"What is aborted is a protoplasmic mass and not a real, live grown-up individual." (Drs. Walter Char & John McDermott, 1972)

"Whenever Jews are left to themselves they bring brutal misery and depravity. They are pure parasites." (Adolf Hitler, 1943)

"A parasite can commit murder, what attention has Catholic thinking or the law given to the fetus's capacity to murder its mother?" (Dr. Natalle Shalness, 1968)

"If it is now pointed out that the Jew is human, I then reject that totally." (Antisemitic speech, Reichstag, 1895)

"It is a wild contention that newborn babies are persons." (Dr. Michael Tooley, 1972)

The Language of Killing

"Fifty-nine thousand persons were evacuated by July 31." (Warsaw, Poland, 1942)

"The uterus was evacuated." (Dr. David Edelman & Colleagues, 1974)

"The Baron de Hirsch ghetto would have to be emptied." (Max Merten, 1943)

"The uterine cavity was emptied." (Dr. A.K. Mukerjee, 1973)

"The removal of the Jewish element." (Hans Frank, 1943)

"Remove the products of conception." (Dr. Thomas Dillon & Colleagues, 1974)

"The treatment was administered to the children of the Haar-Eglfing Institution." (Dr. Pfannmuller, 1945)

"Abortion as treatment for the sexually transmitted disease of unwanted pregnancy." (Dr. Willard Cates & Colleagues, 1976)

"The method of injection is a completely painless method." (Dr. Adolf Wahlmann, 1945)

"Evacuate the conceptus painlessly within 45 seconds." (Dr. Harvey Karman, 1972)

Experimental Exploitation

"If you are going to kill all these people, at least take the brains out so that the material could be utilized." (Testimony of Dr. Julius Hallervordan, 1947)

"In the case of abortion the fetus cannot be 'helped' by being experimented upon since it is doomed to death anyhow, but perhaps its death can be ennobled...when the research has as its objective the saving of the lives (or the reduction of defects) of other wanted fetuses." (Drs. Willard Gaylin & Mark Lappe, 1975)

"The victims of this Buchenwald typhus test did not suffer in vain and did not die in vain... people were saved by these experiments." (Dr. Gebhard Rose, Doctors' Trial, 1947)

"With changes in the abortion laws fetuses as valuable research material is on the increase." (Dr. Leroy Jackson, 1975)

Exerpted from *The Abortion Holocaust*, W. Brennan (Landmark Press, 1983).

How did the change come about?

"The beginnings were at first merely a subtle shift in emphasis in the basic attitude of the physicians. It started with the acceptance of the attitude, basic in the euthanasia movement, that there is such a thing as a life not worthy to be lived. This attitude in its early stages concerned itself merely with the severely and chronically sick. Gradually, the sphere of those to be included in this category was enlarged to encompass the socially unproductive, the ideologically unwanted, the racially unwanted, and finally all non-Germans. But it is important to realize that the infinitely small wedged-in lever from which this entire trend of mind received its impetus was the attitude toward the nonrehabilitable sick."

L. Alexander, "Medical Science Under Dictatorship," *New England Jour. Med.*, vol. 241, July 14, 1949, pp. 39-47

That was in Germany. How about America?
The first public admission of this change of basic ethic was an editorial:

"The reverence of each and every human life has been a keystone of Western medicine, and is the ethic which has caused physicians to try to preserve, protect, repair, prolong, and enhance every human life.

"Since the old ethic has not yet been fully displaced, it has been necessary to separate the idea of abortion from the idea of killing, which continues to be socially abhorrent. The result has been a curious avoidance of the scientific fact, which everyone really knows, that human life begins at conception, and is continuous, whether intra- or extra-uterine, until death. The very considerable semantic gymnastics which are required to rationalize abortion as anything but taking a human life would be ludicrous if they were not often put forth under socially impeccable auspices. It is suggested that this schizophrenic sort of subterfuge is necessary because, while a new ethic is being accepted, the old one has not yet been rejected."

Editorial, *Jour. CA State Med. Assoc.*, Sept. 1970

Doctors really know that abortion kills a human life, don't they?
Perhaps not all of them. Doctors are narrowly specialized. Just because M.D. or D.O. appears after their names, don't assume they know everything about fetal development. Remember, most clergymen aren't scripture scholars, and few attorneys know much about copyright law. Also, few stop to think that 99% of abortions are done on normal, healthy women to directly kill normal, healthy babies for non-medical reasons.

Which doctors are most pro-abortion?
Psychiatrists.

And most pro-life?

Pediatricians, Family Practitioners, and Neo-natologists.

Are there any pro-life medical associations?

Yes. The largest and most effective one in America is the American Association of Pro-Life Obstetricians and Gynecologists (266 Pine Ave., Lauderdale-by-the-Sea, FL 33308). There is also an international association: The World Federation of Doctors Who Respect Life. Their U.S. address is Box 508, Oak Park, IL 60303.

What about nurses, they help with abortions don't they?

Most of them only help with abortions because there are no other jobs available and they need the money. They usually get the dirty end of it. Abortions are particularly upsetting to nurses.

Why is that?

"I saw a bassinet outside the nursery. There was a baby in this bassinet — a crying, perfectly formed baby — but there was a difference in this child. She had been scalded. She was the child of a saline abortion.

"This little girl looked as if she had been put in a pot of boiling water. No doctor, no nurse, no parent to comfort this hurt, burned child. She was left alone to die in pain. They wouldn't let her inside the nursery — they didn't even bother to cover her.

"I was ashamed of my profession that night! It's hard to believe this can happen in our modern hospital, but it does. It happens all the time. I thought a hospital was a place to heal the sick — not a place to kill.

"I asked a nurse from another hospital what they do with their babies who are aborted by saline. Unlike the hospital where I work, where the baby was left alone struggling for breath, their hospital puts the infant in a bucket and puts the lid on. Suffocation! Death by suffocation!

"Another nurse said she had to stop helping with abortions. The little severed arms and legs from a suction abortion were just too much for her to look at."

D. Conklin, "Nurse to Senate: 'Ashamed of Profession,'"
The Miami Voice, May 25, 1979

Can a nurse refuse to assist at an abortion?

It depends. In some hospitals, yes. In others they get transferred and given such lousy hours and duty that they quit. The free standing abortion chambers, of course, do nothing but abortions, so the nurse who works there knows that this is the work she will be doing when she is hired.

What about emotional stress for the nurses?

For salt-poisoning and Prostaglandin abortions, the abortionist gets off easy; he injects the drug and leaves. Later, the mother goes into labor and delivers (usually) a dead baby. The nurses have to cope with the dead, dying, or live baby, as well as attending to the mother, who often becomes hysterical when she discovers that the "product of pregnancy" is in reality, a tiny son or daughter.

"Nurses were more disturbed by amniocentesis abortions (salt poisoning and Prostaglandin) in which they played major roles in supporting the patient as well in her abortion."

N. Kaltreider et al., "The Impact of Midtrimester Abortion
Techniques on Patients and Staff,"
Amer. Jour. OB/GYN, vol. 135, 1979, p. 235

D&E abortions are a newer development. The dilatation and evacuation method spares the mother the emotional trauma of directly facing the fact that she has killed a real baby, but pro-abortion propagandist Dr. W. Cates admits:

"Ossified (bony) parts such as the skull must often be crushed and the bone fragments extracted carefully to avoid tearing the cervix. Reconstruction of the fetal sections after removal is necessary to ensure completeness of the abortion procedure. Clearly, D&E transfers much of the possible psychological trauma of the abortion from the patient to the professional."

J. Roaks & W. Cates, "Emotional Impact of D&E vs. Instillation," *Family Planning Perspective*, Dec. 1977, pp. 276-77

Colorado abortionist Warren Hern, who does these in large volume, writes of:

"... the emotional turmoil that the procedure inevitably wreaks on physicians and staff.... There is no possibility of denial of an act of destruction by the operator.... The sensations of dismemberment flow through the forceps like an electric current.... Some part of our cultural and perhaps even biological heritage recoils at a destructive operation on a form similar to our own...."

W. Hern, "Meeting of Amer. Assoc. Planned Parenthood Physicians," *OB-GYN News*, 1978

"Meeting of Natl. Abortion Federation, San Francisco," *OB-GYN News*, Dec. 1981

What about malpractice insurance for abortionists?

The more dangerous the surgical procedure, the higher the cost of medical malpractice insurance. The State of Florida has always rated its doctors as Class I up to Class VI. On January 1, 1984, a special ultra-risk Class VII rating was created for abortionists. This acknowledged the fact that the risk was greater than that for brain or heart surgery.

"Florida Insurance Reciprocal by PIMCO," *Amer. Assn. of Pro-Life OB & GYN Newsletter*, Jan. 1984, p. 10

How many American doctors do abortions?

Out of over 300,000 physicians in the U.S., there are about 8,700 who are willing to provide abortions.

S. Henshaw, "Competition Cutting into Case Loads," *OB-GYN News*, Sept. 1, 1984

CHAPTER 25

Fetal and Newborn Infant Experimentation

What is fetal experimentation?

Experimentation can be carried out on the living human fetus while he or she still lives in the womb. Experimentation can be carried out on the living human baby after delivery. If the experiment is done for the possible benefit of this specific living human (for example, trial of a drug in treatment), then it is ethical if the parents approve. If, however, the experiment is done with the intention of later killing this living human to find out information from the experiment, then a serious crime is committed against human rights.

But if the mother has the right to abort, why not the right to consent to an experiment? The child can't live anyway.

The U.S. Supreme Court in 1973, and the parliaments in some other nations, debated the conflict of rights between mother and baby. By legalizing abortion, they granted the mother the superior right. Through the surgery of abortion, she can get unpregnant. Once the mother and child are separated, however, if the child is born alive, there is no longer a conflict of legal rights. Besides being alive and human, the child is now separated from the mother and equally entitled to his or her human rights and protection.

"Merely because a developing baby is condemned to death does not give anyone the license to do as one pleases with him or her. To grant such a permission would be to admit in principle that an adult condemned to death for a crime may also be treated in whatever way one wishes. Most people would find this totally unacceptable.

"Non-therapeutic research with discernible risk cannot ethically be imposed on condemned criminals in modern society or on dying children. By the same reasoning, it should not be imposed on aborted fetuses or fetuses marked for abortion."

D. McCarthy, A. Moraczewski, "An Ethical Evaluation of Fetal Experimentation," *Pope John*, Med-Moral Research & Educational Center Publishers: St. Louis, 1976, p. 78

To do so would be to repeat the Nazi era. Remember, Nazi doctors, who did just that, were hanged for it.

But the aborted baby is not viable yet!

Viability measures the sophistication of the external life-support systems around the baby. Viability is not a measure of the aliveness or humanness of the baby. All "pre-viable" babies are viable if left in their natural habitat, the womb (see chapter 9).

Under what conditions can parents give consent for experimentation?

Parents who give consent for experimentation on their children are assumed to have concern for their child's welfare, and the hope has always been that such experimentation will benefit them.

Parents who give consent to have their child in the womb killed obviously have no such loving interest. Legal tradition through our country's history has always forbidden parents to injure or allow others to injure their child. That is what child-abuse laws are all about. If such experiment is not done to preserve the life or health of the baby, the parents should have no right to grant permission.

For purposes of experimentation, what is a "live birth?"

The World Health Organization defines a live birth as the delivery of a neonatal baby with a heartbeat, a pulsating cord, muscular movement, or a respiratory effort.

E. Diamond, "Redefining the Issues in Fetal Experimentation," *JAMA*, vol. 236, no. 3, July 19, 1976, p. 282

Would you regard experiments on live human fetal tissue as ethical?

This is an entirely different question. Such experimentation can be ethical. When we die, some of our tissues can be preserved and classified as "live tissue." Experiments using live human tissue are entirely different from experiments on live humans.

What about using the placenta?

After the child is born, he or she no longer needs their placenta. For many years, hospitals have frozen and sold them to drug companies to extract hormones and other substances. More recently, placentas have also been sold to cosmetic manufacturing companies. This may be distasteful or even revolting to many people. There is, however, no major ethical problem in such use.

What is a "fetus ex utero?"

That is a live-born baby. Such terminology is mere semantic gymnastics to hide the humanity of the newborn baby and to make it more likely that the public will allow experimentation and killing.

It is also a contradiction in terms, as the technical biological name of the being still in the uterus is "fetus," but the proper biologic name, once outside the uterus, is baby or infant.

But don't we need some human experimentation? We can't learn everything from other research.

"With proper design and effort and money, animal experiments can solve almost every fetal problem presently under investigation. A man did not have to be shot into space naked to learn the hazards of unsupported life in the stratosphere."

Eunice Kennedy Shriver, Natl. Inst. Child Health and
Development,
Washington Post, April 21, 1973

Has there been any fetal experimentation in North America?

Dr. A. Ammann, of the University of California, transplanted human fetal thymus glands into two older children. Both donor humans were killed.

Time Magazine, Feb. 28, 1972, p. 54

This happened in South Carolina as well.

"Thymus Implant," *Medical Tribune,* Nov. 3, 1971

Kidneys from aborted babies were used to study kidney maldevelopment at Dalhouse University, Halifax, Nova Scotia. The donor humans were killed.

British Medical News, April 2, 1973

Dr. R. Goodlin at Stanford University, California, did experiments including, "slicing open the rib cage of still-living human fetuses [newborn babies] in order to observe the heart action.... Some as old as twenty-four weeks ... were used."

Sworn testimony of Mark Swedsen, June 1, 1972

"It was repulsive to watch live fetuses [premature infants] being packed in ice while still moving and trying to breathe, then being rushed to a laboratory." Seeing this happening at Magee-Women's Hospital in Pittsburgh, Mrs. W. Dick, Anesthetist, requested to be excused from helping with abortions. Her request "was denied ... with threats of being fired, harassment, intimidation, restrictions in assigned duties, etc." She finally quit her job.

Testimony of Mrs. W. Dick, Anesthetist, Pennsylvania Abortion
Commission, *The Pittsburgh Catholic,* Mar. 17, 1972

Drs. Laphom and Markesbery reported that they took human brains from live aborted babies, 10-19 weeks old, and kept them alive as long as five months in explants [tissue cultures]. The donor babies were killed.

Laphom & Markesbery,
Science, vol. 173, Aug. 1971, pp. 829-832

At Yale-New Haven Medical Center, a live, breathing, and urinating male baby had his chest cut open without anesthesia (thus killing him) after a Cesarean delivery.

Able vs. Markle, Affidavit,
U.S. Supreme Court, 72-56 & 72-730, Feb. 26, 1973

A number of experiments have been done by giving drugs to the mother first, delivering the baby by abortion, then analyzing the drug concentration in the fetal tissues.

Philipson et al., "Transplacental Passage of
Eythromycin & Clindamycin," *New England Jour. Med.*,
vol. 288, no. 23, pp. 1219-1221

How about the other countries?
The most grisly one reported to date was done at the University of Helsinki, Finland, by Dr. Peter Adam, a professor at Case-Western Reserve University in Cleveland.

"To produce those data, the investigators severed the heads of 12 previable fetuses obtained by abdominal hysterotomy at 12 to 20 weeks' gestation. The heads were then perfused through the internal carotid arteries with recirculating Krebs-Ringer bicarbonate medium containing labeled substrates, and were equilibrated continuously with a gaseous oxygen-carbon dioxide mixture. Venous return was obtained from the incised sagittal sinus, and carbon 14-labeled CO_2, evolved from the labeled substrates, was collected in hyamine hydroxide solution." (See below.)

"Post-Abortion Fetal Study Stirs Storm,"
Medical World News, June 8, 1973, p. 21

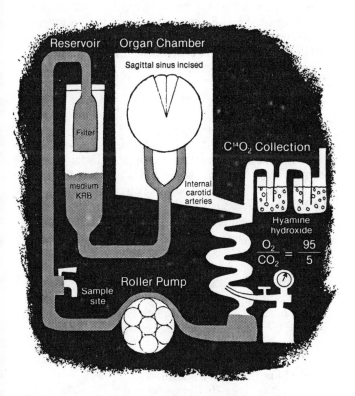

Reservoir   Organ Chamber

Sagittal sinus incised

Filter

medium KRB

Internal carotid arteries

$C^{14}O_2$ Collection

Hyamine hydroxide

$$\frac{O_2}{CO_2} = \frac{95}{5}$$

Sample site   Roller Pump

A six-month-old aborted baby had his testicles transplanted into a 28-year-old Lebanese man who had been unable to become fully sexually active. The surgery was successful, the donor baby was killed.

Reuters News Agency, June 12, 1972

The live, beating hearts of preborn babies (up to 15 weeks) were removed for experimentation at the University of Szeged, Hungary.

Resch. et al., "Comparison of Spontaneous Contraction Rates of In-Situ and Isolated Fetal Hearts in Early Pregnancy," *Amer. Jour. OB/GYN,* vol. 118, no. 1, Jan. 1, 1974

Are there other studies?

With the publication of the above and the resultant public outcry in the U.S. and other countries, most such experimentation has slowed or gone unpublished. For a detailed listing of earlier experimentation, see articles by J. Harrington (Parts I & II), in *Marriage and Family News,* Feb. 1972.

Is there still experimentation in the U.S.?

In April 1974, the U.S. House of Representatives voted 281 to 58 to prohibit research on a human fetus "which has been removed from the womb and which has a beating heart." The U.S. Senate voted likewise, adding only that the ban be reviewed later. A special commission later recommended that the ban be lifted, but maintained substantial restrictions.

The U.S. Congress also denied the U.S. National Science Foundation any funds "to be used to conduct or support research in the U.S. or abroad on a human fetus which has been removed from the womb and which has a beating heart, unless such research is for the purpose of insuring the survival of that fetal baby."

What about more recent studies?

A series of three studies performed up to 1976 at the University of Manitoba in Canada was published and met with intense public outcry. The first involved the delivery of live, normal babies by hysterotomy (mini-Cesarian section) and entailed 54 babies, some as old as 16 weeks' gestational age and as long as 10 inches in crown-rump length. After delivery, the abdomens were cut open and their sex and adrenal glands were examined.

The second study involved 79 babies, up to 26 weeks' gestation, aborted alive by hystertomy, who were killed by heart puncture.

The third study involved 116 babies, up to 22 weeks, aborted alive by hysterotomy, who were then killed by having their hearts punctured, their skulls opened and their pituitary glands removed.

F. Reyes et al., "Studies on Human Sexual Development,"
Parts I, II, III. *Jour. Clinical Endocrinology & Metabolism,*
(I) vol. 37, no. 1, 1973, pp. 74-78,
(II) vol. 38, no. 4, 1974, pp. 612-617,
(III) vol. 42, no. 1, 1976, pp. 9-19

In Arizona in 1981, the E. R. Squibb Drug Company offered free abortions to 14 pregnant women if they would take a certain drug (Naldol) before their abortions and allow their baby's blood to be tested after they were killed. The doctors were paid $10,000.

R. Collins, *Arizona Republic,* Mar. 26, 1981

In Europe a 1983 report to a Committee of the European Parliament by A. Gherto details hysterotomy abortions at 12-21 weeks and subsequent experimentation on various organs. It reports that some of the human remains are frozen and then sold to cosmetic industries.

Cork Examiner, Ireland, Aug. 25, 1983

What do most doctors think of live fetal experimentation?

It cannot be stated strongly enough that the overwhelming majority view this sort of activity as revolting, subhuman, barbaric, and disgusting, and would categorically condemn it. Nevertheless, when the door to abortion-on-demand is open, things like this are bound to happen. Once reverence for life is lost at any stage of human life, practices like this soon appear.

What about experimenting on live human embryos?

Sadly, this may be about to begin. A report of a 16-member government-appointed panel in England recommended that any kind of experimentation on a living human embryo be permitted up to the 14th day of life. They recommended that after 14 days it be a criminal offense. Happily, the House of Lords did not accept this recommendation, and the House of Commons rejected it on a vote of 238 to 66 on Feb. 15, 1985.

M. Warnock et al., *England,* July 18, 1984

What of fetal surgery?

New advances in intrauterine fetal surgery have only added more proof that there are two patients to be concerned with. A recent, dramatic example of treatment of the preborn patient occurred in London's King's College School of Medicine and Dentistry:

"A 28-year-old pregnant woman had a history of four previous fetal deaths from severe Rh disease. In the current pregnancy she was watched closely. At 18 weeks gestation, ultrasound exam showed fetal scalp edema (swelling) and large pericardial effusions (fluid in the sac around the heart) indicating serious Rh trouble.

"Fresh packed blood, group O-Rh negative, was transfused into the baby through the umbilical cord artery at 18 and 19 weeks. During the second transfusion the unborn baby's heart slowed and then stopped. This was detected by ultrasound.

"Under ultrasonic guidance, the mother was turned on her left side and the fetal heart was massaged by the fingers of the doctor. In three minutes, the heart began beating again.

"The unborn baby was transfused again at 23 weeks, 26 weeks, and 29 weeks. At 32 weeks gestation (seven months), a normal infant was delivered."

British. Med. Jour., vol. 288, 1984, pp. 900-901

"Utter helplessness demands utter protection."

Hans Jones, "Philosophical Reflections on Experimenting with Human Subjects, *Daedalus XCVIII,* 1969, p. 240

CHAPTER 26

Infanticide

Abortion leads to Infanticide
like Night follows Day

Why is this so?

One example is all that is needed. Let's assume that a mother has the amniocentesis test to be sure that she is not carrying a Down's Syndrome baby. If it is positive, she definitely intends to have the unborn baby killed by abortion (a narrow majority of Americans agree that for this "hard case" such killing should be permitted). In this instance, the test is normal.

But, when the baby is born, he turns out to have Down's Syndrome. The test was mistaken. Now what? If she had identified the baby's condition before birth, she would have "solved" the problem by killing the tiny patient.

Now the baby is breathing air. Now the diagnosis is definite. Now there is also no danger to the mother as a result of the "procedure."

Why not kill the baby now?

> Same Patient
> Same Problem
> Same Solution

That would be terrible.

But utterly logical! That is the frightening thing about abortion for handicap. The most direct statement on this was by Nobel Laureate, James Watson, the man who cracked the genetic code:

> "Because of the present limits of such detection methods, most birth defects are not discovered until birth.
>
> "If a child were not declared alive until three days after birth, then all parents could be allowed the choice ... the doctor could allow the child to die if the parents so choose and save a lot of misery and suffering."
>
> "Children from the Laboratory,"
> J. Watson, *AMA Prism*, Ch. 3, p. 2, May 1973

• Some of his colleagues disagree. Three days is too short a time. They would prefer thirty days after birth.

• The pro-abortionist, Joseph Fletcher, would use the I.Q. measurement and allow those with an I.Q. under 20 or perhaps 40 to be declared non-human. (Who will bid 60?)

• There are some who think that just being black would be reason enough, or perhaps Jews might be declared "non-persons" again.

• Miss Barbara Smoker, President of the National Secular Society and Vice-Chairman of the British Humanist Association, wrote: "The situation of a newborn baby is very different from that of the same baby, even a few weeks later.... At birth the baby is only a potential human being and at that point it is surely the humane and sensible thing that the life of any baby with obvious severe defects, whether of body or brain, should be quietly snuffed out by the doctor or midwife. This should not be a decision referred to the family who are too emotionally involved; though in borderline cases the doctor's knowledge of the family situation would be one of the factors taken into account."

The Times, January 22, 1973

Is any of this happening — really?

The most famous case was Baby Doe of Bloomington, Indiana, in 1982. He had Down's Syndrome at birth, but he also had a connection between his food-pipe and windpipe (a tracheo-esophageal fistula). There were several surgeons within 50 miles who could have repaired it. Otherwise, the baby could not be fed. Because of the Down's Syndrome, however, the parents refused permission to operate or to administer I.V. feedings or any other treatment. This decision was upheld by the Indiana Supreme Court, and the baby starved to death.

Baby Jane Doe of New York, was born in 1983. She had spina bifida (a partially open spine) and a potential hydrocephalus (water head). Good medical care would have mandated surgical closure of the spinal defect and placement of a shunt to prevent the hydrocephalus. The parents were apparently ready to give permission to operate when they were told that the baby would possibly or probably be mentally retarded. Because of this, they refused permission for surgery. Without closure, such an infant will ultimately die from recurrent meningitis infections which enter through her open spine. Several such infections did occur. However, this little girl's skin spontaneously grew over the spinal defect about three months later, closing it. The parents then consented to the placement of the shunt. But, prior to the parents' consent, the federal government and a private attorney had attempted to step in and have the surgery legally authorized without parental consent. A federal judge, however, held that the parents had the right, in effect, to decide to let the little girl slowly die from these painful infections.

These were landmark cases?

Yes, and tragic ones. Both were similar. Except for the probable mental deficiency, both would promptly have had corrective surgery. In each case, however, because of this undetermined (and undeterminable) mental deficiency, the parents refused, assuring an immediate death in the first case, and (except for spontaneous closure), painful, recurrent infections and death in the second instance.

In both cases, parents' rights to allow death (the right to kill) were granted. The babies were refused ordinary treatment because they had a handicap. Both were discriminated against because of a handicap.

Who sided with the babies?

Many different associations for the handicapped such as the Association for Retarded Citizens (ARC), Right to Life groups or other concerned people, and the U.S. Department of Health and Human Services, which issued regulations to protect such babies.

Who sided with the parents?

The American Academy of Pediatrics, the American Medical Association, and other medical groups who felt that protection of the babies would infringe upon the rights of the doctors to determine treatment. The courts also sided with the parents and struck down the first set of proposed regulations.

Have there been any positive developments?

Yes, one major one. A joint statement in December 1983, by the American Academy of Pediatrics and eight disability rights groups agreed that:

- Discrimination against anyone with a disability, regardless of its severity, is morally and legally indefensible.
- Disabled individuals have the same rights as any other citizens, rights recognized at birth.

- A person's disability (mental or physical) must not be the basis for withholding treatment.
- Anticipated limited potential or lack of community resources are irrelevant and must not determine decisions concerning medical care.
- The individual's medical condition should be the sole focus of the decision.

Pediatrics, vol. 73, no. 4, April 1984, p. 559

Any more bad ones?

Yes. In an earlier issue of *Pediatrics,* a certain Peter Singer wrote that the sanctity-of-life view, the "religious mumbo-jumbo," should be stripped away. "Species membership in *Homo-sapiens* is not morally relevant." If we "compare a dog or a pig to a severely defective infant," he said, "we often find the non-human to have superior capacities." To Singer, quality of life is the only guide.

P. Singer, "Sanctity of Life or Quality of Life?" *Pediatrics,* vol. 73, no. 1, July 1983, pp. 128-129

At the University of Oklahoma, a team of specialists evaluated 69 newborn babies with spina bifida. They admitted that the physical defect could be corrected, but decided whether or not to do so on an evaluation of the child's "quality of life," that is, his or her estimated intelligence, and the support available at home and from society. On this basis, they used "early, vigorous treatment" on 36 of the 69 infants, and they all did well. The remaining 24 babies got a failing grade and were given no treatment, no surgery, no shunt, no antibiotics, not even any sedation when they died (which they all did). This study was published in a major medical journal. It was a callous, cost-benefit analysis test used to determine who should live and who should die.

R. Gross et al., "Early Management and Decision Making in Myleomeningocele," *Pediatrics,* Vol. 72, no. 4, Oct. 4, 1983

A professor of Pediatrics at the University of Wisconsin, a member of the American Academy of Pediatrics' Ethics Committee, sadly stated, "It is common in the U.S. to withhold routine surgery and medical care from infants with Down's Syndrome for the explicit purpose of hastening death."

N. Fost, *Archives of Internal Med.*, Dec. 1982

How does one begin to answer this?

Professor Jerome Lejeune, discoverer of the chromosomal pattern of Down's Syndrome once related to us a story he had heard from a geneticist colleague.

"Many years ago, my father was a Jewish physician in Braunau, Austria. On one particular day, two babies had been delivered by one of his colleagues. One was a fine, healthy boy with a strong cry. His parents were extremely proud and happy. The other was a little girl, but her parents were extremely sad, for she was a Mongoloid baby. I followed them both for almost fifty years. The girl grew up, living at home, and was finally destined to be the one who nursed her mother through a very long and lingering illness after a stroke. I do not remember her name. I do, however, remember the boy's name. He died in a bunker in Berlin. His name was Adolf Hitler."

What if the parents don't want the handicapped infant?

There are organizations like the Spina Bifida Association of America, with over 100 couples on its waiting list, wanting to adopt an infant with spina bifida. (Write J. Grafstron, 1955 Florida Ave., Xenia, OH 45385.) The National Down's Syndrome Society can give you a similar waiting list.

What do parents of retarded children think?

"There has not been a single organization of parents of mentally retarded children that has ever endorsed abortion. We, who are parents of these children and have borne the burden, ask that before you, the legislators, propose to speak for us, by possibly authorizing abortion for fetal abnormality, please ask our opinion first."

Mrs. Rosalie Craig, Testimony before Ohio Legislature, 1971

It is of considerable interest that an unusual number of natural and adoptive parents of handicapped children are to be found among the pro-life activists in all countries.

But isn't it cruel to allow a handicapped child to be born — to a miserable life?

The assumption that handicapped people enjoy life less than "normal" persons has been shown to be false. A well-documented investigation has shown that there is no difference between handicapped and normal persons in their degree of life satisfaction, outlook of what lies immediately ahead, and vulnerability to frustration.

"Though it may be both common and fashionable to believe that the malformed enjoys life less than normal, this appears to lack both empirical and theoretical support."

P. Cameron, Univ. of Louisville, Van Hoeck et al., Wayne State Univ., "Happiness and Life Satisfaction of the Malformed," Proceedings, Amer. Psychologic Assn. Meeting, 1971

But wouldn't care of the handicapped be very costly?

What is your ethic? Do you treat, care for, and help a sick or disabled person, or do you kill him? Do you measure the value of a person's life in money? Or in utilitarian usefulness?

Is keeping these babies worth the cost?

The cost to society to care for all the physically and mentally handicapped among is us would be but a tiny fraction of the cost to society for the morally deformed among us.

What of Down's Syndrome?

"Upwards of 80% of Down's babies will occur to younger mothers" under 35.

Adams et al., "Down's Syndrome, Recent Trends,"
JAMA, vol. 246, no. 7, Aug. 14, 1981, pp. 758-760

The mother is not solely the cause. "In about 30% of the cases, the father has been responsible for the extra 21st chromosome in Down's Syndrome." The older the father, the higher the percent.

Roberts et al., "Midtrimester Amniocentesis,"
Jour. of Repro. Med., vol. 28, no. 3, Mar. 1983, p. 168

Even so:
at a maternal age of 30, 99.9% of babies do not have it
at a maternal age of 36, 99.6% of babies do not have it
at a maternal age of 40, 99.1% of babies do not have it.

There is, we hope, great news coming. A treatment for *this condition* may be found in our lifetime.

Professor Jerome Lejeune, Paris.
Personal communication with authors.

Is it possible to "cleanse the gene pool?"

Any talk about breeding out genetic diseases is a lot of nonsense. Seriously affected persons are unlikely to marry and have children; the genes are passed along by carriers. For instance, there are 40 carriers for every person with sickle cell anemia. If every victim of this disease were eliminated, it would require 750 years just to cut the incidence in half; to stamp it out altogether would require 200,000 abortions for every 500,000 couples. Because each "normal" person is the carrier of three or four bad genes, the only way to eliminate genetic diseases would be to sterilize or abort everybody.

Dr. Hymie Gordon, Professor of Genetics, Mayo Clinic

Will maternal X-rays harm the baby?

"Interruption of pregnancy is *never* justified because of the radiation risk to the embryo/fetus from a diagnostic X-ray exam, abdominal or peripheral."

Policy Statement, Amer. College of Radiology,
AMA News, Nov. 1976, p. 12

How do parents emotionally handle the abortion of a handicapped baby?

Very poorly. One study reported maternal depression of 92% and paternal depression of 82%, plus a 30% incidence of marital separation after the abortion.

Blumberg et al., "Psychiatric Sequelae of Abortion for
Genetic Indication," *Amer. Jour. OB/GYN*,
vol. 122, no. 7, Aug. 1975, pp. 799-780

How are handicapped preborn babies diagnosed before birth?

The mainstay of the "search and destroy" mission is amniocentesis. A new method is chorionic villi biopsy. Another is maternal serum alpha-fetoprotein.

What is amniocentesis?

It involves taking a small amount of fluid from the baby's amniotic sac through a needle inserted into the mother's abdomen and uterine wall. The cells in the fluid are cultured and examined a month later. Certain chemicals in the fluid can also be measured.

Why is it done?

In the midtrimester (middle three months), it is done to diagnose certain conditions. In the third trimester, it is done to treat illnesses of both baby and mother.

Is it safe?

Opinions differ. A very reputable, large English study found that there were 14 fetal deaths in the amniocentesis groups, compared to 5 in the control group; severe maternal bleeding in 37 compared to 12; ruptured membranes in

0.5% compared to none; subsequent spontaneous abortion in 2.7% compared to 1.4%; and Rh antibodies developed in 9 compared to 2. Severe postpartum respiratory distress occurred after birth in 30 compared to 9, with 24 major orthopedic abnormalities compared to 1. The overall increased risk to the baby was 300% and the cumulative overall risk of all negative factors to both mother and child was 9.2% compared to 3.3% in the control group. One must also add to this the false positive and false negative test results which resulted in additional "needless" abortion of normal babies.

Royal College of OB/GYN, "An Assessment of
Hazards of Amniocentesis," *British Jour. OB/GYN,*
vol. 85, Supplement N.2., 1978

Most American studies have found fewer problems, but all studies have found some.

Roberts et al., "Midtrimester Amniocentesis,"
Jour. of Rep. Med., vol. 28, no. 3, Mar. 1983, pp. 167-168

Are there any fetal conditions that can be treated in the midtrimester?
No. (See also March of Dimes, chapter 34.)

Then why do the amniocentesis test?
Solely to make a diagnosis. If a baby with a genetic handicap can be identified, he can then be killed by abortion.

No other reason?
"If abortion is outlawed, amniocentesis programs in midtrimester would close, since the main therapeutic prerogative would have been eliminated."

Golbus, "The Current Scope of Antenatal Diagnosis,"
Hospital Practice, April 1982

What about third trimester amniocentesis?
This is quite different. These are much safer, and they are done to help treat and save the lives of both baby and mother. Then it is done for Rh disease, diabetes, fetal lung maturity, etc.

But what of a child with Tay-Sacs Disease? That child will surely die a slow death of deterioration?

So the new "ethic" says that you should kill him early and efficiently! Does age (younger) and place of residence (in the womb) really change what you are doing (killing)? There are dozens of incurable illnesses, some just last longer than others.

What defects come from Rubella?

Of the 16.9% of children who develop defects when their mothers get Rubella while pregnant:

- 50% had hearing loss, most correctable by hearing aids.
- 50% had heart defects, almost all surgically correctable.
- 30% had cataracts, often one-sided. Most had fair vision.
- Mental retardation was 1.5% compared to 1% in a non-affected population.

Rendle-Short, *Lancet,* vol. 2, 1964, p. 373

What if a woman receives Rubella vaccine while pregnant?

There are no reported cases of significant damage to the babies who were born after such vaccination. For example, "none of the live-born infants had serologic or clinical evidence of congenital rubella."

S. Wyall & K. Herrmann, "Inadvertent Rubella Vaccination of Pregnant Women," *Jour. Amer. Med. Assn.*, vol. 225, 1973, p. 1472

Risk of "infection" of the fetus is "probably less than 5 to 10%." None of the infants born to such vaccinated women had any defects. (They still think she should consider abortion, however.)

"Risk of Congenital Abnormality after Inadvertent Rubella Vaccination of Pregnant Women," *New England Jour. Med.*, vol. 294, April 29, 1976, pp. 972-974

The U.S. Center for Disease Control, U.S. Public Health Services, in a report covering 1971 through 1982, reported on 959 pregnant women who were vaccinated while pregnant. They reported no evidence of Rubella-induced defects. The very few abnormalities found were "expected" in such a large number.

Morbidity & Mortality Weekly Report,
vol. 32, no. 33, Aug. 26, 1983

What is Alpha-Fetoprotein testing, and why is it done?

It tests the mother's blood and can reveal that she is probably carrying a child with either an open spine (spina bifida) or anacephaly.

It must be done on blood drawn between her 16th and 18th week of pregnancy. Of 1,000 women, 50 will have positive results. The blood test must then be repeated. This time, only 30 will be positive. An ultrasound test will then be done and will clear 15, leaving 15 still positive. Then these mothers must have an amniocentesis (2% of babies die from the test). After the necessary four-week wait, the results will pinpoint 1 or 2 babies who have the handicaps, who are 20-22 weeks old, and who weigh 1 to 1½ pounds each.

Even after all of this testing, some of the babies aborted will be normal, and some of the "normals" will be born with the handicap, for the test is not always correct. *The test is available, however,* and is being used. The main problem, even for those who favor abortion, is the level of anxiety created as the elimination process continues. Many, who are "cleared" still don't believe they are "OK" and get abortions on the suspicion that the tests were wrong.

Hasn't abortion reduced infant mortality?

Not so! How is it possible to save one baby's life by killing another? Of course, if you kill one and one-half million babies before they are born, there will be fewer left to be at risk of dying. If we killed everyone over sixty years of age, there also would be a sharp drop in cancer deaths.

The real reason for the actual drop in infant mortality has been the creation of neonatal intensive care units in most major hospitals.

Since When
Do We Kill the Patient
to Cure the Disease?

CHAPTER 27

Euthanasia

Euthanasia is
When the Doctor Kills the Patient

But there are different kinds of euthanasia such as active and passive, direct and indirect, voluntary and involuntary.

Let's clear up this semantic confusion. All of these qualifications are either the product of confused minds, or a direct attempt to change the meaning of the word euthanasia so that we can accept it.

Euthanasia is when the doctor kills the patient.

But I don't want the doctor keeping me alive artificially. Why not a law to permit death with dignity?

No new laws are needed. No doctor in the U.S. has ever been indicted for *allowing* a patient to die a natural death. When a patient is surely dying, doctors may and must use their best judgment when deciding whether to continue or discontinue certain therapeutic efforts that have failed to cure the patient, and that may only be serving to postpone dying. The doctor's only obligation, then, is to keep the patient comfortable and allow a peaceful death.

Doctors have had the confidence of patients in the past because their total effort has been to cure. If and when doctors begin to practice exterminative medicine and begin to kill, then that absolutely essential factor in the doctor/patient relationship — complete confidence — will be destroyed.

What about "Living Wills"?

These are misnamed, for they have nothing to do with living and everything to do with dying. Nor are they wills; they are, rather, "death wishes" or "death directives." Right to Life agrees that anyone who wants to can sign one, but totally opposes making them binding by law.

Why oppose legally binding "death wishes"?

- The Euthanasia Society started the idea, and that should give us pause.
- Informed consent just cannot be given in a generic fashion for an unknown problem at a future time.
- Legislation is not necessary; we have enough government intervention.
- The patient and family can always get another doctor if the present one seems unsatisfactory.
- A conscious patient can always refuse treatment.
- Many patients change their minds. With a signed document that is legally binding, it may be too late.
- What does "terminally ill," or "artificial means," or "heroic measures," or "meaningful," or "reasonable expectation" mean? These definitions change with time and are different in each case.

What do doctors think of these "wills"?

Most informed doctors oppose them. If they become common, the following problem will arise:

Patient "A" has signed a legal "living will." She is seriously ill. There is treatment which could be used that might help her, but it could also leave her partly disabled. Should the doctor use it? Her family loves her and wants the doctor to try, but the patient has signed a legal document. She said to let her die. If the doctor doesn't follow her mandate, she may later sue. So she is allowed to die, even though under the present circumstances she may have wished otherwise.

Patient "B" did not sign such a legally binding document. Clearly, she must want everything possible done to keep her alive. She is gravely ill and in the process of dying. Good medical judgment would be to let natural death occur. But not for her. By not signing, she may all but mandate useless and life-prolonging efforts.

So, with a "living will," doctors are damned if they do and damned if they don't, and it is the patient who will not receive the best medical care.

The Euthanasia Society started these wills?

Yes. The Euthanasia Society and its Foundation have since changed their names to The Society for the Right to Die, which then changed its name to The Society for Concern for Dying. They all have been headquartered at 250 W. 57th St., New York, 10019. On the Euthanasia Society's advisory council as a founding member is Abigail Van Buren, the "Dear Abbey" newspaper columnist, who constantly pushes these misnamed "living wills."

Before his death, Dr. Alan Guttmacher, head of Planned Parenthood World Population was also a prominent member of the Board of the Euthanasia Society of America.

Where does the ACLU stand?

In 1977 The American Civil Liberties Union's Board of Directors stated:

> "Consensual euthanasia involves an act or an omission by a second person, at the request of an individual, for the termination of the latter's life when he or she is either terminally ill or totally and permanently disabled. The ACLU recognizes this form of euthanasia as a legitimate extension of the right of control over one's own body."

> *Euthanasia News,* vol. 3, no. 1, Feb. 1977

What of suicide?

There is a Hemlock Society in America, and an Exit Society in England to aid people in taking their own lives.

Have pro-euthanasia bills been introduced anywhere?

Yes, some frightening ones, by Dr. Sackett in Florida, Senator Halleck in Oregon, Senator Lapides in Maryland, and in the English House of Lords in 1969. A proposed Wisconsin bill would have allowed such killing as young as seven years old. In 1980 such a law actually passed in India.

But a law to allow "Death with Dignity" would not permit euthanasia.

Our mercy killing laws will begin first by legalizing "Living Wills," then death with dignity bills. Next these laws will be expanded to accomplish the real goal, to get rid of people who are a burden on society. (See also Dr. Lois Lobb. In *The Mercy Killers,* by Paul Marx).

Is there an alternative to euthanasia?

The real alternative to euthanasia is to provide loving, competent care for the dying. A new concept for the dying arose in England, where institutions called Hospices specialize in compassionate, skilled care of the dying. This concept has spread to Canada and the U.S., where it has been quickly accepted.

"Once a patient feels welcome and not a burden to others, once his pain is controlled and other symptoms have been at least reduced to manageable proportions, then the cry for euthanasia disappears. It is not that the question of euthanasia is right or wrong, desirable or repugnant, practical or unworkable. It is just that it is irrelevant. Proper care is the alternative to it and can be made universally available as soon as there is adequate instruction of medical students in a teaching hospital. If we fail in this duty to care, let us not turn to the politicians asking them to extricate us from this mess."

R. Lamerton, *Care of the Dying*
Priorty Press Ltd., 1973, p. 99

Why talk about euthanasia in an abortion book?

They both directly kill living humans. They both are done for the same reasons. (See also chapter 28.)

REASON	ABORTION	EUTHANASIA
Usefulness	a burden	a burden
Wanted	unwanted	unwanted
Degree of perfection	handicapped	handicapped
Age	too young	too old
Intelligence	not yet conscious	not really conscious anymore
Place of residence	in the womb	in a nursing home
"Meaningful life"	"does not yet have" Roe vs. Wade	"no longer has" Euthanasia Bills
Cost	too poor	too poor
Numbers	too many children	too many old folks
Marital Status	unmarried	widowed

CHAPTER 28

The German Euthanasia Program

A Brief Look at the Analogy

How did euthanasia come about?

The *original* euthanasia program to "purify" the German race was a creation of certain physicians, *not* Hitler. He simply allowed the use of the tools others had prepared.

The first gas chamber was designed by professors of psychiatry from 12 major German universities. They selected the patients and watched them die. Then they slowly reduced the "price tag" until the mental hospitals were almost empty.

They were joined by some pediatricians, who began by emptying the institutions for handicapped children in 1939. By 1945 these doctors had so lowered the price tag that they were killing bed wetters, children with misshapen ears, and those with learning disabilities.

Wertham, *The German Euthanasia Program*,
Hayes Publishing Co., Cinn: 1977, p. 47

There were internists who helped empty the homes for the aged. Then some doctors went out into the community. Many handicapped and old people were taken from their homes and killed. By 1945 these doctors had even eliminated many World War I amputee veterans.

Few people know that doctors participating in the "German Euthanasia Program" did so voluntarily. Some left the program and received no retaliation. Of course, Hitler approved and exerted specific pressures, but it was doctors who started it.

Hitler, taking his cue from these physicians, after the eugenic killing of almost 300,000 Aryan Germans who were "defective," then used their gas chambers and proceeded to eliminate "defective" races. He destroyed an entire race of Gypsies, six million Jews, and perhaps almost as many captured Poles, Russians, and central Europeans.

ibid, Wertham

But I thought the program started with sterilization.

That's true. The first and fundamental law change was the Law for the Prevention of Progeny with Hereditary Diseases, promulgated by Hitler on July 25, 1933. It was aimed at Aryan Germans and its purpose was to purify the race by eliminating those with supposed heredity diseases. In six years, the law was responsible for the involuntary sterilization of an estimated 375,000 Germans.

W. Deuel, People Under Hitler,
New York, 1942, p. 221

This law also legalized abortion in paragraph 14, for women who were to be sterilized. Later, the "right" to legal abortion was extended to Jews, Poles, Gypsies, and other racial minorities.

ibid, par. 14

But I thought Hitler opposed abortion.

Wrong! Hitler only opposed abortion for "pure blood" Aryan women. He allowed and even encouraged it for others.

In an order to the SS, SD, and police on June 9, 1943, Reichskommisar Kaltenbrunner directed: "In the case of eastern female workers, pregnancy may be interrupted if desired." First, a racial exam was to be done and then, "If a racially valuable result is to be expected, the abortion is to be denied ... if not valuable, the abortion is to be granted."

After the war, the War Crimes Tribunal indicted ten Nazi leaders for "encouraging and compelling abortions," which it considered a "crime against humanity."

"Trials of War Criminals," *Nuremberg Military Tribunal*, Washington, DC: USGPO, vol. IV, p. 610

But no one in America would agree with any of that!

Margaret Sanger, the famous founder of Planned Parenthood, was supportive. She wanted "more children from the fit, less from the unfit."

Birth Control Review, vol. 3, no. 5, May 1919, p. 2

This wasn't only related to contraceptive planning. As editor, she printed grossly eugenic material, approving of Hitler's sterilization program (see *Into the Darkness, Nazi Germany Today*, by L. Stoddard , p. 196).

She believed that "Negroes and Southern Europeans were mentally inferior to native born Americans." She found these people, Hebrews, and others "feebleminded," "human weeds," and called them a "menace to the race." In 1933, her *Birth Control Review* devoted an entire edition to eugenic sterilization.

Sanger's famous "Plan for Peace" was almost the same as Hitler's, even going beyond it to suggest, in essence, concentration camps.

"When the world realized the logical consequences of Hitler's hereditarian-eugenic, totalitarian type of government, Margaret Sanger's birth-control movement had to take a quick step away from its overt eugenic language."

E. Drogin, *Margaret Sanger, Father of Modern Society*, CUL Publications, 1979, p. 28

Do you see signs of this destructive thinking in America today?

Yes, definitely. The last two chapters have spoken of infanticide for handicapped newborns and of the clear preliminary steps toward euthanasia of the elderly and handicapped. We are going down the same road, developing and nurturing the same attitudes in our thinking.

"There is a prevalence of thinking in destructive rather than ameliorative terms in dealing with social problems. The ease with which destruction of life is advocated for those considered either socially useless or socially disturbing, instead of educational and ameliorative measures, may be the first danger sign of loss of creative liberty in thinking which is the hallmark of a democratic society.

"The beginnings [in Germany] were merely a subtle shift in emphasis in the basic attitudes of physicians. It started with the acceptance of the attitude, basic in the euthanasia movement, that there is such a thing as a life not worth living. This attitude in its early stages concerned itself merely with the severely and chronically sick. Gradually, the sphere of those to be included in this category was enlarged to include the socially unproductive, the ideologically unwanted, the racially unwanted, and finally, all non-Germans.

"From the attitude of easing patients with chronic diseases away from the doors of the best types of treatment facilities available, to the actual dispatching of such patients to killing centers is a long, but nevertheless, logical step."

Leo Alexander, "Medical Science Under Dictatorship,"
New England Jour. Med., July 1949

"In 1944, a physician in Germany could participate in genocide with legal sanction; in America he would have been a murderer. In 1977, in America, a physician can perform an abortion with legal sanction; in Germany, he would be a murderer. We have come 360 degrees on the moral compass."

M. Baten & W. Enos, "Questions of Authenticity and
Situational Ethics," Cancer Bulletin, vol. 29, no. 4

Where can I find more details?

Without question, the best source is Dr. William Brennan's book, *The Abortion Holocaust*, (Landmark Press, 1983, $6.95). It describes in minute detail the analogy between the Nazi Holocaust and the abortion holocaust. Complete with charts and fully documented, it is a very valuable book.

CHAPTER 29

Birth Control

What is Right to Life's position on birth control?

The RTL movement limits itself to the protection of life from conception until natural death. It takes no position on the "preliminaries." Therefore, it has no opinion on contraception or sterilization.

What is the difference between contraception, sterilization and abortion?

Contraception and sterilization prevent human life from beginning. Abortion directly kills a human life already begun.

The legal freedom of individuals to use contraceptives has been recognized by most governments during this century. The recognition of such individual freedom of action does not, by itself, make such actions morally either right or wrong. Obviously, there are sharply differing judgments taught by different religions. For example, the Roman Catholic Church forbids the use of artificial contraceptives on the grounds that human persons are no more the arbiters of the process by which human life comes to be than they are of human life already begun. Many other Christian and non-Christian churches hold other opinions. If a husband and wife do decide to use contraceptive methods to plan their family, this decision immediately affects only themselves and their own bodily functions.

Sterilization is a permanent form of contraception. It can never be equated with abortion. It is a permanent termination of one of the body's natural functions. It prevents human life from beginning. It does not kill a life already begun.

Abortion, however, kills another human being. As such it can never be a matter of a mother's privacy or legal freedom of action (as ruled by the U.S. Supreme Court). Once pregnant, a woman is going to have a baby. The only choice open to her then is to allow the child to grow and be delivered or to have her tiny son or daughter killed. It should be the social concern of all citizens to give equal protection by law to all members of society.

How does the "pill" work?

There are over 30 "contraceptive" pills on the market, each differing a little from the others. They "prevent" pregnancy through three separate functions.

1. They thicken the mucous plug at the cervix. If this is the primary effect, then it truly is contraceptive because it prevents sperm from entering.

2. They prevent release of the ovum. If this is the primary effect, then the function is "temporary" sterilization.

3. They render the lining of the womb hostile to the implantation of the tiny new human at one week of life. This effect is abortifacient.

The earlier high-estrogen pills largely prevented ovulation. The newer low-estrogen pills allow "breakthrough" ovulation in up to 20% or more of the months used. Such a released ovum is fertilized perhaps 10% of the time. These tiny new lives which result, at our present "guesstimations," in 1% to 2% of the pill months, do not survive. The reason is that at one week of life this tiny new boy or girl cannot implant in the womb lining (see number 3 above) and dies. These are micro-abortions.

The pill, then, can have a contraceptive or temporary sterilization effect (by far the most common), or it can be an abortifacient.

Willke, "The Physiologic Function of Certain Birth Control Measures," *National RTL News*

In any one month for any one woman, which effect is primary?

For the woman, it is impossible to know.

How does the "morning-after pill" work?

It almost certainly sometimes acts in a sterilizing fashion. The massive dose rapidly affects the ovary, almost certainly preventing any ovulation that might have occurred one to three days after the intercourse. If sperm were still present and active in the woman's genital tract, she might otherwise have been fertilized one to three days after the event. In this case, such treatment (for example, as for an assault rape victim) actually prevents a pregnancy. (Also see chapter 19.)

Like the pill above, this medication also has an antinidatory effect on the endometrium (that is, a hardening of the lining of the uterus), which prevents implantation of the tiny new human being (blastocyst stage).

If, for example, a rape victim had ovulated just before the assault and fertilization had occurred, then the use of such medication after the event would clearly be abortive.

In actual practice, there is no way of knowing if she was fertilized at all, and if so, which effect the medicine had.

What is an I.U.D.?

The intrauterine device, commonly referred to as an I.U.D. or a coil (in Europe), is a small plastic or metal device that is inserted into the cavity of the uterus from below. The purpose of this is to "prevent" pregnancy.

Is an I.U.D. a contraceptive or an abortive agent?

With a few exceptions, almost all scientific papers agree that its effect is to prevent the implantation of the tiny new human being into the nutrient lining of the uterus. This is clearly abortive.

Several papers have suggested a contraceptive action, such as destruction of the sperm by macrophage action (*Acta. Cytol. Balt.*, vol. 14, 1970, pp. 58-64); speeding the passage of the ovum through the tube so as to escape fertilization (T. Mastroianni, *Med. World News*, Nov. 6, 1974). Overwhelmingly, however, other papers, while referring to the process as "contraceptive," typically agree that:

"It is clear that an I.U.D. prevents pregnancy in women by interrupting the reproductive process prior to implantation of the [fertilized] ovum."

Davis & Lesinski, "Mechanism of Action of Intrauterine Contraceptives in Women," *OB/GYN*, vol. 36, no. 3, Sept. 1970

An early, comprehensive collection of scientific papers on this subject was prepared at the Mayo Clinic by Dr. Thomas Hilgers, now Professor of OB/GYN at the University of Creighton in Nebraska. It has been reprinted and made available by Dr. John Harrington, editor of *Marriage and Family Newsletter*.

"The Intrauterine Device, Contraceptive or Abortifacient?" *Marriage and Family Newsletter*, vol. 5, nos. 1, 2, 3, 1974. P.O. Box 190, Midnapore, Alberta, Canada T0L 1J

More recently, the U.S. Food and Drug Administration stated in its official report that the rapid tubal transport theory (above) is not "currently considered to be the mechanism of action." Its effectiveness is "in direct proportion to the quantity and quality of the inflammatory response which it engenders." The report summarizes the various types of I.U.D.s and the various theories of action, and states that there "is one common thread...." They all "interfere in some manner with the implantation of the fertilized ovum in the uterine cavity."

Second Report on I.U.D.s, Dec. 1978, U.S. Dept. of HEW, Food & Drug Administration Document 017-012-00276-5

What about natural family planning?

This is not to be confused with the old (and not always effective) calendar rhythm. Utilizing an intimate knowledge of the woman's bodily functions such as mucous production, body temperature, and other signs and symptoms, this method helps a couple know when her fertile and nonfertile times of the month are. Without using any pills or other artificial means, couples can plan their families by having intercourse when she is (or is not) fertile. The abstinence time can be as brief as one week.

Isn't there a new post-contraceptive pill?

Early reports tell us of a new drug which is supposedly 80% effective in producing a very early abortion. The English form is RU-483. It is an anti-progesterone agent. It has two effects. One is to prevent implantation. The other is to cause the tiny one to "wither on the vine" and die in the early weeks if already implanted.

Lancet, Dec. 8, 1984

But family planning methods don't always work. What happens if a woman becomes pregnant and didn't want to be?

Over a lifetime, statistically speaking, most family planning methods do work. They also do fail in individual situations. Many people who are reading these words have been surprised by an unplanned pregnancy. Most of these originally unplanned pregnancies, however, over a period of nine months, came to be wanted and, after birth, became very cherished and loved children indeed. Truly, family planning, while not always "working" in each individual instance, will, if averaged out over a lifetime of marriage, be very effective in almost all cases in producing a family of approximately the size that a particular couple would desire. In any case, one cannot solve such a "problem" by killing a baby.

What about compulsory sterilization for those who have major, dominant genetic defects which they would be passing on to their children?

Conscientious people with a hereditary defect would be well-advised to refrain from having their own children, but rather to adopt children as their own if they desire a family. Compulsory sterilization for such reasons has already been enacted into law in some states and nations. Not many would agree with this type of law and activity. Even this, however, is something essentially less than the deliberate taking of a human life once conceived, since this involves only that person's body and not the life of another human being (as abortion does).

Would a Constitutional Amendment in the U.S. or a law in Canada or other nation outlawing abortion also forbid the use of the contraceptive pill, the morning-after pill, or the I.U.D.?

No! Such a law or amendment would only outlaw induced abortion. It could not "reach" these drugs, and perhaps not the I.U.D. either. This is because of the legal effect of dual action.

If a drug or device has an illegal action, but also a legal action, it cannot be outlawed or removed from the market. A good example is a butcher knife. This has a legal function in your kitchen. It can also be used as a murder weapon. Because it has both a legal and illegal function, it cannot be outlawed.

The "pill" and "morning-after pill" would still have a legal action (contraception, temporary sterilization), even though the other action (abortificient), would now be illegal. Because of the legal action, the anti-abortion law could not outlaw these medications.

The I.U.D. may also have a dual action. If this is proven, it might not be affected, even though such (contraceptive) action might be only a few percent.

The U.S. Food and Drug Administration has instructed all physicians who insert I.U.D.s to warn women that its use may cause pelvic inflammatory disease and to make their patients "thoroughly aware of this increased risk and its possible interference with future fertility."

U.S. Food & Drug Administration Drug Bulletin, May-June 1978

Is the I.U.D. safe for women?

Not very. The I.U.D., along with prior induced abortion and venereal disease, is also assumed to be one of the principal causes of the 140% increase in ectopic (tubal) pregnancies in the last decade (CDC figures, *Medical World News*, May 14, 1984).

Hallatt, "Ectopic Pregnancy Associated with the IUD,"
Amer. Jour. OB/GYN, vol. 125, p. 754

This is true of all I.U.D.s, but appears perhaps ten times as likely with the "Progestasert" brand.

Medical World News, Feb. 6, 1978
R. Peck, "F.D.A. Advisory Committee on Fertility and Maternal Health Drugs," *Medical Tribune*

The I.U.D. causes infection in the uterus and Fallopian tubes and often seals them off. Dr. R. Burkeman of Johns Hopkins, for example, reported that "nongonococcal salpingitis [pelvic inflammatory disease] is nearly twice as common (47% vs. 25%) in I.U.D. users as in non-users."

R. Burkeman Jr., "I.U.D. Promotes PID,"
vol. 243, no. 24, June 27, 1980

Add to this a "1.5 fold increase in risk of spontaneous miscarriage."

Levin, MA General Hospital,
Family Practice News, May 15-31, 1982

The question of whether an anti-abortion law would forbid the use of the I.U.D. may well prove irrelevant, for it will probably be removed from the market someday because of its damage to women.

Does it cause sterility?

Two studies designed specifically to study the link with infertility "confirm what doctors have strongly suspected for years — that the I.U.D. increases the risk of infertility," said Dr. Bruce Stadel of the National Institute of Child Health and Human Development.

NICHD Notes, Nat. Inst. Health, US Dept. HHS, Apr 10, 1985

Designed by the NICHD, the studies confirmed the higher incidence of PID and resultant sterility, but also showed that "even women who have no signs of pelvic infection with the I.U.D. still have a greater chance of becoming infertile than do those who never used the device."

Different types carried different risks. Most dangerous was the Dalkon Shield (3-7 times) than the Lippes Loop and the Saf-T-Coil (3 times) and then the copper wound types (2 times the risk)

"Tubal Infertility and the I.U.D.," D. Cramer et al, *N. Eng. J. Med,* Vol. 312, No 15, Pg 941-947, Apr 11, 1985

"Primary Tubal Infertility in Relation to the Use of an I.U.D. J. Daling et al, *N. Eng. J. of Med.* vol 312, no 15, p 938, 940, Apr 11, 1985

Do you approve of Planned Parenthood's activities?

To the extent that they help married couples use contraceptives to plan their families, Right to Life has no opinion. Today, however, this is only a small fraction of their work.

Planned Parenthood is now the largest baby-killing conglomerate in North America. In the U.S. it operates 53 abortion clinics, which kill over 83,000 babies a year (see chapter 37).

Remember,
if "Birth Control" is taught to your children in your school these courses often will
promote not just contraception, but also, abortion.

CHAPTER 30

Words — Words — Words

*The words we use are of
incalculable importance.*

Those who support abortion have quite successfully engaged in semantic gymnastics. They have told us that we are for "compulsory pregnancy" and that they are for a "woman's right to choose." "Termination of pregnancy" is "as simple as pulling a tooth." All it does is to gently remove the "products of pregnancy," "the fetus," "the embryo," the "feto-placental unit," "pregnancy tissue," and will "restore her periods." They accuse us of wanting to "impose our morality" and say that she has a "right to her own body," to "reproductive freedom." Most pro-abortionists insist that they "are personally opposed, but ..." They fear a return to "back-alley butchery." They consistently emphasize the problems of "unwanted pregnancy" and "women's rights," while totally ignoring her tiny passenger.

But we call ourselves *Right to Life.* Early on, we who would protect all human life adopted a title that has been startlingly effective. We became "right-to-life." This is the best title. Use it always. We also have said we are "pro-life." This, too, is an excellent title. But many people have used "pro-life" in other ways, changing its original meaning in many minds in an attempt to include those who labor against poverty, against war, against capital punishment, and against nuclear arms. Pro-abortionists have also, at times, claimed to be "pro-life." They have never and will never, however, adopt the title "Right to Life."

Let's be positive, if possible. We are *for* protection for the unborn, the handicapped, and the aged. If possible, don't accept the negative label "anti-abortion." There is nothing negative about being for life. And their label? "Pro-abortion" is acceptable; "anti-life" is best. *Never* use their "pro-choice." If you do, add "to kill" at the end of the phrase.

What grows within? An "unborn baby or child," or perhaps "preborn baby" is better. "Developing baby" is also scientifically and professionally accurate. Sometimes other humanizing terms fit, such as "this little guy." Avoid referring to the unborn child as "it;" use "he" or "she." The terms "the fetus" and "the embryo," fall on the listening ear as "non-human glob." Never use them. If you can't avoid it, speak of "the living human fetus."

Who does the procedure? Never call him/her a doctor. They don't deserve the dignity that "Doctor" calls forth. Also, don't use "surgeon." Call them "abortionists." Never deviate from that title. The word "abortionist" is one of condemnation, of criminality, of killing. That is the label they deserve.

"Termination of pregnancy" is a pro-abortion propaganda phrase. Avoid it like the plague. It masks what is actually happening. It speaks only to the mother's condition, completely ignoring the baby she carries. Furthermore, it is not specific for abortion. Didn't each of you terminate your mother's pregnancy by your birth?

234

Use the word "kill." Use it repeatedly, directly, and often. It is a non-judgmental, accurate, biological description of what happens. We use it when we step on a roach or when we spray crab grass. Use it here also. What of "murder?" This is a much stronger word. One cannot "murder" a dog or an insect, only a human being. To say "murderer" clearly implies that the abortionist knows that this living being is human and kills anyway. Therefore, use "murderer" with caution. Sometimes it may be too inflammatory and even counterproductive. "Kill," however, is always in order.

Who carries the child in her womb? A "mother." Pro-abortionists hate the word. "Pregnant woman" is accurate, but "mother" is much better.

"Womb" is usually a better word than "uterus," carrying a message of love, warmth, and security. "Womb" ties closely with "mother" and leads to "the womb has become a tomb."

Right to control her own body? You might facetiously ask, "Since when has it been out of control?" More to the point, however, it that this is a biologic absurdity, for over half (52%) of the babies born (or aborted) are male. Who ever heard of a woman's body with male organs?

"Right to her own body," if accepted as a feminist credo (*women's* rights), would or should serve to protect the almost 800,000 tiny American *women* whose mothers kill them annually.

"Place of residence" is a catchy and accurate way of remembering that killing in America is legal as long as the baby still lives in his first "place of residence," the womb. We also speak of discrimination on the basis of race, color, age, handicap, and place of residence.

The U.S. Supreme Court Decision of 1973 should always be described as "the tragic ..., the savage ...," and like terms.

Clinic? "Abortion clinic" is strong pro-abortion propaganda semantics. Sadly, this term is commonly used by many pro-lifers. The term is a contradiction. A "clinic" is where you go to be healed. There are even automobile transmission clinics. Use "abortion mill;" "abortion facility" if you must be neutral. Best of all, use "abortion chamber." Why "chamber?" That reminds us of gas chambers — extermination centers — and properly so. Every second human being who enters an abortion chamber, is exterminated (the tiny human inside the womb of a mother). Glad you asked.

The American Civil Liberties Union (ACLU) is accurately described as the legal defense and attack arm of the anti-life movement. Since it is so selective in whose right to live it defends, many call it the "anti-Civil Liberties Union."

Planned Parenthood needs to be explained and named every time you talk of abortion. Sometimes "Planned Barrenhood" may be in order. Planned Parenthood can always be labeled "The Largest Baby-Killing Conglomerate in America." Never fail to mention their over 53 abortion chambers which produce an over 83,000 per year "body count."

"Rape pregnancy" is not specific enough. Always speak of "assault rape pregnancy," which is very, very rare and *is* what we're talking about.

"Euthanasia" comes from two Greek words meaning "good death." Euthanasia proponents use this word to make it sound good. A quick retort is that it no longer means good death; it simply means "good-bye."

236

Similarly, "death with dignity" sounds good, but say it right. We want people to live in dignity until natural death occurs.

"Liberalize abortion?" Horrors! Never use this phrase. For many of us, to be liberal is to be concerned about those who need help the most. Instead, speak of "permissive" or "radical" abortion laws. Similarly, never use "reform" of older protective laws to mean that killing is now permitted.

Pro-abortionists accuse us of wanting to "impose our morality" on women. Turn that around, and say it correctly: "How much longer will our nation continue to allow mothers and abortionists to impose their morality on their helpless babies — fatally?"

"Every Child a Wanted Child" is their slogan. We must finish their sentence: "and if not wanted, kill."

Always say "salt poisoning abortion." Never refer to "saline abortion" or "salting out." These are pro-abortion terms and do not face what actually takes place. Always — and without exception — say "salt poisoning," as that is exactly what kills the baby.

"Interruption of pregnancy" is an absurd and inaccurate use of words. If I interrupt you, it means that I temporarily stop you, after which you resume. Abortion is permanent. It kills.

The abortionist's "curette" is not a "spoon-shaped instrument." It is "a loop-shaped steel knife." The curette doesn't "scrape" the placenta away; it "cuts and slices" it away.

"Person" is defined in one dictionary in 12 different ways. If you use it, define it first. If they use it, ask, "What do you mean by 'person?'" Pro-lifers do much better to speak of "human life."

"Conception?" Some define it as implantation at one week of life. Better to use "fertilization." (See chapter 7.)

"Contraception" is not a Right to Life issue, but I.U.D.s are referred to as contraceptives when in fact, they are "abortifacients." Use the correct word.

Perhaps "untimely" or "problem" pregnancy is better than "unwanted" pregnancy.

Are we "compulsory pregnancy" people? Then they are "compulsory death" people.

They want "reproductive freedom." She has it, and has used it. She is now a mother. She has reproduced. The only question now is whether to kill.

Is abortion a "single issue" in considering a candidate? No. But we do see it clearly as a "disqualifying issue" at the ballot box.

"Therapeutic abortion" always used to mean an abortion needed to save a mother's life. But its use in California's first abortion law, by Canada's "therapeutic abortion committees," and by many pro-abortionists in the U.S. has totally destroyed its original meaning. Now "therapeutic" has come to mean "elective."

For a few "one-liners" consider:

- Abortion is the ultimate child abuse.
- Abortion equals violence; oppose both.
- Intrauterine-battered child.
- Meaningful life? Meaningful to whom?
- It's a slippery slope from abortion to infanticide to euthanasia.
- Quality of Life? Or Equality of Life?
- Back-Alley abortions are now Front-Alley abortions.

"Since men can't get pregnant, they have nothing to say about abortion." If that were true, doctors couldn't treat a disease unless they had it first. How could we train funeral directors when they have never died? How can we oppose Hitler's genocide if we're not Germans or Jews — or slavery if we were not slaves or slave holders? In any case, each child has a father. And 52% of all unborn babies are boys.

If one is "incurably ill," that applies to all diabetics, for they are incurable. Let's speak of "terminally ill" instead.

"Potential" life? No. Rather, this is human life with vast potential.

Did you "come from" a teenager, a small girl, an infant, a female fetus, a female fertilized ovum? No, you once *were* a teenager, a small girl, an infant, *a fetus,* a female fertilized ovum. You were all there at each of those stages of your life. All you've done is to grow up.

"Overpopulation?" Remember, the U.S., Canada, and most of the Western world have had birth rates well below replacement level for over a decade.

"Health" is not what we think it is. As defined by the U.S. Supreme Court, and as interpreted in law throughout the world, it means "social, economic, and physical well being" of the mother.

If a person is "personally opposed, but …," they are in reality, pro-abortion. We'd far rather have a political office holder admit that even though personally in favor of abortion, he or she will vote for the civil rights of the unborn.

Abortion of "handicapped," preborn babies is "killing the patient to cure the disease." Remember, before birth and after birth, it's the same patient and the same handicap. This is prenatal euthanasia.

"Fetal Deformity?" "Fetal Defect?" Why use such "turn off" adjectives when we use "handicapped" for the child already born. The word "deformity" makes us turn away in revulsion. "Defective?" Our culture throws defective things away. "Handicapped" as a word calls forth a helping hand. To use "fetal deformity" or "fetal defect" is to make the killing easier. To use "fetal handicap" is to call forth a helping hand.

Never forget that abortion for rape is "killing an innocent baby for the crime of his father."

An example of the use of words to deceive is shown in the following routine instruction sheets. Both are for the same exam done by the same technician with the same equipment.

Antenatal Testing Unit
Pennsylvania Hospital
Philadelphia, PA 19107
(215) 829-5108

REALTIME ULTRASOUND EXAMINATION

You have been scheduled for realtime ultrasound for your baby. This procedure uses reflected sound waves (similar to sonar) to form a picture of your pelvic organs and your baby. This picture is very important because it can help the doctor estimate your due date, show the position of the baby and the placenta in your uterus, show if your baby is growing well, and show movements of the baby. The ultrasound is a painless procedure. Since the only form of energy used is sound waves, there is no known risk of harm to you or your baby, and this procedure has been used in obstetrics for over twenty years. The sound waves are at a frequency too high to hear.

If your pregnancy is 5 months or less, or if your physician is concerned about the location of the placenta, you will need a full bladder. This is so that we may obtain a more satisfactory ultrasound. Please ask the receptionist or nurse for a cup so you may begin drinking water if necessary.

The doctor will put a washable gel on your abdomen and then place a small plastic instrument on your skin. By running the instrument over your skin a picture is shown on a small screen for the doctor and you to see. The doctor will be able to make some measurements and will go over these results with you. If you have any questions please feel free to ask any of our staff for more information.

Antenatal Testing Unit
Pennsylvania Hospital
Philadelphia, PA 19107
(215) 829-5108

<u>REALTIME ULTRASOUND EXAMINATION PRIOR TO TERMINATION</u>

You have been scheduled for realtime ultrasound to determine how far your pregnancy has progressed. This procedure uses reflected sound waves to form a picture of your pelvic organs and your pregnancy. This picture is very important because it can help your doctor determine which procedure will be appropriate for termination. The ultrasound is a painless procedure and since the only energy used is high frequency sound waves, there is no risk of harm to you.

Since your pregnancy is 5 months or less you will need a full bladder for us to obtain a more satisfactory ultrasound. Please ask the receptionist or nurse for a cup so you may begin drinking water if necessary.

The doctor will put a washable gel on your abdomen and then place a small plastic instrument on you skin. By running the instrument over your skin, a picture is shown on a small screen for the doctor to see. The doctor will be able to make some measurements and will go over these results with you. If you have any questions, please feel free to ask any of our staff for more information.

CHAPTER 31

Opinion Polls

Are they accurate?
Well, it depends...

What factors influence accuracy?

Polls can be set up so that the results will be what the pollster wants to hear, not what public opinion actually is. This is especially true for the abortion issue. It is particularly sensitive to manipulation. There are a number of ways to predetermine the results.

By the words used?

If the wording speaks of "woman's rights," the majority will answer pro-abortion. If the poll asks about rights of the unborn, a strong majority will answer pro-life. Take this question, for example:

> "Should it be possible for a pregnant woman to obtain a *legal* [emphasis in original] abortion?"
> National Opinion Research Center, Univ. Chicago, 1965 (annually)

Note the question is of the woman's rights, with her tiny passenger apparently a nonentity. Note, also, "legal," which is the respondent's mind is matched against "illegal."

When "doctor," or "and her physician," or "medical reasons," or "medical decision" is used, pro-abortion answers are almost guaranteed. The same for "health." But if "abortionist" is used, or if for "social or economic" reasons is used, then a large majority will answer pro-life. "Terminate her pregnancy" brings a strong pro-abortion answer.

Conclusion: Read the question carefully. Is the deck stacked going in?

Give examples of "stacked" questions.

A classic example of leading the respondent by loading the question was a poll done for the National Abortion Rights Action League by Bailey and Deardourff prior to the U.S. Senate vote on the Hatch-Eagleton Amendment.

"The decision on whether or not to perform an abortion rests with the consenting patient, and should be performed by a licensed physician in conformance with good medical practice."

Results? Not surprisingly, more than 90% agreed; less than 10% disagreed.

Market Opinion Research, 1981
Bailey and Deardourff

Note the woman's right to decide, that she is a "patient" of a "licensed physician" who uses "good medical practice." Who wouldn't feel impelled to agree?

The same question, worded differently can return a totally different result, even from the same people. Take the following examples:

1. "Do you think there should be an amendment to the Constitution prohibiting abortions, or shouldn't there be such an amendment?"

Results: Should Be, 29%; Shouldn't Be, 67%

2. "Do you believe there should be an amendment to the Constitution protecting the life of the unborn child, or shouldn't there be such an amendment?"

Results: Should Be, 50%; Shouldn't Be, 34%

New York Times/CBS News Poll.
The New York Times, August 18, 1980, p. 1

Who is asked the question?

You will get a different answer from the readership of *Ms.* magazine than from the readership of *St. Anthony's Messenger.* That is obvious. What is less obvious is that truly professional polling must ask a valid cross section to be accurate.

What does the person who is asked know about the issue? Some questions have asked if the person agrees with the U.S. Supreme Court decision on abortion, when, in fact, only a tiny fraction have a reasonably accurate grasp of what it decreed.

The same is true of a yes or no on a constitutional amendment. What do the respondents know about such an amendment? Which amendment?

Is the question factually accurate?

A frequently used question states: "The Supreme Court has legalized abortion in the first three months of pregnancy. Do you agree?" As our readers know, that statement is flatly false, yet it has been used for years.

In the next questions, the factual error about abortion only in the first three months disqualifies the results, but note also that even subtle differences in wordings bring different results.

1. "The U.S. Supreme Court has ruled that a woman may go to a doctor to end a pregnancy at any time during the first three months of pregnancy. Do you favor or oppose this ruling?"

Results: Favor, 47%; Oppose, 44%

Gallup poll conducted March 1974
The Gallup Opinion Index, Report 106, April 1974

2. "The U.S. Supreme Court has ruled that a woman may go to a doctor for an abortion at any time during the first three months of pregnancy. Do you favor or oppose this ruling?"

Results: Favor, 43%; Oppose, 54%

Sindlinger, "Special Hitchhiker on Abortion," for
National Review, May 1974

The change from "to end a pregnancy" to "for an abortion" changed the results. How much more of a change would there be if "abortionist" were used instead of "doctor;" if the true nine months were stated instead of the incorrect "three months;" or if "to kill her developing baby" were used?

In tracking polls before the 1984 referendum in Colorado on abortion funding, a change from "public funding" to "your tax dollars" added 9% more to those who opposed such funding.

Does the poll contain the Life-of-the-Mother exception?

A *New York Times-CBS* poll asked the same question with and without the exception and found a 15% change in results.

"There is a proposal for a Constitutional Amendment that would make all abortions illegal."

Results: Favor, 28%; Oppose, 63%; Don't know/no answer, 9%

"There is another proposal for a Constitutional Amendment that would allow an abortion only in order to save the life of the mother. All other abortions would be illegal."

Results: Favor, 43%; Oppose, 48%; Don't know/no answer, 9%

New York Times, Oct. 14, 1984, p. E3

Is the question multi-issue?

Does the question mix abortion and contraception? The respondent may well favor one and oppose the other. Is the question placed in context with other loaded questions? Or does it stand by itself so that it can be answered on its own merits?

Can you give an example of an accurate poll?

One done in Ohio by a professional organization on a statistically representative cross sectional sample asked:

"At the present time, a woman may obtain an abortion for any reason during the entire nine months of pregnancy. An amendment to the U.S. Constitution has been proposed which would change the law to protect the right to life of an unborn child. Under this amendment, abortion would not be permitted at any time or for any reason, except to save the life of the mother. Would you favor or oppose such an amendment?"

Results: Favor, 47.1%; Oppose, 44.3%

Incidentally, the breakdown showed that of those favoring the amendment, there were more women than men, more blacks than whites, more younger and older than middle-aged people.

What of comparisons?

When seeking only a percentage difference, a poll can be very useful with a very simple question. For example, just before the 1984 Democratic National Convention, which adopted a strong pro-abortion platform, a poll was conducted which contrasted the opinions of the Democratic delegates with those of a cross section of Democratic voters. It asked:

"Should there be a Constitutional Amendment outlawing abortion?"

This question had all kinds of problems. As mentioned, what are the details of the amendment? "Outlawing" also tilts the answer in the pro-abortion direction. (Who wants to outlaw things? That sounds punitive; does it mean putting women in jail, etc.?) Even so, the answer told us something.

Results: Delegates 9%; Democrats nationwide 46%

Clearly, the delegates did not reflect the thinking of those whom they were supposed to represent.

How about those in the middle?

"Those people who are between the extremes of approval or disapproval, or are inconsistent, constitute one-half to two-thirds of the public."

J. Blake & J. Del Pinal, "Negativism, Equivocation, and Wobbly Assent: Public 'Support' for the Prochoice Platform on Abortion," *Demography,* vol. 18, U. 3, Aug. 1981, p. 312

Blake (who personally favors abortion), examined that middle ground and found that support for the full sweep of the Roe vs. Wade U.S. Supreme Court Decision was rare. "Even among respondents who, on one question, approve all reasons for legalizing abortion," when asked about specifics, 26% disapproved of three reasons, "Medicaid tax funding of abortion; of abortion without the husband's consent; and of abortion after the third month." An additional 29% disapproved of two of the above three reasons, and 27% of one reason, while only 18% approved of all three reasons. Abortion was also "highly unpopular" without parental consent.

ibid, Blake, p. 316

"The fact that high proportions of respondents can be found to approve at least one reason for legalizing abortion does not, apparently, constitute very meaningful public support. People who equivocate, who wish to fine tune the justifications for abortion, are apparently more negative than positive in their views about legalizing abortion. In fact, it may be fair to say that these respondents are 'closet negatives' (i.e., opposed to abortion)."

ibid, Blake, p. 315

Focusing upon the middle majority who said they thought abortion should be legal only under certain circumstances, Gallup asked these questions:

"Now, thinking about the first (second) (last) three months of pregnancy, under which of these circumstances do you think abortions should be legal ... when the woman's life is endangered, when the woman's mental health is endangered, where the pregnancy is a result of rape or incest, when there is a chance the baby will be born deformed, when the woman may suffer severe physical health damage, if the family cannot afford to have the child."

	Life Endangered	Rape/ Incest	Health Damage	Baby Deformed	Mental Health	Can't Afford
1st trimester						
1977	77	65	54	45	42	16
1979	78	59	52	44	42	15
2nd trimester						
1977	64	38	46	39	31	9
1979	66	32	46	37	31	9
3rd trimester						
1977	60	24	34	28	24	6
1979	59	19	33	28	22	4

1977 poll, *The Gallup Opinion Index,* Report 153, April 1978;
1979 poll, *The Gallup Opinion Index,* Report 166, May 1979

That means there is almost no support for the full sweep of the U.S. Supreme Court Decision?

Yes. This was stated very clearly during the hearing on the Hatch-Eagleton Amendment in the U.S. Senate (see chapter 6).

Another thing to consider is whether the question is too general.

"Do you feel that abortion should be a) legal under all circumstances, b) only under certain circumstances, or c) illegal under all circumstances?"

Gallup Poll/National, asked annually since 1975

If read carefully and with thought, the only people in "C" would be those who would not even allow abortion to prevent the mother's death, and the only ones in "A" would be those who even approve sex-selection abortions in the third trimester of pregnancy.

And when details are asked?

A broad, general answer is often rendered invalid (as the next two questions show), when specific details are probed.

1. "As you may have heard, in the last few years a number of states have liberalized their abortion laws. To what extent do you agree or disagree with the following statement regarding abortion: The decision to have an abortion should be made solely by a woman and her physician?"

Results: Agree, 64%; Disagree, 31%

Commissioned by Planned Parenthood and asked in a Gallup poll. *The Gallup Opinion Index,* Report 87, Sept.

2. "Do you think it should be lawful for a woman to be able to get an abortion without her husband's consent?"

Results: Yes, 24%; No, 67%

Commissioned by Blake and asked in a Gallup poll two months after Question 1 above. (1973)

Note also the slanting of the first question: "made solely by a woman and her physician." This guarantees a pro-abortion answer.

Are there other supportive polls?

Yes. Here are two more:

"Suppose you had a fifteen-year-old, unmarried daughter who told you she had recently become pregnant. Would you advise her to have an abortion or not?"

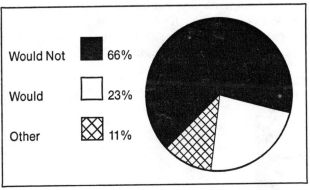

Would Not ■	66%
Would □	23%
Other ⊠	11%

ABC News/*Washington Post* poll, 1981

"Do you think it should be lawful for a woman to be able to get an abortion without her husband's consent?"

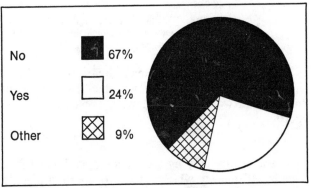

No ■	67%
Yes □	24%
Other ⊠	9%

Judith Blake, *Elective Abortion and Our Reluctant Citizenry*, 1973

What of women's opinions compared to those of men?

The vast majority of polls have consistently reported *more* opposition to abortion from women than from men. This may be due to the fact that women believe earlier that this is human life. Note the following question:

"It is sometimes said that the morality of abortion rests on the question of when one thinks human life begins.... Which of these alternatives best expresses your views? Human life begins ..."

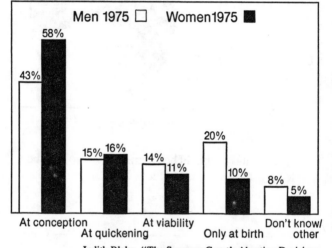

Men 1975 ☐   Women 1975 ■

| | | |
| 43% | 58% | |

15% 16%   14% 11%   20% 10%   8% 5%

At conception
At quickening
At viability
Only at birth
Don't know/ other

Judith Blake, "The Supreme Court's Abortion Decisions and Public Opinion in the United States," *Population and Development Review,* 1 and 2, 1977, pp. 45-62

This has since been confirmed by a *Los Angeles Times* national opinion poll which showed that 51% of men but only 47% of women favor allowing women to have an abortion.

Los Angeles Times, Sept. 1983

And a major study by the Connecticut Mutual Life Insurance Company which asked: "Is abortion morally wrong? Or is it not a moral issue?" (See chapter 32.)

What of age groups?

This is beginning to assume real significance. In the early years of the abortion debate, there was generally substantial approval in the younger age groups and disapproval in the older groups. We are now seeing the young people of yesterday carrying much of their pro-abortion sentiment with them as they grow older. The new generation of young people, on the other hand, are more opposed to abortion than those who preceded them.

In *Who's Who Among High School Students*, the percentage of approval of abortion has dropped from 70% in the 1970s to 39% in 1982.

A 1984 statewide poll in Ohio also showed this U-shaped curve.

Specific questions on parental and husband's consent also generate answers that fly in the face of the oft-claimed majority support for the Supreme Court decision.

Where can I read more detailed information on polls?

We refer you to a study by Professor Raymond Adamak of Kent State University. His analysis has been reprinted and is available from National Right to Life, 419 7th St. N., Suite 500, Washington, DC 20004. Your authors wish to thank Dr. Adamak and National Right to Life for permission to reprint some of that material.

CHAPTER 32

The Secular Media

With a few notable exceptions,
it is overwhelmingly pro-abortion.

That is certainly the shared opinion of pro-life leaders throughout the Western world. Anyone in the Right to Life movement for any length of time can cite numerous examples of pro-abortion bias, ranging from selective reporting of actual facts, to slanting the news, to gross distortion.

Can you give examples?
The U.S. Supreme Court decision of 1973 legalized abortion until birth (see chapter 6). Over a decade later, it is still common in the daily media, to hear or read that it is only legal in the first three months of pregnancy, or only legal until viability, giving the clear impression that it is illegal after that time.

We are called "anti-abortion" (a negative label), while they are "pro-choice" (a positive label).

Large pro-life rallies, marches, picketing, etc., are ignored or grossly underestimated in size. A dozen "pro-choice" protestors, however, will get equal or often much more time on TV or space in print than even tens of thousands of pro-life people.

Anti-abortion "fanatics" are contrasted with pro-choice people with "deep commitments."

It is OK to identify those who oppose abortion as Catholics and in recent years, as Evangelicals, Fundamentalists, or members of Moral Majority. But who has ever heard of a pro-abortion person being identified as a Jew, an atheist, or a homosexual, if such they were.

This is universal?

Of course not. Apart from the religious media, there are a few columnists, daily newspapers, and radio and TV personalities who try to be fair or who are openly pro-life. The point is that they are a very small percentage.

Are there any surveys?

There have been some done to measure the values and convictions of journalists and other leading professionals. The Connecticut Mutual Life Insurance Company did an extensive survey of the general public in the U.S. and contrasted their values with "leaders" including those in the news media.

Table 32 GENERAL PUBLIC
"WHICH OF THE FOLLOWING DO YOU BELIEVE ARE MORALLY WRONG?"

Adultery	85%
Use of hard drugs	84%
Homosexuality	71%
Engaging in sex before the age of 16	71%
Lesbianism	70%
Pornographic movies	68%
Abortion	65%
Smoking marijuana	65%
Living with someone of the opposite sex before marriage	46%
Sex between two single people	40%

Table 35
"IS ABORTION MORALLY WRONG OR IS THIS NOT A MORAL ISSUE?"

	Morally Wrong	Not a Moral Issue
<u>General Public</u>	65%	35%
<u>Level of Relig. Commit.</u>		
Lowest	43%	57%
Low	58%	42%
Moderate	75%	25%
High	78%	22%
Highest	85%	15%
<u>Age</u>		
14-20	65%	35%
21-24	67%	33%
25-34	59%	41%
35-49	65%	35%
50-64	65%	35%
65 or over	75%	25%
<u>Gender</u>		
Male	64%	36%
Female	67%	33%
<u>Region</u>		
Northeast	61%	39%
West	56%	44%
Midwest	67%	33%
South	72%	28%
<u>Place of Residence</u>		
Large City	59%	41%
Small City	66%	34%
Suburb	65%	35%
Rural	71%	29%
<u>Race</u>		
White	64%	36%
Black	73%	27%

Income		
Under $12,000	74%	26%
$12,000 to $25,000	64%	36%
Above $25,000	56%	44%
Education		
11th grade or less	74%	26%
High School graduate	67%	33%
Some college or more	54%	46%
Political Orientation		
Liberal	58%	42%
Moderate	65%	35%
Conservative	71%	29%
Party Affiliation		
Republican	64%	36%
Democrat	68%	32%
Independent	62%	38%

By far the most interesting fact revealed by the study was comparing leaders in various groups with the general public.

Table 136

"IS ABORTION MORALLY WRONG OR IS THIS NOT A MORAL ISSUE?"

	Morally Wrong	Not a Moral Issue
General Public	65%	35%
Leaders-overall	36%	64%
Religion	74%	26%
Business	42%	58%
Military	40%	60%
News Media	35%	65%
Voluntary Association	33%	67%
Government	29%	71%
Education	26%	74%
Law and Justice	25%	75%
Science	25%	75%

"The Impact of Belief,"
Conn. Mutual Life Report on American Values in the '80s

Another and more detailed report was based on "hour long interviews with 240 journalists and broadcasters at the most influential media outlets including the *New York Times, Washington Post, Wall St. Journal, Time Magazine, Newsweek, U.S. News and World Report,* CBS, NBC, ABC, PBS, etc." Among the findings were that 90% said a woman had the right to choose abortion.

Forty-six percent felt adultery was wrong, with only 15% feeling strongly about it, and 76% approved of living with someone of the opposite sex.

On religion, 50% denied any religious affiliation. Twenty-three percent were raised Jewish, but only 14% were practicing Judaism at the time. Only one in five identified themselves as Protestant, one in eight as Catholic. Overall, however, only 8% went to church or synagogue weekly with 86% attending seldom or never.

They were largely male, white, highly educated, with high incomes. They voted heavily for McGovern and Carter over Nixon and Ford. They were committed to the welfare state, to redistribution of income, and were strong environmentalists and desegregationists, Eight-five percent agreed that homosexuals have the right to teach in public schools, etc.

S. Lichter & S. Rothman, "The Media Elite: White, Male, Secular and Liberal," *Public Opinion* Magazine, 1981

In a study two years later of "Television's Elite," 104 network vice presidents, writers, producers, and executives returned similar results. "Ninety-seven percent of the 'elite' agreed that a woman has the right to decide on abortion."

J. Carmody, "The TV Column," *Washington Post*, Feb. 9, 1983

What of journalism students?

In a study of 28 candidates for master's degrees at Columbia University School of Journalism, the leftward bias was much more pronounced, showing overwhelming support of women's rights. To sample one other question;

in 1980, 4% voted for Reagan, 59% for Carter, and 29% for Anderson.

"Accuracy in Media Review," Dec. 82 reporting on Dec. 82 *Washington Journalism Review*

But does this value system show through their reporting?

Not for some, but very obviously for others. With such strong opinions, even the most dedicated professional will show his or her bias only too often.

Is there a pro-life answer?

Yes! For now, take everything you read with a healthy scepticism.

For the future, let's urge our pro-life sons and daughters to seek careers in journalism.

What of Opinion Formers in the performing arts?

A study of the 104 top Hollywood creators of TV shows, each of whom had been associated with two or more prime time series, reported that 97% were pro-abortion. Also, two-thirds said that TV should be a major force for social reform. As with the news media elite, they were well paid (two-thirds over $200,000 per year), white, urban, male, most lived in California and the Northeast, and only 7% went to church once a month.

L. and R. Lichter, S. Rothman, "Hollywood and America, the Odd Couple," *Public Opinion 5,* Dec.-Jan. 1983, pp. 54-58

A study of 149 writers, producers, and directors of the 50 top grossing movies (1965-83) showed 96% pro-abortion, with similar characteristic make-ups as those mentioned above.

S. Rothman & R. Lichter, "What Are Moviemakers Made Of?" *Public Opinion 6,* Dec.-Jan. 1984, pp. 14-18%

Should we give up on the media? Is it hopeless?

Quite the contrary. Our relationship with the media is getting better.

We must get acquainted with media people. They will see us as single issue? True, but they must also see us as well-spoken and professional, not irresponsible firebrands; concerned for the mother as well as her preborn child; broad based, not a single political party or religion or sex; and as a voting block to respect.

We must educate them. Many media people have gross misconceptions of us and what we stand for. When they understand us and our issue better, we will get more balanced reporting.

Most media people are sincere, dedicated, and try to do a job. You should praise their professional work, but constructively criticize their unprofessional reporting. Above all, however, respect them, and continue to work with them. When we do get to know each other, and do continue to communicate, we will get more balance and, sometimes, even favorable treatment.

Reporters and commentators are interested in news, any kind of news. When we make news, we rate time and space and will get it.

A good example of real news that was picked up and aired broadly was *The Silent Scream,* the ultrasound movie of a 12-week suction abortion (see chapter 10). This movie, on the cutting edge of new technology, was news and was given good coverage.

CHAPTER 33

Equal Rights Amendment

The Abortion Connection

Section I: Equality of rights under the law shall not be denied or abridged by the United States or any state on account of sex.

Section II: The Congress shall have the power to enforce, by appropriate legislation, the provisions of this article.

Section III: This amendment shall effect two years after the date of ratification.

When was it originally passed?

On March 22, 1972, by both Houses of Congress. Within two months, 13 states had ratified, within nine months, 22 states; within 12 months, 30 states. Then the tide turned. In the next six years, five more states ratified but five rescinded, leaving the total at 30 of the 38 needed, (assuming that the recisions were valid).

It passed Congress without argument?

Quite the contrary. There was a long series of amendments proposed. The defeat of each of them had immense long term significance. During the debate in the U.S.

Senate prior to passage, this series of amendments was offered to specify that it would not or could not be interpreted by judges to do certain things. They included:

- Women could not be drafted. Amendment 1065: "This article shall not impair, however, the validity of any laws of the United States or any State which exempt women from compulsory military service." It was voted down.
- Women could not be sent into combat. Amendment 1066: "This article shall not impair the validity, however, of any laws of the United States or any State which exempt women from service in combat units of the Armed Forces." It was voted down.
- Women, wives, and mothers would not lose certain privileges that they have always needed. Amendment 1067: "This article shall not impair the validity, however, of any laws of the United States or any State which extend protections or exemptions to women." And Amendment 1068: "This article shall not impair the validity, however, of any laws of the United States or any State which extend protections or exemptions to wives, mothers, or widows." Both were voted down.
- Women would not lose child support. Amendment 1069: "This article shall not impair the validity, however, of any laws of the United States or any State which imposed upon fathers responsibility for the support of their children." It was voted down.
- Schools, seminaries, sports, toilet facilities, etc., could continue to be segregated and have separate private facilities. Amendment 1070: "This article shall not impair the validity, however, of any laws of the United States or any State which secure privacy to men or women, boys or girls." It was voted down.
- Homosexuality would not be forced upon the nation as co-equal legally with the traditional heterosexual family, in education, etc. Amendment

1071: "This article shall not impair the validity, however, of any laws of the United States or any State which make punishable as crimes sexual offenses." It was voted down.

Since the Senate rejected all of these limitations, it was logical to assume that they meant the ERA to allow or even direct that these things happen. This was the beginning of the campaign against the ERA.

But none of these suggested amendments mentioned abortion.

True, although, if the sexes were to be completely equal, then what rights one sex had, the other should also have.

1. Men could have sex and walk away non-pregnant. So, also, if a woman had sex (and got pregnant) she should have the right to also walk away non-pregnant. If she were "forced" to stay pregnant that would be sexual discrimination.

2. If surgical operations peculiar to the male sex (for example, prostate surgery), were paid for with tax money, so also should operations that were peculiar to the female sex (like abortions), be paid for.

But such a connection was still conjecture in those first years after Congressional passage.

Were there other forceful arguments?

There were others, but two were of great importance and worth noting here.

Present Social Security laws give a homemaker benefits because of what her husband earns. Under the ERA, she may also have to pay social security taxes based upon the value of her contributed work at home in order to obtain these later retirement benefits. If homemaker wives are ever required to pay $1,000 or $2,000 a year in Social Security taxes, many or most will have to leave their homes to work.

Another telling argument against the ERA was by Senator Sam Erwin (NC):

"The ERA will transfer from the states to the federal government vast governmental powers which have been reserved to the states throughout our history. By so doing, the amendment will substantially thwart the purpose of the Constitution to create 'an indestructible union composed of indestructible states' and reduce the states in large measure to powerless zeros on the nation's map."

Senator Sam Erwin in a speech to the
NC General Assembly, Mar. 1, 1977

Were there any referenda?

In November 1975, both New York State and New Jersey had statewide referenda. Both decisively defeated their proposed state ERAs. Other referenda (Wisconsin, in 1973; Florida and Nevada, in 1978; and Iowa, in 1980), also rejected the ERA. Most recently, in November 1984, Maine defeated a proposed ERA in a referendum, 65 to 35.

Some states rescinded after ratifying earlier?

Yes. They were Nebraska, Tennessee, Kentucky, Idaho, and South Dakota. The legality of their rescinding was challenged. A Federal Court ruled the rescissions to be legal. This decision was appealed to the U.S. Supreme Court, which ruled it moot (no decision necessary), without commenting upon its merits after the time limit for ratification had expired.

On March 22, 1979, the seven-year limit for ratification expired. Congress then extended the time limit for 30 more months. The constitutionality of extension by a majority vote was questioned, since a two-thirds vote had been needed to send it to the states originally for ratification. Even with the extension, the ERA expired in 1982 without any more states ratifying.

But the ERA was reintroduced.

Yes. In January 1983 the same wording was reintroduced in both the House and the Senate. Hearings were again held.

The prime sponsor of the newly resurrected ERA, Senator Paul Tsongas, testified before Senator Orrin Hatch. "Would the ERA lock the right to abortion and/or abortion funding into the Constitution?" Senator Tsongas' answer: "That issue will be decided in the courts."

U.S. Senate, Subcommittee on the Constitution,
Senate Judiciary Committee, May 26, 1983

To other questions on women-in-combat, private schools, veterans' preference, insurance, homosexuality, etc., Senator Hatch received the same answer. This revealed, in a dramatic and devastating fashion, that the ERA would mean anything the Supreme Court interpreted it to mean, a fact hardly reassuring to anyone who held traditional values.

ibid. above, Hatch, Tsongas

In the meantime, some states incorporated the ERA wording in their State Constitutions?

Yes, and with these came new developments.

Hawaii. In January 1978 Hawaii RTL asked its state court to stop funding elective abortions. Two abortionists and the American Civil Liberties Union intervened. They argued that that state's ERA mandated the use of tax money to pay for elective abortions. The judge ordered that abortions be paid for, but stated that he had not ruled on the basis of the ERA/abortion issue.

Hawaii RTL vs. Chang, 1978

Massachusetts. The Massachusetts Civil Liberties Union asked the highest state court to rule that, "By singling out for special treatment and effectively excluding from coverage an operation which is unique to women, while including without comparable limitation a wide range of other operations, including those which are unique to men, the anti-funding statutes discriminates on the basis of sex, in violation to the Massachusetts ERA."

The judges ruled that taxes must pay for elective abortions without commenting on the validity of the above argument.

Moe vs. King, Sept. 8, 1980

Wisconsin. This state's General Assembly passed the ERA in 1982 but with a preamble which stated "that such an amendment shall not limit in any way the legislature's power to enact legislation prohibiting, regulating, or allowing abortions."

In order to amend that state's Constitution, the General Assembly must first pass the proposal on two successive sessions prior to a referendum vote. The pro-abortion groups woke up, lobbied heavily, and killed the entire ERA in the second session because they could not remove the abortion neutralizing clause, which they called "objectionable anti-civil libertarian language."

What position has Right to Life taken?

Back in the early 1970s, when the first ERA was introduced, the National Right to Life Board did not take a firm position. All members were for equal rights for women, and the abortion connection was not completely clear. As the years passed, and the evidence proving the ERA/abortion connection accumulated, the Board (which is made up of elected representatives from each of the 50 state RTL organizations), took a position of opposition, unless the ERA were amended to render it abortion neutral.

In addition to the above evidence, the final proof came from the realization of what "strict scrutiny" and "unique physical characteristics" would do. The U.S. Supreme Court had clarified this.

Strict Scrutiny?

This was crucially important. In 1977 and in 1980 the U.S. Supreme Court ruled on the constitutionality of the Hyde Amendment to the Labor HHS appropriation bill. It stated that laws forbidding the use of tax funds for abortion were constitutional. The court clearly stated that this was so because they were not based on a "suspect classification" and thus, did not trigger "strict scrutiny" by the courts.

Maher vs. Roe,
U.S. Supreme Court, 432 US 464, 1977
Harris vs. McRae,
U.S. Supreme Court, 1980 at 23

The ERA advocates have emphasized that the ERA's principal legal effect would be to make sex a "suspect classification under the Constitution."

"The most important 'suspect classification' at present is race. If sex discrimination were treated like race discrimination, government refusal to fund abortions would be treated like a refusal to fund medical procedures that affect members of minority races, for example, sickle cell disease which affects only black people."

H. Hyde, The ERA/Abortion Connection,
testimony before Constitution Subcommittee,
U.S. Senate Judiciary Committee, May 26, 1983

In the House hearing, strongly pro-abortion Congressman Don Edwards stated that the ERA would impose such "strict scrutiny" on "pregnancy classification."

Hearings, Judiciary Committee
U.S. House of Representatives, Nov. 9, 1983

So did the Congressional Research Service's legal memo, which, in 1983, suggested that the imposition of "strict scrutiny" on pregnancy classifications by the ERA would invalidate all funding restrictions for abortions.

Unique Physical Characteristics?

"The U.S. Supreme Court has already created a parallel legal doctrine under Title VII of the Civil Rights Act, which prohibits sex discrimination in employment. An employer violates Title VII if he treats an employee 'in a manner which but for that person's sex, would be different.'

"Under the ERA, this doctrine would be applied with constitutional force in every aspect of the law. It would invalidate not only restrictions on funding of abortion, but also any other law that 'discriminates' against such a 'sex-specific' procedure.

"This could include, for example, the 'conscience' laws currently in effect in 44 states, which prevent penalization of medical personnel and institutions for refusing to participate in abortions. The doctrine could also jeopardize the tax-exempt status of, for example, religiously affiliated educational institutions that try to impede abortion-related activities on their campuses.

"Title VII does not require employers to provide abortion 'benefits,' simply because Congress attached to Title VII an *explicit exception* for abortion. The same solution should be applied to the ERA."

D. Johnson, "Proof of Abortion-ERA Link Massive, Compelling," *Natl. Cath. Reporter,* July 6, 1984

If the ERA had been in the Constitution, it is clear that the Hyde Restriction and all of its counterparts would have been judged unconstitutional.

What then?

When the 1983 ERA was introduced, National RTL asked Congress to attach the following abortion neutralizing clause:

"Nothing in this Article (the ERA) shall be construed to grant or secure any right relating to abortion or the funding thereof."

If this had been attached, the ERA would have easily passed by the required two-thirds vote in the U.S. House of Representatives. The radical feminist groups, however, would have none of it. They demanded and got a vote on the unamended original wording — and lost by six votes on November 15, 1983. Without question, the ERA was defeated on the horns of the abortion issue.

Shortly after this, a major court ruling probably drove the last nail into the ERA's coffin.

You mean the Pennsylvania Decision?

Yes. The Commonwealth Court of Pennsylvania in March 1984 ruled that Pennsylvania's ERA required Medicaid funding of abortion-on-demand. The state law had forbidden the use of taxes for elective abortions. Planned Parenthood, the ACLU, and the Women's Law Project had argued that this was "sex discrimination" and was a violation of the Pennsylvania ERA. The Court stated that the ERA

"... is meritorious and sufficient in and of itself to invalidate the statutes before us in that these statutes do unlawfully discriminate against women with respect to a physical condition unique to women."

Fischer vs. Dept. of Public Welfare,
Commonwealth of PA, March 9, 1984

After this decision, all efforts to revive the ERA in the 98th Congress ceased. Just before adjournment, a higher court overturned the lower court's decision. The decision was appealed. The very fact that these courts disagreed and that yet another court must rule gives solid confirmation to the fact that the ERA will mean whatever the courts say it will mean.

Can We Trust the Courts?

CHAPTER 34

Boycotts

What is Right to Life's most important boycott?
The one against the Upjohn Pharmaceutical Company of Kalamazoo, Michigan. It is of great importance, possibly equaled only by the boycott of the March of Dimes.

Why the Upjohn Company?
A decade ago Upjohn held the original basic patents on a newly discovered class of human hormones, the prostaglandins. These held great promise for human betterment. Back then, Upjohn knew that among other functions, different forms of these hormones might a) cure asthma, b) cure many forms of rheumatism and arthritis, c) cure peptic ulcers, d) cause the uterus to contract and cause abortions, and e) correct a congenital heart problem. Their research funds and facilities would not permit a full-scale effort to perfect all these forms at once. Accordingly, they chose, in a fateful decision, to concentrate on the one form whose only function was to kill.

Upjohn spent tens of millions of dollars for research, and finally perfected an intra-amniotic injectable form, Prostin f2a and brought it to the market in 1973. At that time, the U.S. Food & Drug Administration approved it for only one use, "the induction of mid-trimester abortions." Since then, two other forms have been introduced, Prostin E2, as a vaginal suppository and Prostin 15M, for intra-muscular injection. Since their introduction, these three drugs have been recognized as useful in the treatment of several other obstetrically related conditions.

Some of the drug literature for doctors, in detailing its abortion usage, listed as the first possible complication as, "Live birth."

How does it work?

Prostaglandin causes powerful and sustained contractions of the uterus (labor), at any stage of pregnancy, resulting in vaginal delivery of whatever size baby the mother carries. In early pregnancy, the drug always kills the baby. In mid pregnancy, the baby is sometimes born alive — a "complication."

Is the drug safe?

Well, certainly not for the baby! It may be safer at times for the mother than the alternative of salt poisoning, but it is still dangerous (see chapter 14).

Will this be the do-it-yourself abortion?

Upjohn is proceeding as fast as possible to perfect a new vaginal suppository form to be available on prescription. This could be used by the woman herself, in very early pregnancy she could abort at home. Upjohn has tried very hard to label this as anything but what it is. For example, in a recent letter, the company stated that:

"We are doing research on a product which induces a woman's period and which is less physically invasive than suction curettage and potentially useful in abortion before the time when suction is most effective for early abortion."

Letter to President, Michigan RTL, from F. A. Dussling,
Public Relations, Upjohn Co., Dec. 7, 1984

Will the new suppository have any beneficial use?

Yes. It can be used prior to any needed medical D&C to soften the cervix. The problem will be that several suppositories used one after the other will also cause an abortion.

How does the boycott work?

Small wallet cards are used to alert people to ask their doctors or pharmacists if what they are purchasing is an Upjohn product. If it is, they ask for a different company's brand because they don't want to support "a death peddler." These cards are probably available from your local Right to Life chapter. If not, you can write to Cincinnati Right to Life. See reproduction of Upjohn wallet cards on next page.

What about the March of Dimes?

For over a decade, every RTL chapter in the U.S. has endorsed this boycott, and still many who are not informed fail to understand.

The March of Dimes does a lot of good with well over 90% of their dollars. But it tolerates "a little eugenic Auschwitz" on the side. For all of the good that the MOD has done for our society, this evil may, in balance, ultimately do far more harm.

What has the MOD done?

It was they who first funded and set up, all across the country, genetic testing centers. They popularized amniocentesis in the mid-trimester (see chapter 26). This has become a search and destroy mission and has taught a nation that the "answer" to an unborn baby who is handicapped is to kill him or her before birth.

The March of Dimes pays for abortions?

No, they do not. They pay for and facilitate only the search and identify portion, and they stand back and do not protest the almost inevitable (97-98%) killing that then occurs. Right to Life has repeatedly asked them to stop doing mid trimester amniocentesis (not late ones, which benefit both baby and mother). Such testing has only one

purpose: to identify the child's condition. There is no medical problem identifiable in the mid trimester that is treatable in the mid trimester.

But the MOD speaks of two treatable conditions!
The ones that they speak of, both Methylmalonic Acidemia and Biotin deficiency, can be discovered in mid pregnancy. Neither, however, is treatable until later in the third trimester. The testing is not necessary in the mid trimester — unless you want to kill the babies before they get too old.

The MOD argues that by identifying "normals," they often save babies who would otherwise be aborted!
An analogy would have been a testing center outside Auchwitz where suspected Jews would be taken. Some would be found to be "normal" Aryans and their lives would be spared. Of course, the Jews would be gassed. Would you contribute money to such a testing center?

And so the boycott?
Yes. Right to Life suggests that all pro-life people withhold contributions from the MOD until it ceases to be a part of this eugenic death selection process.

You've also boycotted Avon Cosmetics?
Yes, and successfully. They had given funds to several radical, pro-abortion feminist groups who were pushing abortion. They quit, and RTL called off the boycott.

What about the Procter and Gamble and Kellogg boycotts?
Both corporations had given funds to Planned Parenthood. Both quit. We thanked both of them and again buy their products.

How about the United Appeals?
A number of major metropolitan United Appeals have been boycotted for including Planned Parenthood among

their beneficiaries. These boycotts have been successful in Toronto, Tulsa, Calgary, Berks Co., PA, and other places where Planned Parenthood was subsequently excluded. In some cities after a boycott, Planned Parenthood voluntarily withdrew from that United Appeal, as happened in Chicago.

There is still work to do here. One well-publicized target city is Akron, OH. If major religious groups such as the Catholic Diocese and others were to withdraw from the United Appeal, almost certainly that United Appeal would stop funding Planned Parenthood.

How about the U.A. in your city? Best you find out.

CHAPTER 35

Violence — The Answer?

**Since they can't close them,
they burn them down.**

To hear Planned Parenthood officials, abortion prof-
iteer, William Baird, or abortion chamber proprietors
talk, the above is the thinly veiled policy of Right to
Lifers.

Well, isn't this correct?
Absolutely not. There has not been a single instance of
arson or violence against an abortion chamber that has
been proven to be planned or carried out by a Right to Life
group.

Never, not even one?
No, not one. This is remarkable when we know that
there are literally millions of outraged citizens who feel
frustrated and helpless before an all-powerful federal judiciary.

**Our founding fathers, our frontiersmen took matters
into their own hands. Why don't you?**
Because we are nonviolent, peaceful people. Has unjust

and oppressive violence ever really been stopped by more violence? Will the misguided and often, hardened hearts of pro-abortion people be changed or softened by retaliating against their violence with our own violence?

Abortion is violence?

Precisely. The violence is occurring inside the doors of the abortion chambers. Killing of innocent babies is the ultimate violence, and it occurs 4,000 times every day in the United States.

Who throws the fire bombs then?

We believe several have been set by the owners to get insurance after picketers had ruined their businesses.

One incident was caused by a man judged to be insane. Another was by a husband who went berserk in the abortion chamber after his wife had "killed my baby." Others were by a "religious" group (Army of God).

We could also imagine the parents of a minor daughter (who they never even dreamed was pregnant) being called to the intensive care unit of a hospital to find her in critical condition caused by complications from an abortion — an abortion that was legally done without their knowledge or consent. Their beloved daughter, now injured physically and emotionally for life! Can't you imagine that father blindly seeking vengeance against those who did it?

Three fire bombings in Everett, Washington, led to the incarceration of a man who was not a RTL member. Others in Pensacola were charged to four young people who were motivated by religious reasons.

What is the Army of God?

Three men arrested, convicted, and sent to jail have stated that they made up the name and are its only members.

Right to Lifers will never use violence?

We hope not. To adopt pro-abortionists' twisted ethic would be to endorse it.

What about those who picket these places?

They are heroes and heroines. They volunteer their time. They walk in the rain and snow. They endure insults and sometimes assault from the guards that the abortion proprietors hire, and they take it — all in hope of saving one tiny life, in the hope of preventing the physical and psychic damage to one woman.

Do they save lives?

Yes, they do, and that is their reward. They sidewalk-counsel and picket peacefully. When a woman goes through their line to enter, they will offer her literature and help. In a quiet voice, they will say, "Please don't kill your baby. We'll help you in any way you need. Won't you let us?"

But I've heard that the picketers threaten and sometimes physically abuse the women.

Never! In fact, it is the abortion chamber people who frequently do such things. Pro-life picketers have been spit on, pushed, cursed, threatened, ridiculed, hit, etc. All they do is turn the other cheek.

But this picketing does upset some women who have their minds firmly made up. Is that good?

If these women had truly been informed of the full facts of fetal development, of the hazards of induced abortion, and of all the alternatives, there would be no need for picketing. Furthermore, a woman at peace with her choice for an abortion would not be upset by pickets, pictures of babies, and attempted counseling.

Do you mean the picketers give information the women wouldn't get otherwise?

Yes. A good example is the fact that a heartbeat can be heard seven or eight weeks after conception on an office ultrasonic stethoscope. Is this an important bit of information? Should a pregnant mother know it?

In a series of 327 women at the University of Szeged, Hungary, mothers who wanted abortions were allowed to listen to the "fetal heartbeat." After hearing it, 16% refused abortion.

F. Sontag, Third Internatl. Congress of Psychosomatic Medicine, *OB & GYN*, London, 1971

Ask any abortionist, ask any Planned Parenthood official why they *never* tell women there is a heartbeat, and why they would *never* dare to let her listen.

How can the violence be stopped?

The fastest way would be to stop the far more ghastly fatal violence inside their doors. If it were stopped, there would certainly be no more violence outside. As long as the violence against babies continues, while we are saddened to so state, we doubt that the violence against bricks will stop.

CHAPTER 36

Pro-Life Groups

Local

The basic "cell" of the Right to Life movement is the Right to Life chapter in your local area. This may be in a town, small city, a county, or part of a large metropolitan area. It is pluralistic, being made up of all types of people. It should not be affiliated with a specific church, or with a political party. Its function is largely educational, but it must also be active in lobbying. It should also give public witness in parades, picketing, etc. During pre-election times, its members put on another hat and become active in the local Right to Life Political Action Committee. You probably can find your nearest chapter under R in the phone book, since most cells are called "Right to Life of ..." If it is not listed there, write to National RTL for details. If none exists in your community, help start one. Your prime responsibility for personal involvement and financial support lies here and with your local service group which helps pregnant women.

State

In almost all states there is one central RTL organization (a very few states have coexisting similar groups). Local chapters usually elect regional delegates, who comprise the board of the state RTL organization. Usually based in the state capital, its prime function is lobbying the state legislature and helping to start and support local chapters. It also educates, holds an annual state convention, and sees to the necessary administrative needs of a statewide group. Its board elects a delegate to represent it on the board of National Right to Life.

It should have a functional, internal, educational foundation and a similar internal statewide Political Action Committee.

National Single Interest Groups

The central national organization, the *National Right to Life Committee*, has a governing board of 54 members, one elected by each state RTL organization and the District of Columbia, and three at-large members elected by the general membership. It has a central, Washington, DC office and three satellite offices. Because of its structure, its policies closely reflect the thinking and wishes of grass roots pro-lifers nationwide.

It publishes the *National Right to Life News*. It maintains the movement's largest lobbying staff in Washington. It has a national Political Action Committee. Its internal Trust Fund and its Horacio Storer Foundation are educational. Its convention is the major national meeting of the year for the movement. It has multiple other departments to service the movement. The address: National Right to Life Committee, 419 7th St., NW, Suite 400, Washington, DC, 20004 (Phone: 202-626-8800).

Are there other organizations which are also single issue?

There are other independent groups, not a part of the pyramidal membership group above, which make substantial contributions to the pro-life movement. Some of these publish; some are educational foundations; some are church-related; some are political action groups. One does legal research and legal defense. Some are Washington-based and have large mailing lists; others are headquartered in other cities. A few of these are single issue; others pursue multi-issues. Some of them include:

Horatio R. Storer Foundation: A subsidiary corporation of National Right to Life, it is educational in thrust. It publishes a national professional journal, *Issues In Law and Medicine*, sponsors major seminars, publishes books, etc.

March for Life: Its main activity is to put on the large, annual January 22nd March for Life in Washington. It also has a lobbyist in Washington.

Ad Hoc Committee in Defense of Life: Maintains a lobbyist in Washington and publishes *Lifeletter* and the quarterly, *Human Life Review*.

National Committee for a Human Life Amendment: Its primary emphases are lobbying for a Human Life Amendment, lobbying against funding for abortion and also, grass roots development. Its Washington office coordinates its nationwide Congressional District Action Committee (CDAC) groups. It works primarily in the Catholic community.

Action for Life: Based in Chicago, this group reports on and stimulates picketing and other nonviolent direct action outside abortion chambers.

Women Exploited by Abortion: WEBA is made up of women who have had abortions and were injured physically and/or psychologically by them. Primarily giving witness and educating, its members also offer help and counseling to others.

Feminists for Life: A group of dedicated feminists who strongly believe in equal rights for all women, born and unborn.

Professional Groups

The *National Association of Pro-Life Obstetricians and Gynecologists* is the largest, but there also are *Pediatricians for Life, Nurses for Life,* and the *World Federation of Doctors Who Respect Life,* as well as *Scientists for Life, Public Health Workers for Life, Pharmacists for Life, Veterinarians for Life,* and others.

National Political Action Committees

National Right to Life PAC: This is the largest PAC. It works with candidates in every state, both Democrat and Republican. Its less than 5% fund raising overhead is by far the lowest of any RTL PAC. It works closely with the state RTL PACs.

Committee for a Pro-Life Congress: This is unique in that, rather than only giving money directly to campaigns and candidates, it operates as a planning and strategy group. It operates nationally and has been very effective.

National Pro-Life PAC: This is the oldest PAC. It tends toward independent expenditures and operates nationally.

Life Amendment PAC: In 1982 it concentrated heavily on only one political race. It seeks high public profile (for example, publishes a "hit list)." Primarily, it does independent expenditures.

Legal Defense

Americans United for Life: An active and valuable group based in Chicago, it has been active in many states and before the U.S. Supreme Court in defending pro-life interests.

National Right to Life's legal department has been the other part of this effort to date.

State **Right to Life** groups and **Local Right to Life** groups have commonly carried the major part of the responsibility for state and local legal actions.

Multi-Issue Pro-Life Groups

Women's Groups: *Eagle Forum, Concerned Women of America,* and many others have the pro-life issue as a high priority.

Pro-Family Conservative Groups: *American Life Lobby* has pro-life as its foremost issue. It publishes *All About Issues* and maintains a lobbyist in Washington. It has a large nationwide mailing list.

Liberal Political Groups: *Pro-Lifers for Survival, National Pro-Life Democrats,* and *Democrats for Life.*

Conservative Political Groups: *Committee for the Survival of a Free Congress, Conservative Caucus, Heritage Foundation, Republican Pro-Life Impact Committee,* and others.

Religiously Motivated Groups

These groups are growing and increasing in numbers. Most marked recently are Evangelical and Fundamentalist Christian related groups. An older bellwether was the *Knights of Columbus.* Some, such as *Moral Majority, U.S. Catholic Conference,* and *National Association of Evangelicals* are very large and influential. One smaller group, the *Christian Action Council,* has moved from being largely a lobbying presence in Washington to stimulating the development of a large number of crisis pregnancy centers nationally.

International Groups

The *International Right to Life Federation,* is the only single issue RTL group with a central office (in Geneva), an elected board, and broad multinational, international representation. It can be contacted at or through your own national group.

There are other multi-issue and church, or church-related groups as well as caring and medical professional groups.

CHAPTER 37

Pro-Abortion Groups

Planned Parenthood

The Planned Parenthood Federation of America is one of 90 national affiliates of the International Planned Parenthood Federation (London). It gets about two-thirds of its financing through tax money, local, state, and national. It has five regional offices, 174 statewide affiliates, 53 abortion facilities, and 729 local clinics in the U.S. Its total annual cash flow is estimated to be close to one-half billion dollars. It concentrates its efforts on abortion, contraception, and sex education.

What is Planned Parenthood's position on abortion?

In its early years of existence, Planned Parenthood limited itself to contraception and specifically opposed abortion. The following is a quote from an official Planned Parenthood pamphlet:

"Is birth control an abortion?

"Definitely not. An abortion kills the life of a baby after it has begun. It is dangerous to your life and health. It may make you sterile so that when you want a child you cannot have it. Birth control merely postpones the beginning of life."

Planned Parenthood, Aug. 1963
[1]Available from Cincinnati Right to Life, P.O. Box 24073, Cinn., OH 45224, $1. pp.

But Planned Parenthood does abortions now?

Yes. It is the largest unborn baby killing conglomerate in America. In their 53 abortion centers, they killed 83,000 preborn babies in the last reported year, an increase of 539% in eight years.

Planned Parenthood of America, 1982 Service Report

Doesn't Planned Parenthood concentrate mostly on contraception?

In its earlier years, to a much larger extent, Planned Parenthood clinics offered contraceptive advice and aid to married women so that they could more responsibly plan their families. Because of this, it generated widespread support from many areas of our society.

Those days are gone. Today its clientele consists largely of unmarried teenagers. It dispenses medically hazardous drugs (the pill) and devices (the I.U.D.) without parental knowledge or consent. It is the largest provider of abortions in America, again, to teenagers without parental knowledge or consent. It aggressively promotes sex education that, rather than reducing promiscuity, premarital sex, illegitimate pregnancies, abortion, and venereal disease, has almost certainly had just the opposite effect.

J. Ford & M. Schwartz, "Birth Control for Teenagers: Diagram for Disaster," *Linacre Quarterly,* Feb. 1979, pp. 71-811

A. Jurs, "Planned Parenthood Advocates Permissive Sex," *Christianity Today,* Sept. 2, 1982

In its Five Year Plan, it openly stated: <u>Our mission is to serve as the nation's foremost agent of social change in the area of reproductive health and well being</u> [emphasis theirs].

Planned Parenthood Federation of America, *A Five Year Plan, 1976-1980,* p. 5

But all Planned Parenthood affiliates don't agree with abortions or support the ones who do.

Some may not privately agree, but they must do so as a requirement to be affiliated with and to use the Planned Parenthood name. (See Planned Parenthood standards of affiliation article IX, Sect. 1a, 1c, Sect. 2b, Sect. 3c, and Sect. 4a.) They must support the National Federation (Sect. 4d). Failure to do so can result in their disaffiliation (Sect. 7).

That is hard to believe. I've heard that Planned Parenthood is pro-family, pro-life, and pro-child.

Their paid TV commercials say that, but their own official documents, their leaders, and their actions say quite the opposite.

In 1976 the Planned Parenthood's Five Year Plan (see reference above) laid out in detail what their goals were. We quote:

- Objective #2: "Reaffirming and protecting the legitimacy of induced abortion as a necessary back up to contraceptive failure, and extending safe, dignified services to women who seek them."
- Purpose: "To provide leadership in making ... abortion and sterilization available and fully accessible to all."

  "The various activities that we undertake are not 'separate' and certainly not competing. Rather, they are all complementary parts of a single national strategy" (page 5).

  "Services to be made available at *all* clinics include ... *abortion services (or local referral)*" (emphasis in original, page 6).
- Program Emphasis #2: "Keeping abortions legal and accessible to all persons" (page 9).

Is their emphasis still on abortion?

Since the Five Year Plan above, the Planned Parenthood agenda is even more openly and militantly pro-abortion as outlined in their newest action agenda. For example, in

Goal #3, they state that Planned Parenthood will "increase the number of Planned Parenthood affiliates providing early ambulatory abortion services."

Planned Parenthood of America, *Til Victory is Won, 1982, 1984,* p. 16

"Until we reach the millennium ... Planned Parenthood will continue to provide not only sex education and contraception but also abortion."

A. Moran, Exec. V.P., Planned Parenthood of New York City,
New York Times, Dec. 27, 1982

On the 10th Anniversary of the U.S. Supreme Court decision (January 22, 1983), the central news event was a debate arranged by the National Press Club in Washington, DC, that was seen or heard by over 100 million people. To represent the pro-life side, they chose one of your authors, Dr. J. C. Willke, then President of National Right to Life. To represent the pro-abortion side, they chose Ms. Faye Waddleton, then President of Planned Parenthood. Each represented the leading force on the two sides of this national struggle. An audio tape of this debate is available.[2]

[2]Cincinnati Right to Life, P.O. Box 24073, Cinn., OH 45224, $1. pp.

In April 1978 Planned Parenthood circulated a "bigotpack" of cartoons smearing Roman Catholics. One of the cartoons showed a Catholic bishop holding a can of gasoline and a book of matches; the caption said, "Now we're losing the flock on the subject of abortion — but we're not worried ... We've got the faithful out burning down the clinics."[3]

[3]Copies of these cartoons may be ordered for $1. from Friends for Life, 180 N. Michigan Ave., Chicago, IL 60601.

Planned Parenthood has promoted a pro-abortion "comic book," geared for teenagers, entitled *Abortion Eve.* On the back cover is a caricature of the "Assumption of the Blessed Virgin" depicting a pregnant Mary with the idiot face of *Mad* magazine's Alfred E. Neumann. The caption says, "What, me worry?"

What does Planned Parenthood think of Right to Life?
They have an opinion.

"In every generation there exists a group of people so filled with bigotry and self-righteousness that they will resort to any means — even violence — to impose their views on society. Today, such fanatics dominate a movement ironically called 'the Right-to-Life,' a movement which threatens the most basic of all human rights."

Planned Parenthood Pamphlet, the Justice Fund,
810 7th Ave., New York, NY, 10019

But Margaret Sanger, its founder, opposed abortion.
Not so! Not only did she favor abortion, but she proposed forced sterilization for those whom she considered unfit to reproduce. She worked hard for a "race of thoroughbreds" until Hitler's similar "Master Race" made that goal unpopular. She was a true eugenist. For example, her April 1933 *Birth Control Review,* devoted an entire edition to eugenic sterilization.

Who did she consider unfit?
Black people, Jews, Southern European immigrants (especially Italians), but also others of "low I.Q." These "feebleminded" people were a "menace to the race."

E. Drogin, *Margaret Sanger: Father of Modern Society,*
CUL Publishers, 1980, Section 1

Let us quote from her "Plan for Peace," which was little more than peaceful genocide. She wanted the United States:
- "To keep the doors of immigration closed to the entrance of certain aliens whose condition is known to be detrimental to the stamina of the race, such as the feebleminded as determined by Stanford-Binet I.Q. tests.
- "To apply a stern and rigid policy of sterilization and segregation to that grade of population whose progeny is already tainted, or whose inheritance is

such that objectionable traits may be transmitted to offspring.

- "To insure the country against future burdens of maintenance for numerous offspring as may be born of feebleminded parents by pensioning all persons with transmissible diseases who voluntarily consent to sterilization.

- "To give dysgenic groups in our population their choice of segregation or sterilization.

- "To apportion farm lands and homesteads for these segregated persons where they would be taught to work under competent instructors for a period of their entire lives. [Practically speaking, a concentration camp.]

- "[To] take an inventory of the secondary group such as illiterates, paupers, unemployables, criminals, prostitutes, dope fiends; classify them in special departments under government medical protection, and segregate them on farms and open spaces as long as necessary for the strengthening and development of moral conduct." (Again, concentration camps.)

M. Sanger, "Plan for Peace,"
Birth Control Review, vol. 16, no. 4, April 1932

NARAL

Originally, the *National Association for the Repeal of Abortion Laws*, this group was a prime mover in getting the first abortion-on-demand law in New York passed.

Since abortion legalization, and now entitled *The National Abortion Right Action League*, it has been a major force opposing the Right to Life movement.

ACLU

The *American Civil Liberties Union* has been consistently selective as to whose civil liberties it protects. Totally blind to the existence of the preborn baby, it has served as the legal defense arm of the pro-abortion, anti-family movement.

An offshoot of the ACLU, the *John Madison Institute for Constitutional Law* is a small but sharply focused pro-abortion legal group.

N.O.W.
The *National Organization for Women* is a national group of radical anti-life feminists heavily influenced by the militant lesbian faction of its membership. While claiming to seek economic and employment equality for women, three of its first four stated goals clearly show it to be primarily radically feminist. These goals are: a) Lesbian Rights; b) Reproductive Rights (i.e., abortion rights); and c) Legalization of Prostitution.

N.O.W. Natl. Meeting, Oct. 9, 1982

It claims to represent the women of the U.S., but a national poll demonstrated that most women don't see it as representing them.

"Only 28% of women said they thought groups such as N.O.W. and National Women's Political Caucus speak for a majority of American women, while 56% said that these groups represent a 'small minority.'"

Poll, *Los Angeles Times*, Sept. 2, 1983

Religious Coalition for Abortion Rights
This is a collection of clergy and 'religious' groups who are pro-abortion. Probably its best known sub-group is the very small (but very vocal), militantly pro-abortion *Catholics for a Free Choice*, which is largely made up of former Catholics.

YWCA
The *Young Women's Christian Association* was captured two decades ago by a group of radical anti-life feminists. Its policies today are aggressively pro-abortion. For example, in 1973 its 26th National Convention voted "to support efforts to provide safe abortions to all women who desire them." In 1982 it listed as a "priority" the "preservation of the legal option of abortion ... as a right of privacy."

National Education Association

Sadly, this once fine trade organization of teachers is solidly in the grip of national leadership that is dedicated to the pro-abortion cause. To give but one example of its short-sightedness: In the city of Tulsa, every week, three classrooms of future students are killed in their mothers' wombs.

American Association of University Women

In June 1977, AAUW's Biennial Convention voted as a priority issue the "Right to Choose."

National Women's Political Caucus

This supposedly bipartison, civic group has become a platform for pro-abortion activity.

League of Women Voters

At its 1982 National Convention, on a 753 to 472 vote, it stated that "the LWV of the U.S. believes that public policy in a pluralistic society must affirm the constitutional right of privacy of the individual to make reproductive choices." (Ninety-two percent of their chapters agreed).

National Abortion Federation

This is the trade association for operators of abortion chambers.

Network

A group of Roman Catholic nuns who have defied their church's teachings and adopted a permissive attitude toward abortion.

International Planned Parenthood
Pathfinder Fund
United Nations Fund for Population Activity

In the past, all three of these organizations were heavily funded by the U.S. State Department through its Agency for International Development. All three have actively promoted and subsidized abortion in Third World countries. In 1984 President Reagan completed cutting off all funding for the first two unless they completely discontinued their involvement in and promotion of the overseas abortion business.

People for the American Way
This heavily funded group has carried on an effective pro-abortion campaign in the national media under the leadership of Norman Lear.

Clergy Counseling Service
Prior to national legalization of abortion, this small group of Protestant clergy actively recruited women and helped them travel to states where legal abortions could be obtained.

CHAPTER 38

Service

Alternatives to Abortion;
Caring Groups

This book deals primarily with the half of the pro-life movement called Right to Life. The other half, the service effort, is devoted to helping pregnant women and offering them alternatives to abortion. There is also a growing network of helping groups for women suffering from the aftermath of abortion as well as a rapidly expanding number of maternity homes.

Alternative to Abortion and Birthright Groups
These traditional type groups number over 2,000 organizations in North America. Made up of volunteers (usually women), these groups stand ready to offer to the troubled pregnant woman whatever help she needs to continue her pregnancy. This can include medical care, legal or spiritual help, a job, a home, counseling, etc. They also provide help in placing the baby for adoption. If she keeps her baby, they will find her a crib and baby clothes if she needs them. The women who come to these groups usually do so seeking a second opinion other than the pro-abortion advice they have received.

These groups have saved the lives of tens of thousands of babies and have prevented untold psychic and physical problems in women who have been saved from being the abortionist's second victim.

For a directory of these groups, write to Alternatives to Abortion International, 46 N. Broadway, Yonkers, NY 10701 ($6 per copy).

Pregnancy Problem Centers

These are commonly storefront operations. Also entirely volunteer and not under any church auspices, they offer free pregnancy tests. While the woman waits, she is told and shown about pregnancy, fetal development, and abortion and is offered alternatives.

The women who come usually have already decided to have an abortion, and many come to these centers for an abortion. After being fully informed, however, approximately 80% change their minds and carry their baby to term and deliver.

These centers have offered consistent and dramatic evidence to prove that the typical abortion chamber does not tell women the facts of fetal development, of the reality of abortion, or of the availability of alternatives. The ultimate impact of Problem Pregnancy Centers has only begun to have been felt.

Crisis Pregnancy Centers

Similar to the Problem Pregnancy Centers, these differ in that they are usually set up by and through a Christian church. They do counsel mothers, however, of any or no faith. These centers are being rapidly set up throughout the U.S. and Canada.

When these newer helping centers, plus other church and civic groups are added to the traditional Birthright-type centers, there will soon be approximately 4,000 such groups in operation in the U.S.A.

Maternity Homes

In the years immediately following the Supreme Court decision on abortion in America, and after the passage of pro-abortion laws in other nations, many homes for unwed mothers closed their doors.

A rapidly developing and new phenomenon all over the country is the reopening and re-establishment of new maternity homes, mostly under religious auspices. As this is being written, over 50 new homes are under construction.

Post-Abortion Help Groups

There is also a growing network of groups made up of women who have had abortions, suffered through the aftermath, and because of this, have banded together to help other such traumatized women. These volunteers help other women work through these sometimes catastrophic after-effects. These concerned women also volunteer their services to counsel women contemplating abortion.

The charge is often made that RTL people only care for the unborn and not the born. In fact, RTL people are involved, on the average, in far more helping projects than either the pro-abortionists or the population at large. As an example, a poll was taken at a state RTL convention. Two hundred and forty-two attendees were asked what helping activities they were involved in other than abortion. The results were impressive:

- Distribute food and clothing: 158
- Donate blood regularly: 67
- Work on crisis phone lines (drug, alcohol, suicide): 18
- Work in support groups (drug, alcohol, suicide): 32
- Work in programs for abused women: 9
- Work in hospitals, nursing homes, clinics, or hospice programs: 85
- Work in volunteer fire and police departments and neighborhood associations: 45
- Work in Scouting, youth work, or Meals on Wheels: 117

- Work in schools, tutoring, aiding teachers, etc.: 101
- Work on voter registration: 63
- Work in political campaigns: 109
- Work in Sunday schools: 118
- Work on crisis pregnancy phone lines: 50
- Work distributing maternity and infant clothing: 62
- Work in fund-raisers (walkathons, bikeathons, tele-thons) for various social action programs: 149
- Share their homes with a pregnant stranger, elderly, refugees, sick or foster children: 49

"Pro-lifers Do Care,"
Right to Life of Michigan News, Nov. 1983, p. 5

CHAPTER 39

Adoption

What percent of unmarried mothers place their babies for adoption?
Over 90% keep their babies. This is a sharp reversal from two decades ago when the ratio, at least among white mothers in some areas, was almost the reverse.

How long is the wait to adopt a baby?
For newborn white babies, it varies from three to five years to forever. For "special needs" babies and children, it varies from quick to never.

What are "special needs?"
These are some babies of minority or mixed racial backgrounds, those with medical problems, those who were neglected, abused, or disabled, and those over six years old.

People don't want them?
Well, not really. The problems are complex. Let's mention a few.
- The physically or mentally handicapped child who was (unwisely) not placed for adoption as a newborn is much harder to place now that she is older.

This is a tragedy because "Many prospective adoptive parents will accept children [referring to infants] if informed frankly about possible health defects, often even when definite abnormalities have been found."

S. Wolff, *Archives of Disabled Children,* 1974, pp. 49-165

- In some areas minority race babies are another such group.

- One other reason is that many single mothers will not legally relinquish them, even though they cannot care for these children themselves. After several years and a succession of foster homes, the child is sometimes emotionally unstable. If the mother then finally does legally release him, he is hard to place.

What of minority race babies?

Actually, there are enough couples wanting these babies, but, sadly, they sometimes aren't adopted. Reasons include unwillingness of the natural mother to release the child, unwillingness of agencies to allow white parents to adopt them, unrealistically high standards to meet for minority parents to meet in order to qualify, and, one more reason that, if true, is a national disgrace.

What is that?

If a baby is placed for adoption at birth, the social agency gets X number of dollars. For every child in foster care for a year, the agency gets 3X or 4X dollars. The charge has been made that minority race babies are not being placed at birth because the agency needs the additional money it gets for foster care.

"The system has evolved into an industry with perverse incentives for social agencies to maintain children in the system because of the increased revenue. Some 70% of the money for foster care is spent for administrative overhead and services. What we have done, according to the National Council of Family and Juvenile Court judges is 'replace parental neglect with governmental neglect.'"

R. Woodson, "Bureaucratic Barriers to Black Adoption,"
Wall Street Journal, June 26, 1984, p. 34

Isn't foster care good? I know some super people who take these kids and they really try.

You're right. Most foster care is certainly better than either institutional care or some of the inadequate homes they come from, and we warmly thank those generous people who offer their foster-love to these children.

But — and a big but — it is nowhere near as good as one pair of loving adoptive parents from birth. One constant and perhaps unsolvable problem is the reluctance of the courts to take children away from mothers who are clearly unsuitable. Judges quickly place them in foster care, but they seldom legally terminate the birth-mother's "rights" and allow adoption.

J. Kwitng, "Nobody's Kids,"
Wall Street Journal, Sept. 6, 1978, p. 1

Why early placement?

In recent years we've learned a lot about early bonding between parents and child. The father in the delivery room, the baby "rooming in" with the mother, immediate breast feeding, etc., are all part of creating that very special and truly unbreakable emotional tie between this tiny one and her parents.

In adoption, the infant, of necessity, must lose those precious early hours and days with her new parents. That generous birth-mother must have a few days to make her final decision. But then? What is best for the baby?

Without a shade of doubt, that infant *must be* in his or her adoptive parents' arms as early as possible. Some irreplaceable early bonding is gone, but more slips away every day, every week. Whenever possible the baby must go directly from the hospital into those new parents' arms.

But what if the baby is handicapped?

All the more reason for immediate adoption. What if birth-parents have a handicapped baby? Do they give him back? Of course not. What of a handicapped child to be adopted? Should we keep him in an institution until all medical questions are answered? Or in foster care? Then maybe no couple will want him. How cruel! He needs loving parents from the beginning, and maybe even more than a "normal" child.

Please, these infants with handicaps should also be adopted directly from the hospital. There are parents who will take them. Once he is "their baby," they will rarely give him back.

Are there comparisons of children placed in adoptive homes with children kept and raised in a fatherless home?

Children born out of wedlock and kept and raised by their mothers alone show educational failure and psychiatric disorders "far more commonly" than adopted children, as they are commonly exposed to major social and family stress. In contrast, adopted children are rated by parents as no different than natural children in the same social strata. Their teachers rated them as doing only "slightly less well intellectually and psychologically" if at all.

S. Wolff, *Archives of Disabled Children,* 1974, pp. 49-155

What of the unmarried father, if the mother is willing to place the baby for adoption?

In that case, he has the legal right to claim the child. He does, that is, if he comes forward and if she admits his paternity.

What if, in early counseling, the young mother is bitter toward him, says she'll never let him have the baby and flatly states that if she is forced to disclose the father's name, she'll get an abortion?

In that case, if she really means it, most conscientious

counselors unofficially advise her to "not to remember who the guy was." It is true that there is a court decision requiring her to disclose his name. But, if the baby's life is in jeopardy, then the actions necessary to save that baby's life must be taken.

Why do so few mothers place their babies?

In society, customs change. Right now it is the "in" thing to keep your baby. Part of the reason for this has been the overemphasis on women's "rights" (as in abortion) over the baby's rights, and the concept of the mother's "ownership."

A very insidious influence has been the almost condemnation of, and the "poor mouthing" of adoption by many sex educators, Planned Parenthood people, and others. Another reason is money.

Money?

Yes! Here's how it works. A pregnant woman goes to the doctor. She is considering an abortion. She really doesn't want one but can't afford to have the baby. She'll need some living expenses and she wants a private hospital and obstetrician. If these are provided, she will agree to carrying the baby and adoption. The problem is that (in most areas), the adoption agency doesn't have funding to do all of this.

One good answer is to have a private adoption. The doctor contacts another doctor and a lawyer whom he trusts, and a procedure is worked out. The other doctor knows a childless couple who can afford to pass-through the money needed. The lawyer acts as the intermediary. Total confidentiality is maintained if the birth-mother and/or the adopting parents desire it. Assuming the birth-mother does release the child, the infant is taken directly from the hospital as young as legally permissible and given directly to the new parents. Your authors have been involved in many such adoptions, where the baby would otherwise have been killed by abortion.

But isn't that selling babies?

In the vast majority of such cases, the lawyer only charges for her or his professional time, which may cost up to $500 or $800, depending upon whether there was lengthy counseling, etc. This is legitimate.

There are well-publicized cases where childless couples pay huge sums and "buy" a baby. This is not right, and also, the child may not be well served.

The answer is to correct such abuses, if that is necessary. Certainly it is not to abolish private adoption as some suggest. And, after all, what is the greater evil? A childless couple so desperate for a baby to love that they spend an exorbitant sum to get a baby? Or to allow the mother to kill her baby?

Do you prefer private over agency adoptions then?

In general, certainly not. If an agency does most things right (i.e., early placement, etc.), we believe that there is consistently better parent screening, better records, better follow-up, etc. Private adoption can be all of these good things too, but sometimes, is less. We believe that both are absolutely necessary but that both need improvement and the elimination of abuses.

What of open records?

In recent years, organizations have been formed to lobby state legislatures to open previously sealed confidential records. Only three states had never sealed their records — all other states had. One of these three, Pennsylvania, legally closed their records in the fall of 1984. One other, Ohio, opened some in the same year.

About one-third of the states, containing over 50% of the nation's population, have solved the release of identifying information with voluntary mutual consent registries. In almost one-third more, Right to Life groups have worked to defeat open record laws.

The arguments for open records are twofold. There is a very small percentage of adopted children (over 21 years old) and birth-mothers who want reunions. In addition, some of today's young mothers may be reluctant to adopt (and may abort) if there is absolutely no hope of an eventual reunion.

The arguments for confidentiality are also twofold. A high percentage of young mothers in years past placed their babies in adoptive homes only because the law guaranteed a seal of confidentiality on that adoption. Today, many of these generous women are terrified that that confidentiality will be stripped away. Also, some of today's mothers will abort if they know that their privacy will some day be revoked.

What is a mutual consent registry?

It is the compassionate answer to the problems discussed above. Under it, an adopted child over 21 years of age may enter his or her name in the state registry indicating that he or she seeks a reunion. Birth-mothers may also register and request the same. If there is a match, a meeting is arranged. Unless both request it, however, the previous seal of confidentiality is preserved.

> "A more sensible approach, and one that takes into consideration the rights and feelings of other parties in the adoption, is the establishment of registries where sensitive information can be exchanged only with mutual consent."
>
> Editorial, "Unsealing Adoption Records,"
> *Washington Post*, Sept. 10, 1983

What if the right to confidentiality is taken away?

> "More girls will get abortions; perhaps 50% of those who come to our Gladney homes now would do so. Also, many girls who do give birth will lie about their backgrounds to protect themselves, and then we won't get the honest information we need to help the children."
>
> R. L. Piester, Exec. Dir., Edna Gladney Home, Dallas. Interview in *People* Magazine, Nov. 1983, p. 60

How many babies are adopted?

In an average year, according to the National Committee on Adoption, about 65,000 babies are placed for adoption, while between two and four million couples wait with loving arms outstretched and cannot get a child. When one realizes that the average couple would adopt several children if they were available, it is evident that the number of children available, even if abortion were outlawed tomorrow, would never begin to fill the need.

But what of babies with handicaps?

There is a long waiting list for Down's Syndrome babies. For example, when Baby Doe was starved to death in Bloomington, Indiana in 1982, eight couples had asked to adopt him.

There is a national organization of parents of Spina Bifida babies. At this writing, over 100 couples are on the waiting list to adopt such a baby, no matter how severe their problem (see chapter 26).

What is National Right to Life's position?

It will support any reasonable effort to promote the adoption option over abortion. It approves both agency and private adoption, but wants them both well regulated. It opposes completely open or completely closed birth records and supports a mutual consent registry.

National RTL Resolutions, Jan. 20, 1985

CHAPTER 40

Action

The most important thing that you can do is to become personally involved. Unless you do, nothing will change.

Educate

First, educate yourself. Read this book carefully two more times. Then, carry it with you and refer to it. If you haven't seen a pro-life slide presentation, you must. Then, watch one or more of the excellent movies now available.

In addition, there are numerous excellent books that go into depth on any and all aspects of the Human Life issues. There also are less expensive booklets and inexpensive pamphlets. Some additional materials are listed in the back of this book, along with information on where to obtain them.

After educating yourself, then you must educate others.

Lobby, write letters

Subscribe to your local RTL chapter newsletter, to the National RTL News, or to one of the other independent or church-related group publications and stay informed. Then, write letters, write letters, and write letters to your elected officials at local, state, and national levels; to radio and TV stations; to media sponsors; and to others in your community whom you wish to influence. Write, also, to your newspaper and to other civic or religious publications. Visit your public and elected officials. Tell them how you feel about current or proposed legislation regarding abortion, euthanasia, and infanticide.

Vote

Register and vote. Get your family, your club, your friends, your church members to register and vote. Nothing will change until you do. Everything will change when you do.

Volunteer

Volunteer as a member of your local RTL chapter. Can you make phone calls, baby-sit, run errands, type, stuff envelopes? Can you lecture?

Contribute

Some have no time but can give money. This movement is rich in people but almost destitute for funds. If you can give, do so. Be sure that your gifts go to groups that use them wisely and are not largely burned up on overhead and mailing costs. Your first responsibility is to your local RTL chapter, then to your state RTL group, and then to National. Give also to other pro-life groups whose types of action programs you admire and approve. Unless Right to Life groups begin to develop more secure financial bases, nothing will change, for we are fighting the megamillions of anti-life foundations, of Planned Parenthood, of ACLU, and of much of the government.

Pray

Pray as if everything depends upon your prayers, for it just might be so. Pray that God will stay His hand. Do we, will we as a nation deserve His help and His Mercy?

INDEX

N.R.L.C. Library Pack

Abortion, Questions & Answers
Abortion & Slavery
The Abortion Holocaust
The Ultimate Resource
Aborting America
A Private Choice
} all six hardbound $39.00

Handbook on Abortion (Spanish)
Right to Live, Right to Die
Handbook on Abortion
Abortion in Perspective
Germain Euthanasia
Rachel Weeping
Abortion — Silent Holocaust
Psychological Aspects of Abortion
} eight more may be added $48.00

New Perspectives on Human
   Abortion
Death, Dying & Euthanasia
} separate listing $25.00

WALL POSTERS

COPIES

one $2.00
10 . . . . $1.50
100 . . . . $1.10

English

Spanish

COLOR

BLACK & WHITE

HOW BABIES GROW

- For pre-school to adolescent
- A sensitive telling of the beautiful story of conception to birth. 10 min., 18 slides
- 10 min., 21 slides, audible & electronic beeps

$17.95

NEW

by
Dr. J.C. Willke

*"This analogy, far more real to me, is **the** other historical parallel."*
Erma Clardy Craven

Details of slavery that few know . . . how abortion walks in its tracks.

Dr. Willke with his unparalleled knowledge of today's abortion movement has drawn a well documented analogy that is devastatingly convincing.

1 Copy $3.50
10 Copies $2.80
100 Copies $2.45

NEW
8 WEEK FLYER

for mass distribution

— at lectures
— sidewalk counseling
— at fairs
— to school children
— in Sunday school
— in churches
— in mailings

100 copies @ 2.5¢ each
1,000 copies @ 2.0¢ each
10,000 copies @ 1.8¢ each
100,000 copies @ 1.5¢ each

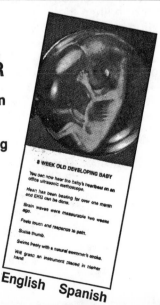

English   Spanish

Pro Life Materials by Dr. & Mrs. Willke

Available in
English
Spanish
French
German
Italian
Portuguese
Dutch
Norwegian
Hungarian
Polish
Japanese
Chinese
Swedish
Turkish

The most widely used
color brochure
in the world.

100 copies ...... 14¢ each
1,000 copies ...... 11¢ each
10,000 copies ...... 8.5¢ each

Supreme Court brochure, available in
English language only, to be used after
they have seen LIFE OR DEATH.
Full color
for mass distribution.

Brief, hard hitting facts on
development in the womb.

Envelope size.

Easy to include with every
letter, bill, or mailing you
send.

**AN ENVELOPE STUFFER
—A MINI BROCHURE** *in En-
glish, Spanish, French, German,
Italian, Portuguese, Croation, and
Swedish.*

Pass out at a sports event,
a fair, a convention, or
at an abortion clinic.

100 copies .... 4.5¢ each plus post.
1,000 copies .... 3.8¢ each plus post.
10,000 copies .... 3.3¢ each plus post.
100,000 copies .... 2.8¢ each plus post.

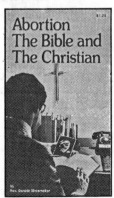

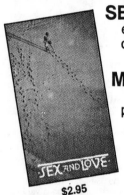